CHICKEN COOKERY
ROUND THE WORLD

CHICKEN COOKERY
ROUND THE WORLD

by Henriëtte Holthausen

WITH DRAWINGS BY J. GROENVELT

Doubleday & Company, Inc., Garden City, New York

1966

To
EDDY
*my perfect guide and companion on
this and many other gastronomic tours*

Preface

THE aim of this book is to give Gallina her rightful place in the limelight, for I consider that the time has come to pay much more attention to the chicken as a source of varied and delicious meals.

I am aware, however, that a cookery book dealing only with chicken would be rather one-sided. I have therefore included many specialities to be found in the countries I have visited, and such recipes do not necessarily include the chicken among their ingredients. To round off the book I have also included some recipes for the sweet course.

May I reassure my readers on one point? I have sampled all these recipes myself, and most of them have been prepared again in my own kitchen in Holland.

My object has been to present a book of recipes for all tastes and all pockets. Sometimes the chicken is treated in a simple, homely manner, while at others the recipes are extravagant, complicated, and difficult to prepare. How could it be otherwise with the universal chicken?

First of all you should become familiar with a variety of herbs and spices, for they play such an important part in most chicken recipes. Once you get to know them I am sure that you will appreciate them as much as I do. I could not cook without them.

Sometimes I use them with a great deal of daring, at others I aim at a delicate, subtle effect demanding caution. Much depends on my mood and my guests, since I try to cook according to their liking.

To-day the chicken is within the reach of most people. It is often cheaper than a joint of good meat, and certainly cheaper than most fish and sea-food. Deep-freeze chickens are good value, as are chicken joints when only a small quantity is needed. And what could be more convenient for the man or woman living alone?

It should be remembered that the younger the chicken, the less time it will take to cook. When using a deep-freeze bird there are various factors that must be taken into account, and these I have summed up in one of the first chapters. I have devoted a whole chapter to herbs and spices as I am sure this is a subject about which too many cooks, amateur and professional, have only the haziest notions.

Special attention has been paid to the general hints on the first steps to be taken when preparing a chicken, for this is so very important.

I sincerely hope that readers will enjoy studying these recipes culled from so many different corners of the world and will be encouraged to try some of them, if only as a diversion from their familiar recipes.

I am grateful to Hermine de Vivanot for her help and advice.

HENRIËTTE HOLTHAUSEN

CONTENTS:

Introduction to Chicken Gastronomy

I HAVE called my book *Chicken Cookery Round the World* because I have, indeed, travelled round the globe in order to discover how the people of our wide world differ in the cooking of this delectable bird. The central figure in this traveller's tale of mine is, of course, the chicken, known to the Romans as Gallina. To-day the numbers of self-sacrificing Gallina needed to meet the enormous demand for chicken dishes are countless.

When reading very old cookery books, especially those dealing with the use made of chickens, we come to the conclusion that neither the Greeks nor the Romans cared much for them. Grilled venison, horses, donkeys, peacocks, swans, and other birds both large and small, together with boars' meat and elephant trunks, were infinitely preferred to chicken meat.

To us moderns the chicken—the boiling fowl as well as the roaster—holds pride of place in our menus. Rich and poor, old and young, the sick as well as the fit, have all learned to appreciate a well-cooked chicken.

Travelling round the world, I have had many opportunities to discover how the different housewives, as well as the chefs in famous restaurants, deal with Gallina. Long before I started on my travels, however, I used to read about the gastronomy of antiquity.

Our early ancestors fed themselves mainly on raw foods, and it was quite accidentally that a Roman general discovered that game tasted far more delicious when cooked. According to the story, this Roman general returned one day, tired after long hours spent hunting. He placed a piece of game by the fire, and then inadvertently fell asleep. A little later he woke to find the room filled with the most delicious smell: the meat was roasting in the heat of the wood-fire! Greatly daring, he tasted the meat and discovered it to be so rich and rare that from then, so goes the story, the Romans began to roast game as well as other poultry, meat, and fish. They also experimented with the roasting of vegetables with or without spices and fresh herbs.

From then on gastronomy evolved steadily, Greeks and Egyptians contributing as well as the Romans. Epicures like Lucullus and Apicius became famous, the one for the fish-ponds in which he used to keep the finest fish, the other for the subtlety of the recipes he invented. The ancient Chinese too should not be overlooked, for did not Marco Polo as early as the thirteenth century learn a great deal from their cookery? They revealed to him not only the magic of gunpowder but also their cunning in the use of herbs and spices. The Chinese, moreover, were the first to prepare ice-sorbets and miedishes (a Chinese form of vermicelli). Marco Polo returned to Italy, his native country, with recipes for vermicelli and ice-sorbets, and both have become world-famous Italian specialities, the one as spaghetti and the other as dessert water ices.

Let us, however, return to the roasting or grilling of meat, game, and poultry. At first it was all grilled quite plainly, but soon the cooks discovered that meat into which either oil or fat had been rubbed became more tender. It also made the grilling process easier, as the meat did not then become too dry or burnt. The next step forward was to make use of fresh green herbs and seeds; roots, dried flowers, and fruit pods or pistils were blended with fat or oil to produce what are now known as spices.

At first all the spices were ground by hand and blended with fresh herbs. To-day this is done by the factories, and flavouring a dish has become a far less personal matter than it used to be, although I have watched with interest housewives and cooks in India and the Far East carefully grinding their own spices in the traditional manner.

And through the centuries Gallina's fame grew. Our gastronomical tour takes us through Italy, France, England, Scandinavia, and many other countries in Europe, as well as through the Near East, the Far East, the United States of America, Mexico, and Africa.

It was a very tiring tour, but I went on because it was so fascinating to discover how many and how varied are the ways in which a chicken can be cooked. And I have tried to give a detailed record of these in the following pages, which I hope you will enjoy as you share my delight in these recipes for chicken dishes complete with their various accompaniments, sweet or savoury, according to each country's taste.

About Herbs and Spices

THE proper use of herbs and spices is a great art which can be learned only with much patience and practice. We have to go a long way before we really know how to give that subtle herb or spice flavour to our dishes. Did not Confucius once say: *"There are but few who can distinguish flavour!"*

I am convinced that every housewife interested in the art of cooking should become used to flavouring her dishes with herbs and spices. If you entertain in your house and serve all dishes, even the most exotic chicken dish, without any special flavour, you not only display a complete absence of inventiveness, but also admit to a great lack of culinary ambition.

To show how many herbs and spices the cook can have at her disposal, a detailed list is given below. The list starts with herbs, a flavour less pungent than that of the spices. I think every one willing to cook in a more international way can get used to the flavour of herbs. With spices this is more difficult. You just have to learn to fall in love with them.

Most of the herbs listed here can be grown in the garden or upon a window-sill or balcony, and it is so useful to have fresh herbs at hand. Herbs are generally herbaceous plants which in some cases have beautiful flowers. Among them there are those that need more sunshine than our climate may provide. This has to be remembered when growing them!

Most spices, on the other hand, grow in warm, tropical countries under a bright sun.

HERBS

Basil. A green plant which needs a fair amount of sun and has to be taken indoors during the winter months. It is a native of the Near East. Its flavour is reminiscent of a mixture of mint and cloves. The plant has white blossoms shading to light pink and giving the impression of being attached to the stalk upside down. Basil is used for soups, meat, chicken, and fish dishes in combination with other herbs and even spices. The fresh as well as the dried leaves have a rather strong flavour, and one must be careful not to use too much.

Bay Leaves. These are leaves from an evergreen tree. They are, when fresh, wax-like, light green, and pointed. They can be used both fresh and dried. The bay leaf tends to dominate other flavours, and is familiar to every housewife everywhere. Be careful when using the dried leaves—even one leaf can be too much. A crumbled part of a leaf is usually enough in one dish. One whole leaf is more than enough for 6–8 helpings of chicken, meat, or fish.

Borage. A plant which grows all over the world and in every climate. The leaf is green, coarse, and a little hairy. The taste of the fresh leaf resembles that of cucumber. Only the fresh leaves should be used. It is a pity that this herb is not more used by cooks.

Caraway Seed. This herb was grown in 700 B.C., and used as a flavouring. The fresh leaves are not unlike the green leaves of the carrot. The seeds are the most important part of this plant, and are grey-brown and oval-shaped like tiny crescents. They give a very special, somewhat old-fashioned, flavour to different dishes (*e.g.*, soups and stews), and are especially good in sauerkraut and other cabbage dishes. Be careful, however, when using these seeds because of their very definite, rather pungent flavour.

Celery. We know the leaves, the stalks, and the root (celeriac). The leaves and stalks give a distinctive flavour to many a dish, a flavour more definite than parsley. A marriage between those two herbs is a very happy one. You can plant both in pots in your kitchen or on a balcony. They can be used in almost every dish from soup, meat, fish, chicken, and game, to salads!

Chervil. This plant, with its white umbrella-like flowers and beautiful green leaves, should be grown in every garden. The fresh leaves give a very delicate flavour to our dishes, as well as a bright green colour. They blend in well with soups and sauces. A chicken prepared in a green-herb sauce gets its special flavour from the chervil leaves. We can use fresh leaves, but cans of chervil are also available.

Chives. A bulb plant with hard, green stalks and violet umbrella-like flowers. Chives is a favourite in many a dish, as it has a faint flavour of onions. We can grow the plant in a pot and place it in the garden, on the balcony, or on the kitchen windowsill. The fresh stalks are cut up finely and are very good for stock and salads.

Cumin Seed. It is difficult to differentiate between the caraway seed and the cumin seed. Cumin seed resembles in appearance caraway seed. The cumin seed is also oval-shaped, but of a somewhat lighter yellow colour. The French call the caraway seed a refined meadow cumin seed with a delicate and very aromatic flavour. The cumin seed has a stronger flavour and is less refined. Both are used with and in special kinds of cheese. Cumin is also excellent in cabbage and sauerkraut dishes, although I prefer using caraway seed for them.

Dill. A pretty plant with sharp-pointed leaves and umbrella-shaped flowers. We can distinguish the stalks with the bronze-coloured flowers in many a jar of pickles, sweet-sour gherkins, onions, and similar ingredients. The fresh plant, which grows in gardens in all countries, as well as the dried seeds, can be used as a somewhat pungent flavour in many dishes. Care must be taken to use it sparingly. This is especially true of the dried dill. It is an excellent flavouring for fish dishes.

Hyssop. A plant with beautiful dark-green pointed leaves and curiously shaped pinkish-white flowers. The leaves can be used either fresh or dried in many meat and chicken dishes. The plant belongs to the mint family and tastes a little like mint, although it is different from the usual well-known mint flavour.

Leek, Onion, Garlic, and Shallot. The most refined, but also the most dominant and ever feared, is garlic; then comes the shallot, and then the most often used, leek and onion. Use the green as well as the white part of the leek for your soups, stew dishes, and vegetable improvisations. If you want a less penetrating garlic flavour, then just do not take off all the skins. Leave the last yellowish skin on it. It then smells less pungent and you may more easily become accustomed to its use. A subtle garlic flavour is wonderful in different soups, meat (especially lamb dishes), chicken dishes, and salads.

Lovage. A plant which grows wild in every garden. Lovage is sometimes called maggiplant, perhaps because its flavour resembles a little this well-known soup and sauces aroma. Personally I would rather compare its flavour with celery leaves and stalks, but then it is somewhat stronger.

Marjoram (Origanum). Usually called sweet marjoram, it is a member of the mint family. The plants have lilac-red flowers and grey leaves and grow throughout Europe and the United States. Marjoram is often seen as a low garden hedge in Italy. The fresh as well as the dried leaves are used. Both have a strong, agreeable flavour, which can be compared with the sage flavour. The leaves are used in innumerable dishes; the dried flowers, in little sachets, are fragrant in the linen cupboard.

Mint. Mint is a widely used green herb known throughout the world. There are several varieties of the mint plant. We use the green leaves, but also the stalks with leaves to flavour drinks, such as the delicious Pimm's. Lamb and mutton dishes are unthinkable without mint, and mint sauce is a very popular sauce in many countries. Personally I love mint both with vegetables and in salads.

Parsley. Every person fond of cooking is familiar with this plant's curly or smooth green leaves. Need I say any more than, "*A good wine needs no bush.*" But does every housewife know that those tiny leaves with the green stalks are rich in Vitamin C? May I therefore advise you to use them as much as possible, and, if you can, chop them just before adding them to the dish, which should be served immediately. Never cook parsley or celery leaves. The stalks should not be thrown away. Tied together into a green bundle, they can be added to boiled dishes, roasts, or stews. We use as a garnish the whole leaves, attached to a tiny piece of stalk, and also leaves cut up coarsely, not chopped.

Rosemary. The name itself sounds like music in our ears, and the flavour is subtle, too. It is a handsome green plant with narrow, spiky leaves and beautiful bluish-pink flowers. The southern countries use this plant very much, both fresh and dried, because it has such a very delicate flavour. It can be used in many fish, meat, and chicken dishes. If the plant gets enough sunshine it grows into a big shrub.

Sage. A greenish-grey plant which grows easily in European and American gardens. Its scent reminds us of mint, and it can be used either fresh or dried. Fresh leaves can be chopped and mixed with cottage cheese. Dried and fresh leaves are good in game dishes, fish extravagancies, meat stews, and forcemeats.

Savory. A distant relative of the mint plant. Even its flavour reminds us of mint. Here again either fresh or dried leaves make a good seasoning for many dishes. Wonderful with broad beans, in salads, soups, and meat stews.

Tarragon. Another plant with a very distinctive flavour. It is used, among other things, to make the tarragon vinegar employed for pickling salads. Its dark-green leaves are pointed, the pale-yellow flowers grow along the whole stalk. The plant tends to spread and needs a lot of sun. The leaves keep their flavour when dried. Tarragon vinegar can be made by putting whole fresh stalks with their leaves in a bottle of white vinegar.

Thyme. The fresh plant has small green leaves and lavender-coloured flowers. It is a beautiful decorative plant in your garden. The fresh as well as the dried leaves (when dried they become greyish) can be used. The flavour is hard to define but very pronounced, and this herb must therefore be treated with great care in cooking. Never use too much in your dishes.

Watercress. A very popular plant with a very agreeable and fresh flavour. It is used as garnish either raw or deep-fried.

This is my homage to the green herbs. You may have noticed that I have made no mention of the powdered form in which all these herbs can be bought. As a matter of fact, if they are not available fresh, I would strongly advise you to buy them coarsely cut up and dried. There are many pots with dried, coarsely chopped herbs which are excellent. It is so pleasing to have a good selection of all these herbs in your kitchen store cupboard in small glass jars.

If I have forgotten some herb you are personally very fond of I hope you will forgive me. I am well aware that a list of herbs or spices never can be complete.

We are now going to have a look at the different spices.

SPICES

IF we have to be careful when using green herbs (especially when these are dried, since, being dehydrated, they are then very concentrated and thus stronger in flavour), even greater care must be taken when using spices. The correct amount of spices to be used can be learned only through long practice, and their use requires knowledge and discernment. Always start by using them cautiously in small quantities—just a little pinch to begin with.

If we use in a dish for 4-6 persons 1 tablespoon of fresh green herbs, we can only use ½ a teaspoon of the same dried, coarsely chopped green herb. And of the pungent-flavouring dried green herbs like thyme or dill the quantity has to be reduced to 1 pinch only.

When using spices we must always add very little to a dish and taste at intervals to check its flavour. We can then judge for ourselves if more of a certain spice should be added. That is, if we use a mixture of spices such as is often prescribed for exotic dishes.

Of course, an exception to this is the use of curry powder and paprika. Here, too, it is necessary to like these flavours, or if we do not then we must try to get accustomed to them. In a curry for 4 helpings, if we do not want too strong and spicy a flavour, 1 teaspoon of curry powder and the same amount of paprika will be ample. To this I must add that from the moment I learned to eat curries in India I got so accustomed to the delicious pungent flavour that by now I add much more of this mixed spice. The same is true of paprika. Once you have eaten paprika dishes in Austria or Hungary you realize that you must add a greater amount of paprika in order to obtain a really well-flavoured dish.

Of spices one could say, "I must get acquainted with them in order to appreciate their flavour!" I hope you'll get as fond of all these flavours as I have become while touring around the world and trying to eat every exotic dish!

Here are some of the best-known spices:

Capsicum. Cayenne pepper, paprika, red pepper, and chili powder all come from the same family called Capsicum. Some of them are used fresh, and others in powder form, or else in the whole pod, dried. These dried capsicum have many different sizes, shapes, and even colours. They are, with the exception of the paprika powder, very hot. The small peppers are used (pickled or dried and chopped without the seeds) for the most exotic dishes. These dishes came to us mainly from the countries of the Far East.

The red and green paprika is made from the sweet and semi-sweet capsicum—the red and green pimentos we can buy in the markets and in most green-grocers. They are excellent fresh and can be used in combination with ground paprika or on their own. When using the other capsicum spices mentioned above we must be careful—especially if we are not accustomed to them. One tiny pinch will do. The Mexican chili powder contains also dried origanum, the wild marjoram. The Portuguese call this red chili—they are very tiny—piri-piri. In this book you will find chicken and other recipes in which these dried capsicum pods are used. In Holland we call the red oblong-shaped chili lombok. It is used in rice recipes. These came to us from the East Indies, now called Indonesia.

Cardamom Seed. This is a spiced seed from the Zingiberaceae family. It therefore has a ginger flavour. We buy the seeds and grind them with mortar and pestle in small quantities combined with other spices. Mortars are nowadays available in wood, and they are very handy if you want to grind your own herbs and spices. Cardamom seeds vary in colour from brown to creamy-white, depending on how they are prepared. In India they use the white whole seed in the preparation of *ghee,* which is goat butter. They also offer you the smaller brown cardamom seeds to suck as you would an acid-drop. Since these seeds are ginger-flavoured, use them with care!

Cinnamon. This comes from a tree with leathery green aromatic leaf. It is a native of Ceylon and India. The cinnamon comes from the bark of the smaller branches. These are dried, and the bark, when peeled, becomes curly. It is preferable to buy cinnamon in quills and not ground. Its flavour is very delicate and subtle. It must, however, be handled with great care and not overdone, as it can be much too pronounced as a flavour. It is used in savoury dishes as well as in sweet ones.

Clove. Buy whole cloves. They are the unopened buds of an evergreen tree from the Moluccas, an archipelago of Indonesia. They also come from India, Ceylon, and Malaya. A clove has a rather pungent flavour, but is excellent if handled with care and knowledge. It is perfect in combination with sweet ingredients such as pears, apples, pineapples, when stewed, or as a special flavour in an exotic chicken recipe, or in soups and other dishes.

Coriander. Like the celery seed, it belongs to the Umbelliferae family and like aniseed, which belongs to the same family, it has an anise flavour. Do not buy it ground but as seeds. The smell is reminiscent of a combination of aniseed with lemon, delicate and aromatic. It originates in the Far East, North Africa, and also the United States. It is a big, green plant, the leaves of which remind us of the parsley plant. The tiny seeds are yellow-coloured. They give a wonderful flavour, if properly used, to most of the exotic dishes.

Ginger. This comes from the same family as turmeric, belonging to the Zingiberaceae. It originates in about the same countries—the East Indies, India, China, and other tropical countries. In these countries fresh ginger is used as well as its dried form. In Europe we are familiar with peeled and unpeeled ginger. The dried, unpeeled ginger root must be scalded in hot water and then peeled. Only small pieces of such ginger root are used. I do not think that I ate many dishes in Hongkong-Kowloon to which no ginger was added. If a dish requires ginger I sometimes use crystallized ginger or ginger preserved in syrup. What a wonderful combination this sweet ginger makes with some other hot spices! Be careful, however, with dried ginger as it is much stronger than when preserved.

Mace. Every cook should have some dried mace in her store cupboard, and this goes for housewives all over the world. Do not buy mace in powder form, but rather in little dried brownish pieces. They smell better and are more easy to use. Use tiny parts of these pieces and check up to see that the flavour is not too strong in your dish. The mace comes from the nutmeg tree. This is a beautiful tree with plenty of green leaves and fruits. The aril of the fruit is carefully removed and gives us the horny pieces of mace. Mace is normally used in combination with the bay leaf, cloves, and onion. It has a wonderful flavour and adds interest to many recipes.

Nutmeg. This is the ripe fruit of the nutmeg tree. We buy it as a dried whole seed, but it has to be grated shortly before serving the dish. I regret to say that Dutch housewives use nutmeg too much and too often in their meals. This spice has a very pronounced flavour, and thus must be used with great care. Never let it boil or roast with a dish.

Pepper. Black pepper is the dried fruit of a plant called *Piper nigrum;* white pepper is obtained by peeling off the outer dark coating from the dried mature peppercorns. Both are well known, and I would suggest that they should be used freshly ground. Have a peppermill handy, for the result will give a much finer flavour. Grind shortly before adding in small amounts to the dishes. There exist special dishes to which we add coarsely ground pepper seeds.

Saffron. This is an orange-yellow coloured spice, coming from the dried pistil of the *Crocus sativus*. Saffron adds a wonderful flavour to a dish and gives it a most beautiful deep-yellow colour. It is a very expensive spice, and in India it is often replaced by turmeric. Turmeric might be described as the poor man's saffron. Saffron must be bought only in tiny quantities—not only because it is expensive, but also because it loses its colour and flavour when kept a long time in stock. Saffron is essential in many fish-soup and chicken recipes.

Turmeric. This powder comes from the East Indies, India, China, and many other warm countries. It is ground from the root of a plant which, when dried, has a beautiful yellow colour. In all these countries it is used not only to add colour to food but also as a dye. In Europe we buy it as a powder, for the root as a whole is very hard to grind. You can, when visiting spice markets in the East, recognize this root very easily by its strange shape and its hard yellow colour. Turmeric plays a leading part in every well-mixed curry powder.

Curry Powder. It was in India that I learned to appreciate fully the use and the flavour of a well-mixed curry powder. No self-respecting inhabitant of that lovely country would dream of buying this many-flavoured condiment ready made. It is only in Europe that we buy bottles and jars filled with the yellow powder. In India every one buys all the seeds, herbs, and spices separately and unground. They pound all ingredients in a mortar, and thus prepare an individual curry powder. As a result every curry dish you eat tastes different from the last. In Europe we know only one special flavour. But in India you learn a quite different side of the curry powder story. The following is a favourite mixture:

Mild curry powder for a recipe giving 8 helpings:

¼ inch or 1 teaspoon
   powdered turmeric
2 cloves of garlic
4 peppercorns
1 tiny, dried red chili

¼ inch ginger or 4
   cardamom seeds
4 coriander seeds
¼ inch cinnamon
6 caraway seeds

Red Paprika Powder. As I said at the beginning of this chapter on condiments, the sweet and semi-sweet paprika powder are prepared from the well-known green and red vegetables belonging to the Capsicum family. In my opinion the best paprika powder comes from Spain, North Africa (which also provides us with the stronger paprika powder), Portugal, and (last but not least) Hungary. The flavour is so varied that there is a paprika for every palate. Several paprikas are sweet, others strong and sharp. Make your own choice. We have become more and more familiar with paprika, and I really do not know many cooks who do not have it in their store cupboard. How right they are! How could we prepare a good paprika chicken or goulash without flavouring it with paprika and, if in season, combined with fresh sliced pimentos?

In North Africa I learned to appreciate another powder mixture with which I think you should be familiar. If you want to try it out here is the recipe.

Ras el Hanout. A wonderfully flavoured mixture of some twenty-seven different blended herbs, spices, and seeds. The Ras el Hanout contains three different specimens of capsicum, then cinnamon, caraway seeds, cumin, turmeric, belladonna, four different kinds of pepper, further rose leaves, rosebuds, ginger, allspice, lavender, iris leaves, nutmeg, bay leaf, and many other flavours.

In Europe allspice is often mistaken for *quatre épices.* Allspice is the dried blue berry of the Jamaica pepper tree. Its flavour is reminiscent of clove, cinnamon, and nutmeg. *Quatre épices* is a combination—thus a blended flavour—of white pepper, cloves, ginger, and nutmeg.

General Hints for Preparation of Chicken

A CHICKEN, whether a spring chicken or an old boiling fowl, can be prepared in many different ways. I should like to begin with the frozen chicken and to point out that you can prepare it in precisely the same way as a fresh one. With a frozen bird, however, we must take into account the following points:

(1) A frozen chicken must thaw while still in the plastic in which it has been packed.

(2) When thawed, wipe with a clean cloth, in order to make it completely dry.

(3) Then prepare in precisely the same way as if it were freshly killed.

(4) The chicken, if we roast it, must not be salted in advance. Only rub the inside of the bird with a little salt, then brown it as quickly as possible in the oven or upon the gas or electric stove. Only when it is browned on all sides is salt added.

(5) After the browning process add all the ingredients indicated in the recipe.

(6) We must, however, remember that a frozen chicken is more quickly cooked than a fresh one.

(7) A frozen boiling fowl, when thawed, is put in the pan and covered with cold water to which flavourings are added.

These are given in the recipe you intend using. Before serving chicken soup skim the water if a clear stock is needed. We should also skim off any fat.

It is a sound idea for the housewife, who may have to deal with unexpected guests, to keep such a frozen fowl in the freezing chamber of her refrigerator. She can then prepare a very good chicken dish even for unexpected guests.

Deep-freeze chickens are also a little less expensive than fresh chickens.

And here is the first tip for the preparation of the fresh fowl.

Boiling and Poaching. For both these use what are known as boiling fowls. They weigh from 3½ pounds to 5 pounds. For a chicken sauté it is better to use a tender, lean cockerel. We do, however, use a boiling fowl when preparing croquettes, bouchée fillings, and little snacks, as well as for chicken salads. We can also prepare quite a good stew with a boiling fowl, but in this case we must make sure to cut off all the yellow fat before boiling it. If we forget to take off the fat beforehand we must skim it off when the liquid has become cold, as the fat then comes to the surface and is easy to remove. Always remember that taking off the fat makes all dishes so much more delicate in flavour.

Fat chicken stock should never be used for a soup or for a stew. Indeed, no dishes, however simple they may be, should be too greasy.

Now for the boiling. We put the fowl in a not too small pan and add the correct flavourings according to the recipe chosen. We then pour enough water over it to cover the chicken and the flavouring, which consists mainly of different vegetables. Herbs, and sometimes even spices, are essential in many chicken recipes. I will give you a detailed description of these with the appropriate recipes.

If we are using a boiling fowl for croquettes, stews, hors d'oeuvre dishes, or bouchée fillings we boil it in less water. Use just a little more than the amount you will need afterwards to make the sauce. This will give your dish a stronger stock and thus a better flavour. And may I point out that a chicken, especially a boiling fowl, is no water bird? Cooks often overestimate its power to give you a strong stock. If we really want a strong stock we should use, in addition to the fowl, a veal knuckle or some beef bones with or without lean meat on them. Then we can be sure of a good and tasty stock.

Poaching. If we cook a boiling fowl with flavourings scarcely covered with water we call this poaching. Poaching means to simmer a fowl or some other ingredient in as little water as is necessary for this process. So allow just enough liquid to cover all the ingredients in order to have them well done and tender. The resulting stock is mainly used for sauce. It is the perfect way to prepare a delicious chicken stew, sauté, or filling for bouchées. This way of cooking is particularly suitable for people with delicate digestions. Before serving, however, skim off all the fat and do not use spices or too much salt or pepper. Fresh green herbs are allowable in most cases.

Roasting. A tender roaster should be used. We roast in butter, margarine, or other fat. The pan in which the bird is roasted should not be too large, nor yet too small. Its size must correspond with the size of the chicken. If your pan is too large the roaster will feel rather forlorn, and the fat in which it is being cooked will spread away from it. In a smaller pan the chicken lies in the hot fat and cooks better.

First brown the chicken in a very hot oven and as quickly as possible. Then reduce the oven heat a little and salt the chicken.

The roasting process now must go on regularly. Yet we must see that the chicken does not turn dark, nor must it become too dry. We therefore baste it at intervals with a kitchen-spoonful of the dripping. To prevent the gravy turning brown we add a tablespoonful of water or, even better, stock.

As I said before, we salt only the inside of the chicken before roasting. After the chicken has browned we add more salt, and if prescribed in the recipe we add also herbs, vegetables, and perhaps spices. Before a housewife starts cooking she must first make sure that she has in her kitchen cupboard all the ingredients required for the recipe she has chosen.

Pan-roasting. The housewife who has no oven, or does not want to use it for the roasting of just a chicken, can roast it on the gas or electric stove. This is done in an ordinary, heavy iron meat pan with lid.

We roast the whole chicken in butter, margarine, or fat which has first been browned. For this, contrary to what is done in oven-roasting, we must turn the chicken over several times. When it has browned on all sides we add salt to taste and whatever special ingredients are needed for the recipe. Then we put the lid *aslant* on the pan and cook for 50–60 minutes for a 3-pound bird.

During this roasting process we must

(1) Add from time to time some water or stock, but not too much. It is better to use a tablespoon for this operation.

(2) Be careful to see that as the liquid evaporates the gravy does not burn or become too dark brown. It is to avoid this that we must add liquid from time to time during the roasting process.

We can roast a chicken also in a covered pan, but that is called roasting only as a courtesy. Steam develops in a covered pan, and we should therefore describe this form of cooking more correctly as simmering or stewing. A well-browned crisp chicken soon loses its brown colour and crispness through the action of the steam, but we can try the following trick.

About 10 minutes before the chicken is ready take off the lid. Turn the heat up and let the watery gravy reduce by evaporation in the uncovered pan. The chicken then dries and will become brown and crisp, but be careful, or there is a danger of over-cooking the chicken and of the gravy becoming too dark. However, if you control the reducing process carefully you will succeed in serving up a nicely browned roasted chicken.

A chicken is well roasted if we can carve it easily and the meat, though tender, adheres to the bone. When the meat comes off the bones too easily the chicken is overdone.

Only in certain chicken recipes, most of them Eastern in origin, is the meat allowed to be overdone and taken from the bones.

As a last word on roasting let me say that the best way to roast a chicken is in the oven, but, as is the case with many other things, roasting in the oven is a matter of getting accustomed to that kind of cooking.

Sautéing. If we are going to stew a fowl we first divide it into 4 to 6 or even more pieces. This will, of course, depend upon the size of the bird. A sautéed fowl or roaster can be prepared in many different ways. Its flavour and even its name depends on the recipe; that is to say, on the herbs, spices, and other flavours we are supposed to add. Sometimes we must brown the chicken, and sometimes it need only be as pale as ivory. We sauté the chicken in a medium-size saucepan and always without a lid. After having obtained the correct colour we add all the ingredients needed and then put the lid on the pan.

From now on the chicken should simmer slowly until done. I have tried to give you in each recipe the correct time needed for the chicken to become tender and well done.

Much will depend on the bird itself, its age, and the tenderness of its flesh. Very often sautéed chicken specialities need the addition of sherry, whisky, brandy, or other spirits. Wine, either red or white, is excellent used with chicken. I am fully aware that many housewives cannot open a bottle of wine just for the pleasure of preparing a special chicken recipe. If there are no left-overs of red or white wine, then a mixture of water and port, whisky, or sherry makes a suitable substitute.

Soy sauce, tomato ketchup, and Worcester Sauce are also used in many chicken recipes.

Grilling. One could write pages and pages about this wonderful way of preparing dishes, especially chicken dishes. There are so many possibilities in this domain of cooking. While on my tour around the world I have learned that correct grilling depends mainly on your own imagination and handiness. First and foremost, grilling is best done on a wood or charcoal fire. To grill on a barbecue on a wood or charcoal fire is really exciting. In the Far East I saw little boys and girls doing it just in the streets on very little home-made baking-tins which were filled with burning charcoal. They had made little iron grills upon which they put the spits. The result was wonderful. The little pieces of meat, chicken, or lamb were combined with eggplant, marrow, tomatoes, or paprikas. To these they add fresh green herbs and well-chosen spices. It is a pity that so few cooks have such a grill at their disposal.

Of course, we can also grill on an electric or gas grill, and this is nowadays included in a modern gas or electric stove. It is very important to put the chicken immediately into direct contact with the heat. Only when the chicken has turned dark brown can it be taken away a little from the direct heat. A spring chicken is well grilled in approximately 15 to 20 minutes; a bigger roaster needs more time—30 to 45 minutes. The simplest way of preparing a chicken for grilling is to rub the flesh with oil (olive oil does very well), butter, or fat. Personally I always use oil.

Here too at the beginning we salt only the inside of the bird. Only when the chicken is browned do we add salt to the outside. Let me now explain why. Salt turns into moisture, and any ingredient that we are going to roast or grill should be absolutely dry. We even dry it with a cloth before putting it into the grill or on the barbecue or in the oven. If we salt the whole bird at the beginning we certainly take a risk that the fowl will become moist. It will then not brown as quickly as is necessary. From this too slow process it will dry out and become tough instead of tender.

The grilling of a chicken on a modern barbecue can easily be done in a garden or on a balcony. I have done this myself for years, not only with great pleasure but also with good results.

You can also grill very well on an electric grill with a rotating spit. I have, in fact, succeeded in grilling in just an ordinary oven. Rub the chicken well with oil on all sides, and in the meantime keep the oven full on for about 10 minutes before we put the chicken on the oven rack. This rack is also rubbed with oil. The oven remains on full for the first 15 minutes. We do not completely close the oven door, but put some small object between door and oven so as to keep it open about 2 inches. Thus the steam can escape, allowing us to grill the chicken quite simply. Underneath the rack put a large baking-pan. The gravy from the chicken will drip into it. By doing it in this way your oven will not become too dirty. In a very hot oven you can reckon 30 minutes for the grilling of a whole spring chicken. If cut into two or four parts, it needs only 15 to 20 minutes.

But remember that once the chicken is well browned you must reduce the oven heat, and do not forget that whenever grilling you must baste the chicken occasionally with oil or butter. For this you can use a little brush dipped in oil. You can buy these brushes in every well-equipped household shop.

Imitation Grilling. If you want to grill a piece of tender chicken or a steak, a lamb chop, a slice of fish or vegetable, here is another and very simple way. I found it out by accident.

Use a heavy iron omelet pan with handle. In Holland we call such pans 'Grandma's saucepan.' Rub the inside thoroughly with oil and do the same with the ingredient you are going to grill. Put the omelet pan on a high gas flame or electric burner upon the stove. Let the empty pan heat up, and when it looks really hot put in it the oil-rubbed piece of chicken or meat or whatever you wish to grill. Shake the pan and let the piece of chicken or meat brown on one side. Turn it over and have the other side browned. Add salt only now.

Reduce the heat, rub more oil, and allow about 10 minutes for the grilling. Do not add any liquid, but just rub once in a while with oil or butter.

You will be surprised how well you can grill in such a simple heavy iron pan.

Deep-frying. To deep-fry a chicken cut into 2, 4, or 6 pieces, we use a heavy iron deep-frying pan in which a good amount of oil has been poured. The chicken must be coated with egg and breadcrumbs. As a matter of fact, such a chicken must swim in oil to be well fried. It then cooks rapidly and becomes wonderfully crisp. In Austria I had the best deep-frying lessons in the cookery school in Vienna. In the subsequent recipes you will read much more about this way of preparing a chicken. I think you will like it very much, for it tastes delicious and it is really quite easy to prepare.

Before concluding this chapter I should like to insist once more that when you roast, grill, or deep-fry a chicken, whole or in pieces, it must be absolutely and completely *dry*.

Experience has also taught me that a frozen chicken browns perfectly only if, before putting it in the fat, we roll it in flour. The reason is that a frozen chicken has a tendency to become soggy if steps are not taken to prevent it.

By now you have probably become a little impatient and want to get on with the recipes. Let us therefore now follow Gallina on her tour around the world.

FIRST TOUR:
Europe

FRANCE

IF a person is occupying herself with the preparation of food in general, and the chicken in particular, she will undoubtedly arrive in France, the country which throughout the ages has become very famous for her mastery of the art of the cuisine. At the beginning of this book I have described some of the culinary achievements of people long ago. Although their method of cooking was primitive, our ancestors possessed the special gift of being able to add to their dishes the most wonderful flavours, and this they did with a very special subtlety.

We know, for instance, that onions, garlic, and many raw vegetables and fruit were often combined with fresh green herbs, and spices played an important part in their methods of cooking. Combinations used in recipes of the past were, fortunately, written down by contemporary authors, and are, therefore, still available for us to study. Through the years the use of herbs and spices has developed into the fine art that we know to-day.

It was only during the reign of Henry IV (at the end of the sixteenth century and at the beginning of the seventeenth century under the combined influence of Marie and Catherine de Médicis) that the Italian and French master-cooks and *pâtissiers* changed completely their way of cooking. It is in this period that the first real cookery books were written. One very famous author of this period was the French cook *La Varenne*. He wrote the first cookery book in 1651, during the reign of Louis XIV. In his book entitled *Cuisinier Français* he puts down, as Massialot was to do later, new rules for cooking and gives a very clear explanation of them.

It is here that for the first time we read about the making of special sauces, heretofore a completely unknown culinary item. La Varenne was also the first to use special pots and pans for cooking and to advocate working in a well-equipped kitchen. Up to that time the cooking was done in the living halls. From then on meat, fowl, game, fish, and, indeed, all food, was prepared according to well-defined recipes and rules.

It was in this period that it became customary to name dishes after famous persons. We still read in cookery books and on restaurant menus names such as Sauce Béchamel (the well-known white sauce), Conti dishes (made with mutton in combination with lentils), Muttonchops à la Maintenon, and other dishes all named after some well-known person of the court.

Henry IV has become very famous as the inspiration of a special soup. It was he who was once said to have declared that he could feel happy only if he knew that all his subjects would have chicken broth on Sunday. This soup, then, is called Poule-au-Pot or Poule (chicken) Henri IV. And it is with this very tasty chicken soup that I should like to start our tour around the world.

Poule-au-Pot or Poule Henri IV

for 6 servings we need:

1 lean boiling fowl
1 pound lean shin of beef with or without bone. It will give us a good strong stock
2 pounds soup vegetables, including ½ pound not too small carrots
1 onion
some leeks
½ small celeriac, or some stalks of French celery

a bunch of herbs (parsley and celery stalks)
Fasten on to the onion one bay leaf and a tiny piece of mace, using 2 cloves as 'nails'
1 peeled clove of garlic
salt to taste
5 peppercorns
enough water to cover all these ingredients

In a deep, broad pan we put the whole chicken (first of all we take off all the yellow fat; this is very essential), together with the shin of beef with or without a bone and the washed, cleaned vegetables cut in finger-lengths, the herbs, the garnished onion, and the garlic. The leek we cut into two parts lengthways, and these two parts are again cut up into four short pieces. We pour the water on these ingredients until they are well covered. About 8 cups in all would be needed. When the water boils we add salt to taste, but, please, not too much to begin with. We can always add more later if necessary, but, once in, it is so difficult to take salt out! Last of all we add the coarsely crushed peppercorns.

When the water has come to the boil we thoroughly skim off the greyish scum that comes to the top. If we fail to do this the soup won't be clear when we are serving it. Scum always makes a stock cloudy.

This poule-au-pot must boil slowly for about 1½–2 hours, in a moderate heat, until the chicken and the beef are tender.

How shall we serve this soup? Personally I think the following is the best way. First we must prepare a

White Sauce. With less than 2 cups of the hot chicken stock, 3 tablespoons of butter, and a little less flour or cornflour we prepare a well-mixed homogeneous creamy sauce. Use a saucepan for the cooking of the sauce. To the sauce we add (off the fire) some tablespoons of thick cream and the juice of ½ a lemon. Conclude by adding salt and pepper to taste and a little nutmeg freshly grated. The chicken is taken out of the stock, divided in several pieces, and boned and skinned.

The meat of the beef bone is used some other day to make meatballs, when we can add some fresh minced meat, herbs, spices, some slices of white bread, and one egg. This makes a perfect mixture for meatballs.

Now on each plate we place a piece of chicken and some of the vegetable supplemented by some cooked rice. The recipe for cooking rice is given on p. 48. The white sauce is served separately in a sauce-boat. Beside each plate place a soup cup filled with chicken stock. A very good soup indeed for a Sunday meal.

Let us now have a look at cold chicken appetizers.

Canapé de Volaille (Chicken Canapé)

Garnished canapés are one of the favourite French hors d'oeuvres. For the canapé we use thin slices of toasted white bread. They can be given different shapes. The nicest is to halve the slice diagonally. You thus obtain two pretty three-cornered canapés.

Cut into thin slivers a boiled or roasted cold chicken, using preferably the skinned and boned breasts. We need as well slices of smoked tongue (also cut up into thin slivers), mayonnaise (home-made or from a jar or bottle), and butter, blended with mustard. The recipe for a good mayonnaise is on p. 57.

You already have the canapés, which, after being toasted, are allowed to become cold. The butter should be creamy, so that it can easily be blended with the mustard. For a quarter of a pound you need as much mustard as is necessary to give it a dark-yellow colour.

Butter the canapés with this savoury butter. With the strips of tongue you make a circle on each canapé. In the middle you put the slivers of chicken. Garnish with mayonnaise and chopped parsley. If you prefer a very well-seasoned mayonnaise you can add a few drops of Worcester Sauce.

This canapé is a very good appetizer and is easy to make. The approximate quantities for about 6 servings are as follows: the breast-meat of 1 boiling fowl or roaster, ⅓ pound of cold tongue, and about 1 cup of mayonnaise.

The meat of a roaster is to be recommended for this snack as it is more tender than the flesh of a boiling fowl. You can, of course, also use the meat of a boiling fowl if you have removed all the fat.

You can use the drumsticks the next day for a sauté dish. The recipe for it you will find on p. 47.

If you would rather not prepare the toast for the canapés yourself, then just buy ready-made toast or barquettes. Barquettes are hollow pastry shells. They are very handy and look charming. If you prefer you can also mix the thin slices of chicken with the tongue and the mayonnaise all in one. It then makes a different kind of garnish. Less elegant as regards colour, but it is quicker to prepare.

Cocktail Eliane

Mix boiled or roasted chicken—without skin or bones—cut up in tiny squares with asparagus tips (tinned or fresh) and/or green peas with slices of bananas and parts of hard-boiled eggs. Be careful not to make a mash of all these ingredients, for then the cocktail will not look very attractive. A fork is best for mixing.

For this cocktail use the following *Cocktail Dressing*. Blend ½ cup of mayonnaise with 2 teaspoons of Worcester Sauce;

double the amount of tomato ketchup and soy sauce; at least 2 tablespoons of thick cream; 1 tablespoon of port or sherry and ½ tablespoon of brandy. Add to taste salt and cayenne pepper. Pour the pink dressing over the chicken, which should be put in a large glass dish, lined with crisp, dry lettuce leaves. Garnish with pieces of chicken, reserved for this purpose, and surround with a ring of stuffed olives, cut in halves. This cocktail can also be served in individual glasses.

Poulet Froid à la Gelée (Cold Chicken in Aspic)

This is a delicious hors d'oeuvre, typically French. Every good and honest cook will tell you that it is difficult to make a good aspic. Besides, it is expensive and takes quite some time to prepare. In France you can buy ready-made aspic which is well flavoured and of a good brown colour.

Chefs in restaurants prepare such an aspic from strong brown stock, the main secret of which lies in the clarifying. The stock after having boiled slowly for 3–4 hours must be clarified by adding to it egg-shells and egg-whites. These must boil in the stock for at least 15 minutes. The stock then becomes completely clear and is poured through a strainer and a cheese-cloth into a bowl. Add some brown but absolutely de-greased gravy to the stock, from which the aspic then gets its brown colour.

We can also give the stock a good dark colour by first roasting the meat and vegetables in the pan before pouring the water on it. When the water comes to the boil we shall see that it is a rich brown colour.

Skim off the scum and fat and then reduce the heat. If you wish to make an aspic, then you can use the following recipe. It is not very complicated.

Aspic. Simmer for about 15 minutes in 2 cups of water, 1 pinch of dried thyme, a small piece of mace, ½ a bay leaf, and 5 coarsely ground peppercorns with ¾ cup of soup vegetables. Towards the end of the 15 minutes add 2 tablespoons of white wine and 1 tablespoon of flavoured vinegar. Finally dilute two soup cubes in the liquid. Strain this liquid through a sieve, lined with a flannel-cloth (rinsed in water and wrung out).

Prepare a mixture with 1½ tablespoons of gelatine powder, dissolved in 2 tablespoons of port. This mixture is added to the strained liquid by stirring well with a wire whisk. Let it come to the boil again and then take off the stove and allow it to cool completely and lightly set. You may have noted that we have not added salt. As a matter of fact all soup cubes are salted, and we therefore should always be careful about adding salt when using cubes.

We now come to the use of the chicken, boiled or roasted the day before.

Roast Chicken. For this we use the home-made aspic described above to which is added for colouring some of the chicken gravy from which the fat has been skimmed. The chicken is skinned and boned and cut up in 6–8 equal pieces. These pieces are put on a serving dish, the bottom of which we have covered with crisp, well-dried lettuce leaves. We garnish the pieces of chicken with hard-boiled eggs, cut in halves, and slices of tomato. The slices must be solid and above all not watery. When our aspic begins to set we pour it upon the garnished chicken. If the aspic is the correct thickness it will not run, but will cover the pieces of chicken. Allow the dish to stand in a cool place for 4–5 hours to enable it to set properly.

Boiled Chicken. If we use boiled chicken meat for this aspic recipe we make the aspic with the skimmed chicken stock. We work in the same way as indicated earlier (p. 42), but using the chicken stock instead of water. We have to skim off the fat as otherwise it would not make a clear aspic, which would be a pity as a well-prepared aspic should be a transparent gold colour.

This poulet-froid should certainly delight your guests. You serve it with hot toast and butter, and if celebrating a special occasion a glass of white wine would not come amiss.

When serving this dish myself I put on the table little dishes filled with capers, stuffed olives, sweet-sour gherkins, onions, and pickles.

Now we must proceed and prepare a good French chicken soup.

Crème de Volaille (Cream of Chicken)

for 6 servings:

1 not too fat boiling fowl	½ cup thick cream
about 8 cups stock prepared the day before with some shin of beef or a veal knuckle and salt	1 egg-yolk
	4 full tablespoons flour or cornflour
	3 tablespoons butter
1 leek	½ cup milk
1 garnished onion (see p. 46)	
small bundle of celery and parsley stalks	

Our first task is to make the stock with the beef or veal and the leek, onion, celery, and parsley. This we must make the previous day. When the stock has become cold we must take off all the fat. This is easy with cold stock, for the fat has all 'set' on the surface and can be skimmed off with a kitchen spoon. We are now ready to proceed.

Let the stock come slowly to the boil again, strain it, and pour it on the chicken.

If the stock boils again we must thoroughly skim off the scum. The heat is lowered and the chicken simmered for 1½–2 hours. The cooking time depends on how long the boiling fowl will need to become tender without becoming overdone. The meat of a well-boiled fowl must stick to the bone in such a way that it can be easily cut off. It should not fall off the bones.

At least about 6 cups of stock are needed to cover one boiling fowl. You may well ask why we have to make a stock with meat if we also use chicken? The answer is that one boiling fowl cannot give us a strong enough stock. That is why we prepare the stock the day before, for by doing so we obtain a basic stock which will increase in flavour and strength by cooking our fowl in it the following day. Generally speaking, it is the chicken which gives us the thinnest and most colourless stock! Chicken stock can be prepared in a pressure cooker in about 35–40 minutes. The same applies for stock made with beef, veal knuckle, or only soup bones. A pressure cooker saves a lot of time.

But to continue. The stock is now ready, the chicken is thoroughly done, and the meat firm. We skin and bone the fowl, carving the breast only into fine slivers. These we put in a dish partly covered with a lid and let the meat cool.

The meat from the legs is chopped into very tiny pieces. Now we must prepare a white or Béchamel sauce.

Sauce Béchamel. Melt 2 tablespoons of butter in a pan. It should not turn to brown. To it we add the 3 tablespoons of flour and stir with a wire whisk. The mixture should become thick but not lumpy. Stirring well, we dilute with some scalded milk to which we have added just enough of the stock to obtain a smooth sauce. To this sauce we add the chopped chicken meat.

The chicken stock is then brought to the boil and the sauce is added to it. We stir well while the pan remains on the stove with the heat turned low. The chicken soup must come again to the boil, and only then must we add salt according to taste, pepper, and finally the white slivers of chicken meat. Allow 5 minutes for the meat to get hot. In the meantime beat smooth the egg-yolk with the thick cream. Take the pan from the stove and while stirring with a wire whisk very slowly add the egg-cream mixture to the chicken soup. We now have achieved this creamy, delicious French chicken soup. Ideally, it should not be thick but just lightly creamy. After having added the egg-yolk and cream this soup must not be allowed to come to the boil again. If it does it will curdle.

Next let us prepare an exquisite white chicken dish called

Poulet à la crème (Creamy Chicken)

for 4 servings we need:

1 tender roaster, divided into four, or 2 spring chickens, divided into halves	¼ cup stock
	1 liqueur glass brandy
	1 garnished onion
5 tablespoons butter	1½ tablespoons cornflour
at least ¼ cup cream	salt and pepper to taste

Let the butter melt in a large meat pan and become hot but not dark. It should be a deep golden colour. The best colour is that of an unpeeled peanut! The pieces of chicken are sautéed in the butter, and when they have become light brown we add the garnished onion. This is an onion to which is fastened by means of 2 cloves a piece of mace and a tiny bay leaf. When the onion has also become pale gold we add salt to taste. If, however, we intend later using salted stock or water with a meat cube we must be very sparing when salting the chicken in order to avoid overdoing it.

We now put the lid on the pan and reduce the heat. The chicken must simmer for about 30–40 minutes to become tender yet not overdone. Again, the meat must not be allowed to fall off the bones.

In the meantime we make in a little dish a smooth mixture of the stock or water with the meat cube and the cornflour. To this mixture we add the cream with or without a beaten egg-yolk. The more cream we use the smoother will be the dish.

We now take the pieces of chicken out of the pan and keep them warm on a plate. We also remove the onion. Stirring well, we add the flour-cream-water mixture to the chicken gravy. While stirring with a whisk we let this creamy sauce become very hot, but don't let it boil.

The result should be a creamy yet not thick sauce to which we add the brandy. Before serving we taste to see if there is enough salt and pepper in it. We pour part of this sauce upon the pieces of chicken, which are put in a hot shallow dish, and the rest of the sauce we serve in a sauce-boat.

With this chicken dish is served rice-pilaff, the recipe for which is on p. 48.

And here is the recipe for the chicken legs which we did not used in one of our hors d'oeuvre dishes. And we always can, if we prepare a chicken soup, keep the dark chicken meat for the day after.

Poulet-champignon à l'Estragon (Chicken-mushrooms with Tarragon Sauce)

for 2 servings:

2 left-over chicken legs (roasted or boiled)
¼ pound fresh mushrooms
3 tablespoons bacon, cut up in squares
½ coarsely chopped onion
1 tablespoon brandy

2-3 tablespoons coarsely chopped tarragon leaves
1½ teaspoons flour
1 tablespoon butter
2 tablespoons water or stock if you have some available

Brown the bacon in a sauté pan with the butter and add to this mixture the two chicken legs and the washed and well-dried mushrooms. Let both turn nicely brown as quickly as possible. Add salt to taste and the onion. By the time the onion is also browned the chicken legs and the mushrooms should be thoroughly hot. Now add the flour to the gravy and stir with a wooden spoon. Then pour in as much water or stock as is necessary to obtain a thickish sauce. This sauce should not become too thick or stodgy. The correct consistency is that of a lightly whipped cream.

Remove the pan from the stove and add the tablespoon of brandy with the chopped tarragon leaves. It is now ready, but before serving we must check to see if we have added enough salt. Some pepper can be shaken over it with advantage. Put the chicken-mushrooms into a hot shallow dish and cover with the creamy tarragon sauce. With this chicken recipe too the pilaff is an excellent accompaniment, and well-boiled, not too big potatoes are also good. If they are in season small potatoes are perfect. Do not cook the new potatoes too long. We cook new potatoes by covering them with boiling water and then allowing only 10 minutes' boiling time.

We serve this with finely chopped parsley.

Pilaff (Rice-dish)

for 4 servings we use:

1 cup rice	1 small finely chopped onion
3 tablespoons butter or oil	water

Let the butter or oil become hot, without burning, and sauté the onion till it is pale gold. It is essential that the colour of the onion should remain pale. We then add the uncooked rice, stirring it with a fork. Every grain of rice should turn a golden colour, and only then do we add cold water. The water must barely cover the rice—½ inch high. Putting the lid on the pan, we let the water come to the boil. Then we reduce the heat to a minimum, and even put an asbestos mat under the pan to ensure this. We must not remove the lid to look at the rice or attempt to stir it. Just put the kitchen-timer on, set for precisely 17 minutes, for this is the amount of time the rice needs to cook completely dry. Each grain should be separate from its neighbours. This, as a matter of fact, is the way rice is prepared in many foreign countries, particularly in France. I will give you later on another recipe for rice, given to me by a very helpful cook in New Delhi. At the end of 17 minutes you take the lid off the pan, otherwise the rice will become soggy, for a lot of steam will develop in the covered pan. If we cannot serve the rice at once we must cover the pan with a cloth folded in four, reduce the heat to the lowest point, and leave the pan on an asbestos mat. In this way the rice will keep warm and remain dry.

By sautéing the rice first the hot butter or oil makes each grain glossy and separate. Sticky rice does not taste so well and does not blend happily with a sauce.

Here is another chicken dish which has become rather famous.

Poulet Sauté Chasseur (Hunters' Chicken)

for 4 servings:

1 roaster, cut into six
8 peeled whole shallots
4 tablespoons white wine or
4 tablespoons stock or
water with a meat cube
1 tablespoon brandy or, if
you prefer, lemon juice,
according to taste
3 tablespoons tomato purée
or 1 pound fresh peeled
tomatoes

1¼ cup sliced mushrooms
(fresh or canned)
½ cup butter
1 garnished onion
1 pinch cayenne pepper
1 pinch thyme and marjoram
salt to taste

We melt the butter in a deep pan, letting it become dark brown, but it must not burn. In it we sauté the pieces of chicken with the whole shallots and the garnished onion. When they have all become a nice brown colour we add salt to taste, the peeled tomatoes, divided into parts (or the tomato purée), and all the spices with a pinch of cayenne pepper. All these ingredients we stir through the butter with a fork and then add the white wine or whatever else we have chosen as a liquid. We now put the lid on the pan and reduce the heat.

The chicken needs about 30–45 minutes to be well cooked. Of course, you will understand that it is always necessary to check to see that the meat is not going to be overdone. The time given for the cooking of the chicken depends very much on the age of the bird and, of course, also on the heat you allow for the 'stewing' in the closed pan.

When the chicken is tender all through and the meat still firm, take the pieces of chicken with the garnished onion out of the pan and keep them warm. The sauce must first cool off a little in order that we may skim off all the fat covering the surface of the sauce.

The de-greased sauce must be brought to the boil again in an open pan and allowed to reduce a little by evaporation. For this reducing process we must, of course, turn up the heat. When the sauce has reduced somewhat we must add the pieces of chicken with the mushrooms and the brandy. Both must become very hot. Taste the sauce to see if enough salt and pepper have been added and put the chicken in the sauce in a deep dish. With this chicken we serve boiled potatoes and cauliflower, green peas, butter beans, or any other vegetable that may be preferred.

Blanquette de Poulet (White Chicken Stew)

for 4 servings:

1 small lean boiling fowl or	4 peppercorns
1 roaster	1 egg
1 leek	the juice of 1 lemon
5 carrots	⅛ cup cream
1 bunch celery and parsley	2 tablespoons flour
stalks	4 tablespoons butter
1 bay leaf	salt to taste
2 cloves	

Divide the chicken in halves. Melt the butter in a pan and sauté the chicken in it, until it is pale gold. If you use a boiling fowl take care that, before sautéing, every piece of yellow fat has been removed.

To this sautéed chicken we add the leek, well washed beforehand and cut up into lengths; the cleaned carrots, cut in thin slices; the bay leaf with cloves; the bunch of herbs, and salt to taste. We now mix the flour through the butter and the vegetables.

Now pour about 1½ cups of cold water on the chicken, but it should scarcely be covered by it. Let it come to the boil, then put the lid on the pan and allow to simmer on a low heat—a roaster for about 30–40 minutes to be well done and a boiling fowl (if it is a young one) about 60–90 minutes.

When the meat is tender take it out of the pan with a strainer. We work the boiling liquid with all the garnish through a sieve or Chinese strainer. As the vegetables have in the meantime become tender they can easily be worked through the sieve. The strained vegetables will thicken the sauce and flavour it. The sauce must now boil for about 5–8 minutes in an open pan in order to reduce it a little. Stir occasionally.

Now dilute the egg with the cream, take the pan from the stove, and, with a wire whisk, add the egg-and-cream mixture to the sauce, which is now off the boil, being careful not to let the egg turn as this would sadly spoil the appearance of the dish.

Taste to see whether the somewhat creamy sauce has enough salt. If you care for it add freshly ground pepper and a dash of Worcester Sauce.

Now put the two halves of the chicken back in the sauce to let them get warm again. This chicken is served as follows:

Having at the same time cooked some dry rice, we put this into a deep and pre-warmed dish. On it we put the pieces of chicken and pour a little of the sauce over it. The rest of this sauce is served in a sauce-boat.

Mushrooms are also excellent in this chicken dish. If you do not add pepper or Worcester Sauce or cream, this recipe is especially to be recommended for persons with stomach complaints or weak digestions. Children usually like it very much.

I could, of course, give you many more chicken recipes from France but we must continue our tour, and our next stop is Belgium.

BELGIUM

I THINK you will agree that, even when described in a very concise way, the gastronomic highlights of the Belgian cuisine are fascinating. One of these is the manner in which most Belgian housewives prepare their own mayonnaise. They very seldom use bought mayonnaise.

Another thing worth considering and imitating is the perfect manner in which they prepare French-fried potatoes, and by no means least are the delicious 'green' herbs in which they serve the meat, fish, and chicken specialities.

These green-coloured dishes, believe me, are delicious.

Let us start by preparing a very simple yet authentically Belgian chicken salad.

Salade de Poulet Wavre (Chicken Salad)

for 5–6 servings:

1 small boiling fowl	1 pinch pepper
2 onions	salt to taste
2 carrots	1 bunch green herbs
1 leek	(parsley and celery stalks)
1 bay leaf	4 cups water
1 tiny piece mace	

Cut off all the yellow fat and put the fowl in a pan, cover it with water, and let it come to the boil. Now add all the other ingredients. The onions and the carrots are cut into not too small pieces; the white as well as the green of the leek is divided into thin, long strips; the spices with salt are added to taste and, of course, the bunch of green herbs. When the water boils put the lid on the pan and reduce the heat. The chicken needs about 1½ hours to be well done. In a pressure-cooker this time is naturally much shorter, and we should allow about 30–40 minutes for the same boiling fowl.

When the chicken is tender but not overdone—the meat must remain firm—we take it out of the stock with a skimmer. When the fowl has cooled off sufficiently we should then skin and bone it. Do this so carefully that the chicken can easily be divided into 10 whole pieces of good firm meat.

These 10 pieces we now put into a marinade, prepared as follows:

Marinade

3 tablespoons wine vinegar or lemon juice	1 pinch pepper
½ cup oil	some salt
1 tablespoon not too strong mustard	a great quantity of chopped green herbs, among which tarragon is most important

Each piece of chicken must be turned over in the marinade and left for about 1 hour in a covered pot. In the meantime we must prepare more than about ½ cup of mayonnaise. You have already thoroughly washed a crisp yellow heart of a lettuce. Be careful not to break its leaves and put them whole into a wire salad basket so that they can drip. When dry cut this yellow lettuce heart *en julienne* (fine strips) and garnish the bottom of a glass bowl with them. A wooden or china bowl will do as well, but glass makes the dish look more attractive.

Spread a layer of mayonnaise over the lettuce, and on it you now put the pieces of chicken from the marinade. Place them in the shape of a pyramid on the mayonnaise and cover this pyramid with a further layer of mayonnaise.

This chicken salad should be garnished as follows:

Cut slices of hard-boiled egg and put them, with slices of well-washed unpeeled tomato, in a circle around the chicken pyramid. Garnish the slices of egg with de-salted, rolled-up anchovy fillets. To de-salt the anchovies we put them in milk for about an hour before using. You will certainly be complimented on this salad.

If, instead of an hors d'oeuvre, you want to use this dish as a main course you should serve with new potatoes, boiled and garnished with chopped parsley or French-fried. This combination of cold chicken and hot potatoes is a very happy one, as you can experience for yourself.

The chicken stock which was left over we can use to prepare a good chicken soup, in combination with the contents of a packet or a can of soup. We can also mix the stock with a sauce made with flour, some butter, and milk. It gives us a creamy soup which is even more tasty with some canned asparagus added.

We now come to the recipe for mayonnaise.

Mayonaise à la Minute (Instant Mayonnaise)

for 4–6 servings:

about 1½ cups oil
1 raw large egg-yolk
2 teaspoons mustard
1 pinch freshly ground
  pepper

some dashes vinegar,
  preferably wine vinegar
the same quantity of water

Put the raw egg-yolk in a soup-plate and blend with the mustard, the pepper, and salt to taste. Use a small whisk or fork for this. Let the oil run drop by drop in this egg-mustard mixture while beating thoroughly with the whisk or fork. Oil trickles best out of the bottle if you first cut a lengthwise nick in the cork and then put it back on the bottle. The oil will then come out drop by drop. Only in this way will you succeed in making a firm yet creamy mayonnaise. If the oil is poured in too quickly your mayonnaise will never thicken properly.

If at the beginning of the operation the egg-mayonnaise blend becomes too thick you can dilute with a few drops of water. Afterwards the oil can be allowed to run more quickly into this mixture. When you have enough mayonnaise you should add some more water and vinegar to taste. This will make the mayonnaise smoother. Moreover, by adding water to the vinegar the mayonnaise will not curdle.

When you have finally prepared this mayonnaise you taste to see if

(1) it is flavoured enough or whether it needs more mustard, vinegar, or lemon juice;

(2) there is enough salt and pepper in it.

Almost every day in a Belgian family the housewife prepares a small quantity of mayonnaise, for every kind of salad is dressed with it. She uses an ordinary soup-plate and a fork, for to her it is only a question of a few minutes' work. She always uses one egg-yolk for enough mayonnaise to dress a salad for 4–5 persons. I believe that the mayonnaise they serve in Belgian homes looks and tastes so good because a very small quantity is made every day and because the housewife knows precisely how to make it.

How then do we prepare a good mayonnaise?

(1) We need one big egg-yolk for less than 2 cups of mayonnaise.

(2) The oil must not be too cold. Room temperature is required.

(3) At the beginning the oil must fall drop by drop on the egg-mustard blend.

(4) Take care that the egg, vinegar, or lemon juice and also the water have the same room temperature.

If we keep these four points in mind we are sure to make a perfect mayonnaise. We add water in order that the mayonnaise should keep the proper consistency and not curdle.

Variations on the basic mayonnaise (each using about 1½ cups of oil):

Mayonaise Verte (Green Mayonnaise). Take a handful of spinach leaves, wash, chop coarsely, and then bring to the boil with the adhering water for about 4 minutes. Put the spinach with the water into a strainer. This green and rather dry spinach pulp is worked through the mayonnaise, which acquires a fascinating green colour.

Mayonaise Aurore (Red Mayonnaise). Blend the mayonnaise with 1–1½ tablespoons of tomato ketchup or 1½ teaspoons of tomato purée.

Mayonaise Mousseline (Cream Mayonnaise). Blend the mayonnaise with the stiffly whipped white of an egg and 1 tablespoon of thick cream.

Mayonaise Collée (Sticky Mayonnaise). Blend a little more than ¼ cup of warm meat gravy, without any fat on it, with 1 tablespoon of gelatine powder. Work this mixture through the mayonnaise and leave 3–4 hours in a cool place to get a little but not completely set. This mayonnaise is excellent as a cover for cold chicken salads when served as hors d'oeuvre. We pour this mayonnaise over the salad while still runny. It will then set completely as a thick, creamy yellow coating.

Another typical Belgian recipe follows. It is a national dish named

Pommes Frites (Belgian-fried Potatoes)

For this dish—the same as the well-known French-fried—we use good-quality white potatoes which are not too small in size. Moreover, they should not vary too much in size. Peel the potatoes and cut them up in equal slices. They should not be too long, too thick, or too big. As a matter of fact, the size of a normal ring-finger is about right.

All the slices are wrapped up in a dry cloth so as to keep them completely dry. The best plan is to pre-fry them for the first time in the morning for the evening meal. For this you use a big, heavy iron deep-frying pan, well filled with a good-quality oil or vegetable fat. The choice is yours. I advise using olive oil, which is very good for deep-frying. It is one of the oils which does not absorb the flavour or odour of the food cooked in it. If you fry fish in olive oil and immediately afterwards fry meat or potatoes, you can do this without any risk of their tasting of fish. Moreover, olive oil does not cause any disagreeable oil smell in your kitchen.

Another important general point in using oil is that it stands a high degree of heat without any risk of burning. On the other hand, fat is apt to burn easily and must be clarified more often than oil. To do this you must drain it through a cheese-cloth to get it clear again and to get rid of any sediment.

Last but not least, fat has to be renewed more often than oil and is, therefore, more costly in the long run.

Place the deep-frying pan on the gas or electric stove and heat the oil or the fat until it becomes hot, but not so hot that a bluish smoke rises from it. In this first frying we give the potatoes only sufficient time to cook through. This takes about 5 minutes. This first frying should not brown them; the correct colour is yellow, and about 325° Fahrenheit is the right heat.

We must have enough oil in the pan to fry a good quantity of potatoes at one time. If we have too little oil to deal with the amount of potatoes to be cooked the result can be very disagreeable. The moisture which comes out of the potatoes when they are in contact with the warm oil will make the oil rise in the pan and overflow. A very disagreeable experience indeed!

When the slices are done—we try one to see—we take them out with a skimmer or the wire basket which goes with the deep-frying pan. In the wire basket they can cool and drip satisfactorily.

In the evening, just before serving the French-fried potatoes, we again heat the oil in the pan. The temperature must now be raised to about 450° Fahrenheit. Only when the oil has reached this temperature do we put the pre-fried slices of potato in it. We can now put larger quantities in the oil than the first time. The potatoes are completely dry, so there is no danger now of the oil coming out of the pan.

Allow a few minutes to turn brown. Take them out and serve immediately.

Pommes Frites à ma Manière (French-fried Potatoes My Way)

for 3 servings:

1 deep-frying pan with wire basket, about 17 inches	2 pounds potatoes, cut into squares, not slices
3 pounds vegetable fat	

Heat the fat to 300° Fahrenheit, and put the squares of potato into the wire basket. Place the wire basket in the fat and leave the gas high on. In precisely 10 minutes the potatoes will be ready and well done. They should be a nice light brown in colour but not dark brown.

If all the squares are put into the fat at once they will cool it off immediately. The fat needs some more time to become hot again, and while this process goes on the potatoes have the opportunity to get slowly but surely cooked. In the meantime the water in the potatoes evaporates gradually. Towards the end of the 10 minutes the dried and cooked potatoes brown automatically and are ready to serve. This is, of course, a much easier way of bringing nice French-fried potatoes to your table. This method cannot, however, be used for potatoes cut up in slices. They would be cooked too quickly without having the opportunity to turn brown. Besides this way of frying potato squares is only to be recommended when making them for a few people. If preparing a large quantity of fried we need to pre-fry as explained earlier.

We will now prepare the

Poulet au 'Vert' (Green Chicken)

for 4 servings:

1 roaster	½ cup stock or a soup cube
about 8 tablespoons chopped,	dissolved in water
fresh green herbs, such as	¼ pound mushrooms
chervil, celery leaves,	1 pinch thyme
parsley leaves, chives, and	1 pinch pepper
lovage	salt to taste
1 egg-yolk	6 tablespoons butter
2 tablespoons thick cream	

Blend the chopped herbs with the well-washed and chopped mushrooms, the thyme, the pepper, and a pinch of salt. Put these ingredients into a dish and pour over them the ½ cup of stock or water with the cube. If you use a cube you had better be careful with the salt. Let the butter brown well in a meat pan and then sauté in it the chicken, which you have previously divided into four pieces. Brown well on all sides, turning the pieces with a fork. When they are a good brown colour you should add salt to taste. But don't add too much salt, for the blend of herbs and flavours which you now add are already salted. Bring to the boil again, reduce the heat, and put the lid on the pan. If a big bird has been used let it simmer for about ½–¾ of an hour in order to have the pieces of chicken nicely done. With a small bird only about 30 minutes is required.

Check to see if the meat is tender and comes off the bones easily and then remove it from the richly flavoured sauce. Keep the lid off the pan and turn the heat up. The sauce should now reduce a little. It must not be watery but rather thickened by the green herbs. Taste again to see that there is enough salt in it and then take the pan off the stove. Blend the egg-yolk with the cream and with a whisk slowly add the mixture to the sauce. Leave the pan to stand a few minutes on a very low heat on an asbestos mat in order to have the sauce thicken but not burn. Put the pieces of chicken again in the sauce to warm up.

Serve the chicken in a warm deep dish and pour the creamy sauce over it. Creamed potatoes, with quickly roasted tomatoes, first cut into halves, scooped out, and filled with green peas, go wonderfully with this dish.

For my last Belgian recipe I recommend

Waterzooi (Concentrated Chicken Soup)

for 6 servings:

2 tender, not too big roasters, each of which is divided into 4 parts

5 cups stock made with the giblets, 1½ pounds shin of beef, cut up into rather large squares, 3 thick slices white bread, 1 bunch parsley and celery stalks

1 celeriac
2 garnished onions
6 peppercorns
salt to taste

The day before we need this dish, prepare the stock with the cups of water and all the ingredients with the exception of the celeriac and the two roasters. Let it boil slowly for about 1½–2 hours. It must become a well-flavoured stock. We must watch to see that the water boils very slowly.

On the day this dish is served we start by skimming off the cold stock. All the fat lies on the surface and is easy to take off.

Let the stock then come to the boil and drain through a sieve. From the boiled ingredients we take out all the giblets, which we then bone, and the green herbs and onion. Next we add the meat obtained from the giblets to the ingredients in the sieve and work them through the sieve. This 'fine mash,' well thickened by the bread, is added to the drained stock.

We have already peeled and washed the celeriac. It must be twice washed, once before peeling and again after peeling, and then cut into small squares. The stock is put back on the stove, and now we can add the celeriac squares with the two roasters, each divided in four, and salt to taste. Let this come to the boil, reduce the heat, and allow about 20–30 minutes for the cooking. The waterzooi is now ready. We taste to see if it is well salted and add some freshly ground pepper.

Serve the waterzooi in soup-plates. Believe me, after this rich and delicious meal all that is needed is a good cup of coffee.

I regret that we must now leave Belgium and come along with Gallina to see what Holland has in store for us.

HOLLAND

WE have now arrived in my own country, and if I am to give you Dutch chicken recipes we must go back to the years before the Second World War. In those days our ways with chicken were simple. The Dutch housewife if she ate chicken—it then ranked with the more expensive meals—was happy with just a plain roast chicken (and she loved a spring chicken) or a sober yet well-prepared clear or creamy chicken soup. The French way of preparing a chicken was not yet accepted by the Dutch housewife, and only in the more expensive restaurants were French dishes available. The Second World War was to change many things, and in the years that followed our country became quite a tourist centre. What was even more important to us was that the numerous re-established Dutch travel bureaux organized holidays to many different countries at prices acceptable to all classes of the population. In this way our people became familiar with the customs of other countries and learned about international cookery.

It was not long before the restaurants and hotels in Holland found that they had to live up to the cooking standards of other countries, and Dutch housewives, who had enjoyed many specialities while on holiday abroad, soon tried their hand at cooking in a modern and sophisticated way.

The chicken dish soon became popular and was served more often than before the war. Now chicken is no longer considered an extravagant, expensive meal. On our tour through Holland, therefore, I shall describe for you some of the original Dutch recipes as well as other more international ways of cooking in Holland.

There are some rather exotic recipes among these, but they are only really good imitations. You will find the original recipes given in the countries where they were first cooked. There are also recipes which will remind you of Italy or Spain, but they have always been adapted to the Dutch taste. I am also giving you some Indonesian recipes, adapted for European kitchens.

Here is a very original Dutch chicken dish which I discovered in a very old Dutch cookery book, *Aaltje-Alie, The Economical Cook*. This recipe is for the housewife who has to work on a tight budget and yet who wants to give her family a treat.

Kippesoep Aaltje-Alie (Chicken Soup)

for 4 servings:

1½ pounds boned chicken divided into pieces	celery and parsley stalks
	salt to taste
4 cups water	1 egg
1½ tablespoons rice	1 tablespoon water
1 meat cube	2 tablespoons flour

Put the chicken meat into the water, let it come to the boil, and then turn down the heat and simmer for about 30 minutes. Meanwhile wash the celery and parsley and chop off the small stalks and the leaves and put them to one side. The remaining stalks, tied in a bunch, are added to the chicken in the stock.

When the chicken meat is tender we remove it with the herbs from the stock. First we skim off the fat, then we add the rice with the meat cube. Allow to come to the boil again and the rice should be cooked in 20 minutes. Add salt and pepper to taste. Beat the egg with the flour and water to a smooth cream, using a whisk. Add this mixture to the hot chicken soup, which must not be allowed to boil any more. Finally add the boned and skinned chicken meat. Let it become warm and remove the pan from the stove. We now add the chopped celery and parsley leaves and serve the soup.

The following is a good chicken soup and very easy to prepare.

Gebonden Hollandse Kippesoep (Creamy Dutch Chicken Soup)

for 5–6 servings:

1 boiling fowl, not too fat	1 pinch basil
8 cups water	salt to taste
3 carrots	3 tablespoons butter
1 leek	4 tablespoons flour
1 bundle green stalks	1 egg
½ cup vermicelli	¼ cup cream or condensed
1 tiny piece of mace	milk
1 pinch thyme	

Having removed the yellow fat, put the chicken in a stew-pan and add the washed vegetables, coarsely cut up, to the water with salt to taste. Bring to the boil, put the lid on the pan, and let the contents simmer on a low heat. Allow about 2 hours for the chicken to become tender. Take out the chicken, cut off the breast and bone it. Prepare in a little saucepan a smooth mixture of the butter (you had previously put it near the heat so it has become soft) and the flour, adding a little of the hot chicken stock. Let it stand for a while.

After you have skimmed off the fat put the stock with the vegetables on the stove again and add the vermicelli. On a moderate heat the vermicelli will be soft in about 15 minutes. (If you prefer rice you can add it to the stock instead of the vermicelli. Rice must boil 20 minutes.)

For this chicken soup we use only the meat of the breast, and this we cut up *en julienne* (fine strips). We first wait for the vermicelli or the rice to be done; then with a wire whisk we mix the butter-flour blend into the soup. We let the soup come to the boil again, then turn off the heat immediately and add the white chicken strips.

We taste to see if there is enough salt in it and add some freshly ground pepper. Finally we add the chopped leaves we had taken off the parsley and celery stalks. Using the soup tureen in which the soup is to be served, we beat in the egg with the cream, and upon it we pour the chicken soup while still beating with the whisk.

Serve immediately.

The chicken legs are left for another day, and you will find on p. 47 a recipe designed for the purpose but only for two persons.

You can also use these two chicken legs for the Ajam Roedjak on p. 73 but then, of course, you must use only half of all the ingredients mentioned in this recipe.

Gebraden Kip Holland (Dutch Roasted Chicken)

for 4 servings:

1 big cockerel
⅓ cup butter
pepper and salt to taste

Rub the inside of the cockerel with a little salt and add to it about 2 tablespoons of butter. Let the rest of the butter brown in a stew-pot. Stir in the butter with a fork so that it will brown smoothly.

The roaster should brown on all sides in the butter. To achieve this we turn the bird several times until it is brown all over. Only then do we sprinkle salt to taste on it, add some tablespoons of water to the butter, put the lid aslant on the pan, and reduce the heat. But the chicken must continue roasting and the butter remain very hot. We can also roast the chicken on the stove if we use a partly covered pan from which the steam can escape. Once in a while we turn the chicken over to see that the gravy does not get too dark and is not in danger of burning. You may have to add a few tablespoons of water now and again to the gravy. To get a chicken nicely roasted we should allow about 1 hour for a very big roaster. In the oven this roasting process needs only about 30–40 minutes. The oven gives us a more regular heat, and I prefer to roast chicken and meat this way. However, if the gravy reduces too quickly and burns to a dark-brown sticky mass we should add some water. In order to prevent such a thing happening we must baste the chicken very regularly and add a tablespoon water or stock. Sometimes more butter can be used to advantage.

In America they wrap up the chicken in a piece of foil once it has become brown. This is a very convenient way of roasting —but can we call it roasting? A disadvantage is that during the process the chicken loses its brown colour. I work with foil only when I am in a hurry and have no time to control the oven as I should. Fifteen minutes before serving the chicken I remove the foil, turn the heat very high, and let the chicken brown by spreading some butter on it.

But to return to our pot-roast chicken. The chicken is tender and done, and we put it whole on a serving dish. The legs are garnished with a paper frill. Skim off part of the fat from the meat juices in the pan and add some boiling water. Serve in a gravy-boat.

In Holland we usually serve with roast chicken a compote of fruit, either freshly prepared or canned. (I prefer a fresh compote or apple sauce.) And, of course, boiled potatoes topped with chopped parsley. Green peas or asparagus also are often served with roast chicken.

Kip met Rijstrand (Chicken in a Rice Border)

for 6 servings:

2 small cockerels
¼ pound coarsely cut-up
   soup vegetables (carrots,
   leek, celeriac, and others)
1 garnished onion
salt to taste
piece of mace

1 pinch marjoram
1 pinch dill
the juice of ½ a lemon or
   1 tablespoon tomato
   ketchup
2 cups rice
about 4 cups water

FOR THE SAUCE
4 tablespoons butter
3 tablespoons flour
1½ cups stock

Divide each roaster in halves and put these in a pan. Pour the cups of water over them, add salt to taste and all other ingredients, with the exception of the rice and the lemon juice (or tomato ketchup). Let the water boil, then reduce the heat and allow about 20 minutes for the chicken to be well cooked. See whether the meat is tender, but not so tender that it will fall off the bones. Strain through a sieve and put the stock on one side. When cool skim off all the fat.

Dutch Rice. The rice is cooked in about 2 cups of the stock. But we only pour enough stock upon the dry (not washed) rice just to cover it. Let the stock boil, reduce the heat to a minimum, and put an asbestos mat under the covered pan. Allow precisely 17 minutes for the rice to be cooked and dry. Salt need not be added as the stock has already been salted to taste. When the rice is cooked we take off the lid and cover the pan with a folded cloth. Now the steam which is apt to develop can escape and the rice will remain dry and not become soggy.

While the rice is cooking we skin the chicken-halves and prepare the sauce.

Melting the 4 tablespoons of butter in a saucepan, we add the flour and stir in order to obtain a smooth paste. We dilute this paste with as much chicken stock as is required to make a smooth sauce. It should have the consistency of thick cream. We can now add to this sauce the lemon juice or the tomato ketchup, or both if preferred.

To serve this dish we put the well-boiled dry rice in a savarin mould which has been greased beforehand, pressing rather hard on it. Then we turn this mould into a warm dish. The centre of the rice ring is filled with the chicken, which in the meantime we have divided into smaller pieces. Part of the creamy sauce is poured over the chicken. What is left we serve separately in a sauce-boat. And if we care for some variety in our dishes we can add to the sauce in the sauce-boat two tablespoons of thick cream. We have now prepared a not too thick sauce covering the chicken ragout and a very creamy sauce in the sauce-boat.

Three ounces of mushrooms, cut up in slices and cooked in the sauce, will add a particularly subtle flavour to this dish, and a glass of white Alsatian wine or Rhine wine will go down very well with it.

Now here is a recipe to prove to you that in Holland we prepare a chicken dish under the influence of that international gastronomy of which nowadays we hear so much.

Kip Oriental (Oriental Chicken)

for 4 servings:

1 big roaster, divided in four
4 tablespoons butter
the contents of 1 small can
   of pineapple
1 tablespoon curry powder
   (this according to taste)
1 pinch basil
1 pinch crushed cardamom
   seeds

garnished onion
some tablespoons of
   pineapple juice or stock
½ tablespoon Worcester
Sauce
2 tablespoons chopped
   parsley, chervil, and/or
   celery

Melt the butter in a casserole and let it get a good brown colour. Stir once in a while with your fork in order that it may brown uniformly. Then we sauté the pieces of chicken, which have been lightly floured, in the brown butter. When brown we add salt to taste with the garnished onion, the curry powder, the basil, and the crushed cardamom seeds. All these ingredients should also become pale brown. Then we add 2–3 tablespoons of pineapple juice or stock. If you like a sweet-relished pineapple flavour you use the juice, but if you prefer a more European flavour then use the stock. This is entirely a matter of taste.

The slices of pineapple are put in a sieve to drip. The chicken sauté must come to the boil; then we reduce the heat and put the lid on the pan. This sauté should simmer gently for about 35–40 minutes. If the roaster was tender this is enough time for the meat to become well cooked. For this dish the meat is supposed to come off the bones very easily. As a matter of fact, you should be able to eat it with a spoon and fork instead of a knife and fork.

When the 35 minutes have gone by we take the lid off the pan and see whether the chicken is done. If it is we remove the pieces from the sauce and keep them warm. We increase the heat, and in the uncovered pan we reduce the sauce a little. It should not be too liquid, and that is why we let it evaporate.

Do not forget that the flour in which the pieces of chicken were rolled will thicken this sauce, but that the steam from stewing in a closed pan will have thinned the sauce, which must therefore be reduced.

We have also taken out the onion. To this thickened sauce we add the slices of pineapple. Allow two slices per person. Turn the heat low and taste to see if the sauce has enough salt. Add some freshly ground pepper and let the slices of pineapple get thoroughly hot. Put the pieces of chicken back in the sauce to make sure that you serve them very hot, allowing 2–3 minutes for this operation. Have a warm deep dish ready into which to put the sautéed chicken with the slices of pineapple. Remove the pan from the stove and add the Worcester Sauce with the chopped fresh herbs. If you add 1 tablespoon of yoghurt it not only makes the sauce smooth and more creamy, but gives the dish an authentic Oriental flavour. Cover the chicken and pineapple slices with some of the sauce. The rest you serve in a sauce-boat.

With this dish we eat cooked rice or spaghetti. The rice which goes especially well with this chicken dish is prepared as follows:

Exotische Rijst (Exotic Rice)

for 4 servings:

a little more than 1 cup rice	*1 finely chopped onion*
1 thick slice cooked ham	*1 teaspoon turmeric to give*
(about ¼ pound)	*the rice a yellow colour*
3 tablespoons oil	*1 pinch pepper*

Cook diced ham in the very hot oil. When the ham turns a golden colour add the chopped onion with the turmeric and the rice. Stir with a fork in order that every grain of rice becomes golden but not brown—pale gold, that is the required colour. When we have obtained this we pour cold water on it, using just enough to cover the rice with ½ inch.

Let the water come to the boil; then reduce the heat to its lowest point, putting the lid on the pan and an asbestos mat under it. Allow precisely 17 minutes for the rice to get well boiled and dry. At the end of 17 minutes take off the lid immediately and cover the pan with a folded cloth in order to keep each grain dry and separate.

We always serve boiled rice in a pre-warmed deep dish.

Ajam Oppor Bali (Indonesian Chicken Dish)

for 6 servings:

1 big, lean boiling fowl (we have cut out all the yellow fat before preparing it)
¼ pound grated coconut
1 cup milk in which we soak the coconut overnight
6 tablespoons peanut butter, diluted in ¼ cup of water
1 pinch grated nutmeg

1 crushed clove of garlic
1 finely chopped onion
1 pinch ginger-powder or 4 crushed cardamom seeds
1 crushed small bay leaf
salt to taste
5 tablespoons butter or vegetable margarine
1 cucumber

Pass the milk plus coconut through a cheese-cloth, and then bring the thickened milk to the boil. Add the water in which the peanut butter is diluted with the other ingredients listed, including the butter, but with the exception of the chicken and the cucumber.

You have previously divided the chicken into about 6–8 parts, and when the coconut-water-milk mixture has come to the boil you put the chicken parts into it. Let this boil again, then put the lid on the pan, lower the heat, and allow this Ajam Oppor chicken dish 1½ hours at least to get well done and extremely tender. Of course, you watch to see if there is enough sauce in the pan to let the chicken simmer slowly. If the liquid is very concentrated you can add some water, milk, or lemon juice, according to taste.

When 1½ hours have passed ascertain whether the chicken meat has become very tender. If it has, then taste to see if there is enough salt in the sauce and add some pepper. Serve the chicken and sauce in a deep dish, preferably a glass fire-proof dish. With it goes plain boiled rice. Cook this rice as indicated for the Dutch rice (p. 69). Peel the cucumber if it is an old one; if it is young and fresh then wash it well and do not peel. Divide lengthways and take out the seeds, if there are any. (Only old cucumbers show these seeds.) The two halves are divided once again lengthways and cut into fingers. Place in a bowl and serve without any dressing. Dip the crisp fingers of cucumber in the sauce. With this Indonesian dish it is customary to serve little saucers of freshly roasted peanuts, some mango chutney, Chinese soy sauce, and Worcester Sauce, as well as tiny jars of Indonesian 'sambals.' Sambal is prepared commercially from very hot ground chilies blended with oil, garlic, and different spices. It is red and has a very distinct flavour.

I usually serve sautéed bananas with this chicken dish. Peel the bananas, cut them lengthways, and sauté them in hot butter, then pour some lemon juice on them. You will certainly like it. Allow one banana for each person.

The Indonesian way of serving chicken with rice is always greatly appreciated. This is due to the fact that the chicken is accompanied by so many side-dishes. Here I have given only a very few examples.

Another Indonesian chicken dish is

Ajam Roedjak

for 4 servings:

1 tender roaster
½ tablespoon sugar
1 pinch salt
2 teaspoons paprika powder
2–3 chopped shallots
1 crushed clove of garlic
2 tablespoons soy sauce
1 piece ginger root (½ inch length)

½ tablespoon dried tamarind
½ cup butter or vegetable margarine
1½ tablespoons boemboe roedjak, an Indonesian ready-made spice to be replaced by curry paste
¼ cup condensed unsweetened milk

Skin the roaster and cut up in small pieces. A pair of kitchen scissors is useful for this. Peel the piece of ginger root and put in boiling water for 5 minutes. Cover and let stand. Do the same with the tamarind, which need not be peeled, only soaked in some water. Drain ginger root and tamarind. Chop. Have a stewing-pan ready and in it brown the butter or margarine. Lightly brown the boemboe roedjak in the butter, and then add the pieces of chicken with the sugar, salt to taste, and the paprika powder. The pieces of chicken should also turn light brown, and only then add all the other ingredients except the condensed milk. Stir with a wooden spoon; then put the lid on the pan and reduce the heat.

The chicken should stew very slowly and become very tender. The sauce should not reduce too much, but if it does than add some tablespoons of the condensed milk from time to time. We allow 45 minutes' cooking-time.

This Ajam Roedjak is served with its sauce in a deep warm dish. Dry cooked rice and again, as in the previous recipe, fingers of raw cucumber are served with it. We also put on the table the chili sauce, the soy sauce, and Worcester Sauce.

Slices of lemon and pickles add a special flavour to this recipe. In Holland we drink beer with it.

And here is a recipe for chicken livers, given to me by the chef of a restaurant in 's-Graveland, a wonderful riverside place in Holland.

Kippelevers (Chicken Livers)

for 2 servings:

½ pound chicken livers, well washed in lots of cold water. We remove from each liver the impurities such as fibres and little yellow spots

4 tablespoons butter

¼ cup cream

1 pinch dried thyme

2 teaspoons dried tarragon or 2 tablespoons fresh coarsely chopped tarragon

1 tablespoon tomato ketchup

salt to taste

¼ teaspoon paprika powder

The butter should become dark brown in the saucepan, and in it we sauté the whole chicken livers. Stir with a fork in order to brown the livers on all sides equally. Add salt, the thyme, and the paprika powder to taste. The livers should be done in about 10–15 minutes. Then the tarragon water is poured upon them. For this 'tarragon water' we soak the fresh, coarsely chopped tarragon leaves or the dried tarragon in just enough water to cover. Strain in a sieve with muslin cloth in it.

When the livers with the tarragon water have come to the boil again, reduce the heat, and add the tomato ketchup with the cream. Allow just a few more minutes and then taste to see if it is well salted. Serve with rice or spaghetti, both accompanied by a bowl filled with a compote of cranberries or blueberries.

Spaghetti Koken (How to cook Spaghetti)

for 2 servings:

½ pound spaghetti
about 6 cups water
1 tablespoon salt

Bring the water to the boil in a large pan and put in the unbroken spaghetti. In the boiling water it will become soft and fall back into the water by itself. Keep the water boiling and allow exactly 10 minutes for the spaghetti to cook. Drain then in a colander and let cold water run over it. This will make it firm again. Toss the spaghetti in hot butter before serving, but do not allow to brown!

When serving add grated Gruyère or other suitable cheese, shaking the pan. With it we drink a glass of Chianti.

Kip op mijn Manier (Chicken My Way)

for 4 servings:

1 *big roaster*	*about 2 tablespoons port*
1 *small can peaches*	*6 tablespoons butter*
2 *bananas*	*2 tablespoons stock or water*
½ *cup cream*	*salt to taste*
1½ *tablespoons cornflour*	*1 pinch freshly ground pepper*

The roaster is divided in 4 equal parts. After sautéing the chicken in browned butter—now and then turning the pieces—we add salt to taste, with the port and the stock or water. Let this come to the boil and put the lid aslant on the pan, so as not to have too much steam, which would add too much liquid to this dish. Reduce the heat and let the chicken simmer slowly in the sauce. In 30 minutes the chicken should be done.

Only if the sauce reduces too much during the simmering process do we add more stock or water.

Remove the pieces of chicken—if well done—from the pan and take the pan from the stove. Make a smooth mixture with the cornflour and the cream and blend with the chicken juices. Now return the pan to the stove on a low heat. Place an asbestos mat under the pan and allow the sauce to thicken. We have in the meantime added the chicken to the sauce in order that it may become quite hot.

Heat 2 tablespoons of oil in a saucepan. Sauté the halved bananas in this for a few minutes. Turn the heat right down and add well-drained peaches.

Before serving the chicken check that there is enough salt and add the pepper. Those who care for a very delicate flavour now add some more port. Put the pieces of chicken in a warm dish and decorate with the peaches and the bananas. Part of the sauce is poured upon the chicken, the rest goes into a sauce-boat. We can serve rice with it, or boiled potatoes with green peas or French beans. If new potatoes are served—the small kind—we cook them in as little boiling water as possible and in as short a time as possible. When ready sprinkle generously with chopped parsley.

I always serve celery, fresh or canned, with this dish. If fresh, it should be boiled, then drained and butter added before serving. Canned celery I warm up in butter.

When rice is served, stir either fresh or canned peas into the cooked rice. Stir in the peas with a fork in order not to make a mash of the rice, and add lots of chopped parsley, chive, or celery leaves, and a generous lump of butter.

Now let us go with Gallina to Italy.

ITALY

ANYONE loving sunshine, art, and an abundance of flowers and trees, to say nothing of a very tasty cuisine, will inevitably go to Italy. While the mind will be enriched by the country's innumerable art treasures, the gourmet's palate too will appreciate the masterpieces of Italian cookery.

Perhaps it is because of the sunshine and the warm climate that the ingredients of Italian dishes, especially the fruit and the vegetables, look so colourful and are so rich and full in flavour.

Tasty, well-prepared dishes are served both in the luxury restaurants and in the humblest trattorias. They might resemble one another too much at times, but then we should not forget that all Italians are great eaters of farinaceous foods (spaghettis, noodles, tagliatelli, canelloni, and others), with or without seafoods, meat, or chicken.

Their way of preparing fish is skilful indeed, especially when they grill it on a bed of fennel herbs, while their deep-fried seafood dishes are equally delicious. The chicken also plays a leading part in an Italian menu. When prepared with fresh herbs and spices the result is an exquisitely aromatic chicken dish.

A chicken prepared with fresh green peas and tomatoes is among the surprises a gourmet can encounter in Italy.

Many Italian men and women are born cooks and are particularly clever at blending herbs and spices. Never in my life have I enjoyed such perfectly grilled chicken as at Capri. One of these grills, called the 'Pollo alla Diavolo,' will be described in this chapter, but since the Italians also use the chicken for different salads and soups we shall start by preparing the salad.

Insalata Morra (Morra Salad)

for 4 servings:

¼ pound boiled white
chicken meat (the breast
meat cut in strips)
¼ pound ham in shreds

¼ pound shredded celeriac
1 lettuce
mayonnaise

From now on we will no longer talk about strips or shreds, but will use the culinary name for this way of cutting up ingredients, which is 'julienne.'

We already have a julienne of white chicken, ham, and celeriac. The celeriac is washed, peeled, washed again, and cut into slices. These slices are cut in a julienne. Before doing so, we pre-boil the slices for about 2 minutes in plenty of boiling water, drain, and allow them to cool before slicing. Then we put them in a dish and pour on the juice of 1 lemon. This we do in order to keep the slices of celeriac from discolouring.

We mix the julienne of chicken, ham, and celeriac in a large dish and add as much mayonnaise as is necessary to obtain a smooth and tasty salad, adding a little cayenne pepper and Worcester Sauce. In a salad-bowl we make a 'bed' of the cleaned and dried lettuce leaves, using for preference the tender inner leaves. Upon this lettuce bed we spread out the Morra salad and garnish it with slices of radishes and tomatoes.

As a second Italian *capriccio* I can recommend the following.

Crema di Pollo con Riso e Piselli o Asparagi (Cream of Chicken with Rice and Green Peas or Asparagus)

for 5 servings:

1 or ½ boiling fowl (according to your choice)	2 tablespoons rice
¼ pound cut-up soup vegetables	½ cup fresh shelled green peas or 1 small can asparagus soup
1 bay leaf	salt to taste
2 cloves	1 pinch pepper
1 pinch thyme	1 egg-yolk
1 pinch basil	2 tablespoons cornflour
6 cups water	½ cup cream

First cut off all the fat and place the chicken with the vegetables, herbs, salt, and the water in a pan. Let it come to the boil and then reduce the heat. The chicken must simmer with the lid on for about 1½ hours, when the meat should be tender but not overcooked. Strain in a colander and take out the chicken, which must now be boned and skinned. Cut the meat into fine pieces.

The strained stock is put back on the stove without all the other ingredients. Skim off any fat that may remain on the surface and allow to boil again before adding the rice with the fresh green peas. If we use canned peas or asparagus, open the can and drain the contents. We allow the rice 20 minutes and the fresh peas 15 minutes to cook.

Meanwhile, blend the cornflour with the cream and the egg-yolk to a smooth paste. We use a wire whisk for this. A pinch of nutmeg still further improves the flavour. When the rice and the peas are done stir in the creamed egg and cornflour and then add the chicken with the canned vegetables, if these are used. The soup, now ready, must on no account be allowed to boil again! Taste to see if it is salted enough and add some ground pepper.

Let the guest have grated Gruyère or Parmesan cheese with this soup and slices of warm crisp bread. Sometimes guests like tomato ketchup or Worcester Sauce with such a cream soup, and so have some handy on the table.

Here is a cold chicken dish.

Pollo Lesso in Insalata (Boiled Chicken Salad)

for 4 servings:

½ boiling fowl, with no fat
   at all
¼ pound soup vegetables
about 4 cups water, enough
   to cover the fowl

a little salt and pepper
1½ cups mayonnaise

FOR THE GARNISH
   fresh tomatoes
   2 lettuce hearts
   cucumber
   green peas

capers
chives
some parsley

Having cut off any fat there may be on the fowl, we place it in a pan with the vegetables and pour over enough water to cover it. Allow it to come to the boil and cook on a low flame for about 1–1½ hours, when the fowl should be done. Of course the time given depends very much on the age and weight of the boiling fowl.

The time will be less if we use a pressure cooker. We should then allow about 30–40 minutes for a whole and 20–30 minutes for half a fowl. When the chicken is done we take it out of the stock (which can be used either to make soup or just as stock). After the fowl has cooled off a little, skin and bone it.

Divide the flesh into pieces, which should not be too small. Cut the lettuce hearts into julienne and place at the bottom of the dish. Then lay the chicken on it, this time using both the breast meat and the dark meat from the drumsticks. Blend the meat with about 1–1½ cups of mayonnaise, adding the freshly boiled peas, the capers, and the asparagus if any are used.

Garnish with peeled sliced tomatoes and peeled pieces of cucumber, and decorate with mayonnaise and chopped parsley or chives. If you are interested in colour, add some tomato purée or tomato ketchup to the mayonnaise.

We now come to a recipe which, to me, is particularly delicious.

Pollo alla Diavolo (Devilled Chicken)

for 2 servings:

1 very tender roaster or
  spring chicken
about 2–3 tablespoons
  mustard, blended with
  about ½ cup oil

½ teaspoon pepper
salt to taste

We grill this chicken in a very hot oven on the rack of a roasting tin or, even better, on a barbecue or in a modern gas or electric grill.

First we split the chicken down the back, but do not separate entirely. We spreadeagle the bisected bird and place it on a slab with a heavy object pressing it flat. Leave the spreadeagled chicken for about 1 hour to allow it to become very flat and then brush all over with the mustard-oil mixture, keeping some for use later when we are grilling the chicken.

Pre-heat the oven for at least 10 minutes. It should be very hot. Put the chicken very close to the heat and let it brown as quickly as possible. When it has become well-browned reduce the heat a little. This flat chicken should be done in about 15–20 minutes. While grilling from time to time rub the chicken with a brush with the mustard-oil mixture. If the legs turn brown too quickly cover them with a piece of grease-proof paper or with foil. We need to baste uncovered legs more frequently.

This grilled chicken is put on a dish and garnished only with parsley and slices of lemon.

With it we can serve sauté potatoes or deep-fried potatoes and, of course, an Italian mixed salad. In Capri they serve a wonderful white or red Chianti with this meal.

Insalata Composta (Italian Mixed Salad)

If possible use a wooden bowl for this salad. Mix the dressing in a bowl:

2 tablespoons chopped onion
2 tablespoons chopped sweet-sour gherkins
2 tablespoons fresh pimento, cut in julienne
1 pinch dried basil or ½ tablespoon chopped fresh basil

1 good pinch pepper
salt to taste
1 clove of crushed garlic
2 teaspoons mustard
½ cup olive oil
3–4 tablespoons wine vinegar

All these ingredients must be well blended. Put some lettuce leaves in the salad-bowl with unpeeled tomatoes cut in quarters and boiled but cooled beetroots (summer or winter beetroots) cut in squares. Add well-washed chicory cut up several times lengthways and, to finish, thin slices of carrots, cucumber and radishes. This will indeed make a beautiful colour composition.

Five minutes before serving pour the salad dressing over all these vegetables, first tasting to see whether the dressing has enough salt. If you want a really exquisite-looking salad garnish with pieces of hard-boiled eggs, each cut into four, some capers, and slices of orange or apple.

In place of wine vinegar many Italian cooks use fresh lemon juice, which provides a palatable source of Vitamin C.

Another Italian chicken speciality is the

Pollo alla Romana (Roman Chicken)

for 4 servings:

1 *tender and not too small roaster*	4 *tablespoons chopped boiled fat ham*
2 *tablespoons tomato purée*	4 *tablespoons butter or ⅓ cup olive oil*
5 *large peeled tomatoes*	
½ *leek, finely chopped (the green and the white)*	1 *glass Italian white wine*
	1 *clove of garlic*
3 *carrots, cut up in slices*	*salt and pepper to taste*
1 *garnished onion*	

Heat the butter or oil well in a roasting-pan, together with the chopped ham, and in this brown the chicken, divided into quarters.

When the pieces have turned light brown we add salt to taste and some pepper. Then we put in the peeled and crushed clove of garlic with the garnished onion, the peeled tomatoes cut up in quarters, the tomato purée, the slices of carrots, and the finely chopped leek.

Stir with a fork so that the ingredients may become well coated. Only then do we add the glass of white wine (if preferred stock or water with a cube can be used). This liquid, however, should first be reduced a little in the open pan.

Put the lid on the pan, reduce the heat, and let the chicken stew slowly for about 30 minutes. The time will depend on the age and the weight of the roaster. We now take the chicken out of the sauce, which is then worked through a Chinese strainer. It is preferable to remove the bay leaf and the cloves before straining. The sauce is now somewhat thickened by the vegetables, but it may be a little watery, owing to cooking in a closed pan.

Return the sauce to the pan and if necessary reduce once more until it has thickened. This *sugo*, as the Italians call it, should resemble a thick tomato sauce, and the less we have left over after reducing, the better it will taste. If you care for a more highly flavoured sauce you can add during this reducing process a pinch of basil, thyme, and dill. Put the pieces of chicken back into the sauce, reduce the heat, and let them warm thoroughly.

Serve the chicken in its sauce in a deep dish. The Italians, of course, eat spaghetti or noodles with this dish. They also add grated Parmesan cheese to the spaghetti or the noodles.

If you want to make it a real Italian meal, then serve a glass of Lacrima Christi wine.

And this reminds me. Have you ever had 'Bitter Campari' as an aperitif? If not then try it with a slice of lemon and some soda water. Very good indeed, especially on a very hot day, since this Campari quenches the thirst.

Insalata di Pollo e Pimento (Chicken and Paprika Salad)

for 6 servings:

1 *boiling fowl*	½ *lettuce*
1 *red and 1 green paprika*	*about 1 cup mayonnaise*
(*pimento*)	1 *tablespoon tomato ketchup*
3–4 *tablespoons chopped*	½ *tablespoon Worcester*
sweet-sour gherkins	*Sauce*
3–4 *tablespoons sweet-sour*	
onions	

First remove all the fat and boil the chicken, barely covered with water, to which you have added again some cut-up soup vegetables, salt to taste but not too much, a pinch of thyme and marjoram or oregano, 1 bay leaf, and 1 little piece of mace. In the pressure cooker allow only 20–30 minutes; in a cooking-pan on the stove about 1½ hours. Take the chicken from the stock and skin and bone it. Let it cool off and then cut the meat into julienne. The paprikas are washed and cut in halves. We take out all the seeds as well as the thin and thick membranes. They can sometimes make the paprika very 'hot.'

Also cut these paprikas in fine julienne. Add the paprikas, the chopped gherkins and onions, and the tomato ketchup to the chicken julienne and as much mayonnaise as is needed in order to make a smooth yet not too 'heavy' salad. It is best to blend all these ingredients with a fork, for it will not make a mash as spoons are apt to do. We have washed the leaves of the lettuce, only taking off the outer tougher leaves. We separate the others and use them after we have dried them as a foundation on which we dress this salad. As garnish we use halved hard-boiled eggs, slices of fresh or canned pineapple, and slices of red radishes. Here and there we place a green olive, preferably a stuffed one.

This salad should look very gay, and special care should be given to the colour scheme. Personally I use only a very little mayonnaise to bind the salad, as not every one cares for mayonnaise. Instead I serve mayonnaise separately, so that my guests can please themselves. If I use this salad as an entrée, fresh-made toast or French bread and butter are served with it, and a glass of sherry is very acceptable.

Gallina Bollita con Riso (Boiled Chicken with Rice)

for 4 servings:

1 big roaster	4 whole carrots
4 cups water salted to taste	5 tablespoons butter
1 big onion (garnished with	¾ pound rice
1 bay leaf, 2 cloves, a	1 extra onion
piece of mace)	grated Parmesan cheese
1 bunch green herbs	

Use a pan in which the roaster fits comfortably and cover the chicken with water. You will need about 4 cups. Now add all the vegetables with salt to taste and let the water come to the boil. Reduce the heat, cover the pan, and allow 30–45 minutes for the roaster to be done. (A boiling fowl needs longer.)

Heat the butter in a saucepan and let it barely colour. Add the chopped onion and the unwashed rice. Onion and rice should turn yellow, and then we add the required amount of chicken stock (see p. 48 on rice cooking). We must, of course, first skim off all the fat from the stock. Let the stock come to the boil, reduce the heat, and allow 17 minutes on a very low heat in the covered pan for the rice to be well cooked. In the meantime keep the chicken warm in the remainder of the stock. When the rice is cooked skin the chicken and divide it into 6 pieces. The rice will look very shiny owing to the butter. We add some freshly ground pepper to it (stir again with a fork), a pinch of nutmeg, and some paprika powder. Put the rice in a warm deep dish and the chicken on top of it.

Serve with grated Parmesan cheese and a glass of white wine or beer for those who like it.

This is an easily digested chicken dish, since it is served without any gravy or sauce. If you care for it then add some Worcester Sauce and soy sauce to the rice. Mango chutney also goes very well with this dish.

We now take our leave of Italy and follow Gallina to Spain.

SPAIN

ITALY is a wonderfully gay and sunny country, and the same can be said of Spain. We should also note that the Spaniards are a people who enjoy dancing and singing and highly flavoured gastronomy. Chief ingredients in this country's cookery are fish and meat, mutton and lamb being great favourites. Chickens, too, are the mainstay of a number of delicious dishes.

As in Italy, the Spanish cook has quantities of fresh fruit and vegetables available, and the excellent quality of the country's olive oil, the fat white cloves of garlic, and the Spanish pimento to be found in every kitchen are most useful adjuncts. Turmeric colours many dishes bright yellow, while saffron gives its own very special flavour to innumerable fish, soup, and chicken recipes, including paella, the national speciality.

Last but not least, the Spaniards believe in using a great variety of fresh herbs. The foreign tourist will particularly appreciate the sea-food, especially if he is staying on the coast. It holds an important place in the daily menu of every Spanish housewife, and a wide variety is always served in many restaurants.

Strange as it may sound, I thoroughly enjoyed their habit of combining fish, shellfish, and other sea-foods with chicken. Spaniards take it as a matter of course, and it is the basis of the paella, that dish for which every region has its own pet recipe. Although potatoes are served with certain dishes, Spaniards much prefer rice. In the matter of cooking they display a remarkable ingenuity, which I can only describe as culinary *avantgardisme*. They combine fruit and vegetables in a manner that proves they are not afraid of the unusual, even the unlikely. Thus they cook fresh young peas and a variety of garden herbs together with fish, meat, or chicken. The peas are not served separately as a vegetable, but form an integral part of a dish that is both colourful and unusual.

But let us now follow Gallina on her tour through Spain, beginning with an excellent broth.

Sopa de Ave (Chicken Broth)

for 4 servings:

a little less than 6 cups clear chicken broth made from ½ boiling fowl or 1 packet or can chicken broth	pepper and salt to taste
	1 pinch paprika powder
	1 pinch thyme
	1 pinch marjoram
½ cup skimmed gravy	1 pinch dried tarragon or
2 egg-yolks	some more if fresh
some cream	1 tablespoon Worcester Sauce
1 glass sherry	

Prepare the clear chicken broth according to your own taste, using the boiling fowl or a packet or can of chicken broth. When the skimmed gravy has come to the boil we take it off the stove and add all the given ingredients, including the beaten egg-yolks and some cream. This mixture is then added to the chicken broth, stirring well with a wire whisk. The broth should be very hot, but must not come to the boil any more or the egg-yolks will curdle. Before serving taste this very delicious sopa de

ave to check if you have added enough salt and pepper. If you
have used half a boiling fowl use the meat later on for an hors
d'oeuvre or for a ragout.

With this chicken broth we serve bread. Chopped parsley
should be added as a garnish.

And here is a cold chicken salad just for one person.

Ensalada di Live (Chicken Salad)

for 1 only:

¼ pound cooked chicken meat	1 dash Worcester Sauce
	the heart of a lettuce
3–4 tablespoons mayonnaise	1 banana
1½ teaspoons paprika powder	1 tablespoon chopped parsley
pepper and salt to taste	or celery leaves

Mix all the ingredients mentioned smoothly together except
the lettuce heart and the banana. Take the former and wash the
crisp yellow leaves. Dry them and garnish an individual dish
with these leaves. Only then do we add the banana, cut up in
slices, to the chicken mayonnaise, put it on the lettuce leaves,
and the salad is ready. Serve it with fresh-made thin toast and
butter. With this dish you will enjoy a glass of dry Spanish
sherry.

Many other chicken dishes are available in this country, but
I should like you to join me in preparing the national dish of
Spain which, however, has innumerable variations. Chicken is
but one of the ingredients, which include several kinds of meat,
for there seems to be no end to variations on the paella theme.
As, however, we are interested mainly with the chicken in this
book I will confine myself to a Gallina recipe.

Paella

for 4 servings:

1 lean roaster, divided into 6–8 pieces

1½ cups rice (if your guests are hungry use some more)

1 small can crab and/or 4 frozen prawns

1 small can cuttle-fish or fresh if available (optional)

¼ cup mussels or 1 pound raw mussels in the shell, already well washed and cleaned

¼ pound pork meat cut up in squares

VEGETABLES

2 fresh paprikas, preferably 1 red and 1 green, or 6 red paprikas (canned in oil, which is to be drained off)

1 large onion

¼ pound fresh peas (weight shelled) or 1 package frozen peas

4 large peeled tomatoes

SPICES

1 teaspoon turmeric

1 teaspoon paprika powder

1 pinch black or cayenne pepper

1 pinch thyme

1 pinch saffron

FOR THE WHOLE

⅓ cup olive oil

about ½ cup water

salt to taste

As you will see from the recipe, the list of ingredients is pretty formidable and suggests that this is a difficult dish to prepare. In actual fact once you have collected all you need and have it ready to hand preparing the paella is simple. It is cooked in a large, heavy iron frying-pan, preferably one with a rounded bottom such as is used in Indonesia to cook rice or noodles, though I have also seen them in shops in other countries. An ordinary pan can, of course, be used, but the danger of the food sticking to the pan is greater, and one has to stir more often to avoid this.

Start by letting the olive oil get quite hot. Then sauté in it the raw pieces of chicken and the squares of pork. Add the chopped onion and tomatoes cut in fours. Stir and then add the uncooked, unwashed rice. Simmer these ingredients in the uncovered pan for about 5 minutes, then add all the spices and the fresh peas, but not the frozen variety if these are used. Cook for a further 10 minutes and then add the frozen prawns, washed but not shelled; the raw mussels in their shells, the fresh cuttle-fish cut in thick strips, and the two paprikas cut in fair-sized slices.

Stir and add just enough water barely to cover all the ingredients. Cover the pan, reduce the heat, and allow the paella to cook for 12–17 minutes. See whether the chicken is done. If it is cooked the paella is ready.

If frozen peas and/or canned crab and cuttle-fish are used

drain well and only add at the last minute, about 5 minutes before serving, stirring them in carefully with a fork in order not to break up the grains of rice. It is customary to serve this dish in the pan in which it was cooked. In Spain they use a very heavy, rather shallow pan.

For a somewhat more sophisticated paella the following can be added to our list of ingredients: pieces of boiled lobster, in their shell; artichoke hearts; slices of the Spanish sausage known as chorizo, though if we lack these chipolatas will do; and chicken peas (which have been soaked overnight) or butter beans.

Remember the paella must be served piping hot. In Spain a glass of local red or white wine is the accompaniment of every paella.

Another Spanish chicken dish, the best I ever tasted, is the

Pollo al Oporto (Chicken in Port)

for 4 servings:

1 roaster
4–5 tablespoons butter
2–3 tablespoons red port
½ cup clear broth or water
    with a meat cube
1 pinch marjoram
1 tiny piece of cinnamon
salt to taste but not if you
    use a cube

1 pinch freshly ground pepper
1 garnished onion (i.e., an
    onion to which a bay leaf
    is stuck with 2 cloves)
½ pound mushrooms of equal
    size

Divide the roaster into four pieces and sauté them in an ordinary meat-pan in the butter that has been allowed to brown. Add to it the garnished onion with the marjoram, the cinnamon, and pepper and salt to taste. Pour in the red port and the broth or the water with the cube. Allow to come to the boil, then reduce the heat and just cover the pan. We put the lid aslant on the pan in order to let the steam come out. In a covered pan the sauce would become too liquid. In less than 30 minutes this dish will be ready. But after 20 minutes we add the whole mushrooms. They are done in 10 minutes. Serve the pieces of chicken in their sauce, first taking out the garnished onion. With this chicken dish we should serve deliciously fluffy mashed potatoes.

Puré de Patata (Mashed Potatoes)

for 4 servings:

8 raw, not too small potatoes of equal size	1 tablespoon chopped parsley
3 tablespoons butter	salt and pepper to taste
1 egg-yolk	1 pinch nutmeg
⅓ cup scalded milk	cream to taste

Wash but do not peel the potatoes. Dry them thoroughly and put them on a baking-pan. Rub them first with oil and do the same with the baking-pan. When the oven is very hot bake the potatoes in it for about 30–45 minutes.

Now take them out and split them open lengthwise. Scoop out the inside with a spoon and put it in a pan. Mash the potato with a wire whisk and blend over a low heat with the scalded milk mixed with the butter, the egg-yolk, salt and pepper to taste, and the nutmeg. Do not use too much nutmeg as its flavour is rather pungent and apt to be overpowering. When the mixture has become creamy you take it off the heat and add the chopped parsley to it. Add cream to taste. As you see, it is not difficult and the result is delicious.

Even without an oven you can prepare this form of mashed potato. Boil the potatoes in their jackets in a steamer or in the pressure cooker. If using a pressure cooker reckon about 12 minutes, if a steamer is used about 30 minutes.

I assume that most housewives are familiar with the use of

the steamer. A steamer lessens the risk of overcooking the potatoes and having them a soggy mess.

On a visit to Mr. Pepe in his Spanish restaurant in London I
learned how to prepare the following Spanish chicken dish:

Pollo alla Catalana (Catalan Chicken)

for 4 servings:

1 tender roaster, divided into 4 pieces	1 clove of garlic
	1 bay leaf
8 poached deep-frozen prawns in their shells	1 chopped onion
	⅓ cup butter
16 boiled mussels also in their shells	salt and pepper to taste

FOR THE SAUCE

1 small can tomato purée	1 pinch sugar
1 cup stock or water with a meat cube	about 2 tablespoons cornflour

Brown ⅔ of the butter in a deep pan and sauté the chicken
quarters in it, allowing them to become light brown. The
chicken should be done in about 30 minutes. This sautéing
should be done in the morning. Before dinner-time we sauté, in
the remaining butter, the chopped onion, clove of garlic, bay
leaf, with the prawns and the mussels both in their shells. We
reduce the heat and let these ingredients simmer slowly. In the
meantime we prepare the tomato sauce. For this we use half
the chicken gravy and bring it to the boil. It is then blended
with the tomato purée, the cornflour, and the hot stock or water with a cube. Use a wire whisk. Bring this sauce to the boil, reduce the heat, and let it boil slowly for about 5 minutes. Taste to
see if the sauce needs some more salt or pepper; add the sugar
and for extra flavour a dash of Worcester Sauce. This dish is
served as follows:

The sautéed pieces of chicken are put into a shallow dish and
on top of them we put the sea-food and cover the whole with

the tomato sauce. With this we serve boiled potatoes liberally strewn with chopped parsley and freshly ground pepper. I drank an excellent Spanish wine with this dish called Marques de Muriete—Vinos de Tiola.

Arroz con Ave (Rice with Chicken)

for 6 servings:

⅓ cup oil, preferably olive oil
1 lean boiling fowl cut up in 8 pieces
2 onions sliced thinly
1 small can tomato purée

1 clove of garlic
1 teaspoon paprika powder
1 teaspoon turmeric powder
salt and pepper to taste
1½ cups uncooked rice

FOR THE GARNISH
1 can pineapple slices
2 tablespoons butter

½ cup raisins
juice of 1 lemon

If some fat remains, remove it and divide the chicken into eight pieces. Let the oil become quite hot in a casserole and sauté the pieces of chicken until they are light brown. Then add all the ingredients except the uncooked rice and those needed for the garnish. Stir with a fork in order that the slices of onion may also become brown.

Add just enough water to cover the ingredients, reduce the heat, cover the pan, and allow to simmer for about 1–1½ hours.

The chicken dish should not be quite cooked as the rice is prepared in the same casserole. We add the rice to the chicken and check if there remains enough liquid to let the rice cook well and become dry and done at the end of 17 minutes. This time the rice should be somewhat glossy owing to the oil in the sauce. The rice will look less dry than when boiled in water. We cover the pan with the lid and reduce the heat to very, very low. At the end of 17 minutes the pieces of chicken are nicely tender. While the rice is boiling we open the can of pineapple slices and put them in a sieve.

We wash the raisins and simmer them in boiling water for

about 5 minutes. They then join the pineapple in the sieve as both must drain well. Finally we brown the two tablespoons of butter in a frying-pan and sauté the slices of pineapple and the raisins in it; then we add the lemon juice. We are now ready to serve the chicken dish, first checking to see that enough salt and pepper have been added. With a fork we blend the rice with the chicken and then put this mixture in a warm dish. Cover with the fruit garnish.

With this dish a glass of Spanish red wine is delicious.

We must now leave Spain and follow Gallina on her tour through Portugal.

PORTUGAL

From Spain to Portugal *il n'y a qu'un pas* . . . and yet how different are these two countries! We could say of Portugal that it still is a somewhat simple land with beautiful landscapes. It is mainly this simplicity, combined with the friendliness and helpfulness of the people and the beauty of the countryside, that makes Portugal so very attractive to the traveller.

I cannot state precisely what makes this country so cheerful and agreeable to be in, but one thing is certain—I left it taking with me marvellous memories.

Were it not that in this book we deal especially with the chicken I would pay homage here to the many sea-food dishes, which include lobster, shrimp, crawfish, and mussels for which Portuguese cooks are famous.

I have not come across any other country in which all this sea-food is available in such abundance and for so little money. Inevitably this makes Portugal a particularly attractive place for sea-food 'gluttons.' I can never forget the exquisite bacalao (dried codfish dishes). They were prepared with such refinement and such fascinating culinary imagination. The codfish I ate there, prepared with eggs, chopped fresh herbs, and fried potatoes, was the best I was ever served anywhere in the world.

And, last but not least, we must not underestimate the Portuguese wines (among which the sparkling wines are indeed good). The white wines are also particularly attractive.

But do not think that Miss Gallina does not keep her own important place in Portuguese gastronomy. In every restaurant, whether expensive or simple, and in every kitchen the chicken is a real prima donna. The Portuguese would rather prepare a chicken than a meat dish, for, with the exception of lamb or mutton, meat is of inferior quality.

Let me start by describing a Portuguese chicken soup.

Sopa com Frango (Soup with Chicken)

for 5 servings:

½ boiling fowl cut in small
pieces
6 cups water
about 1 pound vegetables,
among which leek, carrots,
onions, celeriac, and, if
available, some stalks of
dill and tarragon tied to a
bunch with parsley stalks

¼ pound spaghetti
2–3 tablespoons olive oil
1 generous pinch pepper
salt to taste

Wash the vegetables and cut them up in not too small pieces. After letting them drain for about 10 minutes sauté them in the hot olive oil till light brown in colour. Then, and not before, pour 2 cups of water over them and let it come to the boil. Cover the pan and reduce the heat.

Meanwhile we put the pieces of chicken in the other 4 cups of water with salt to taste and the bunch of green stalks. Let these also come to the boil, allowing 1–1½ hours for the fowl to be done. The vegetables should be ready in 20 minutes or even less. Check to see and then work them with the liquid through a pointed sieve. When the chicken is done take the pieces out of the stock, skin and bone them, and cut the meat into squares. Put them back into the stock and add to it the vegetable purée with the liquid.

Bring to the boil again and add the spaghetti you have previously broken into smaller pieces. In less than 8 minutes your soup will be ready.

Add some freshly ground black pepper and see if the chicken soup is salted to your taste. When serving this soup we place a bowl with a little quantity of grated cheese next to the plate of each guest.

After this very nice nourishing soup very little else will be needed.

Frango Piri-piri (Chicken in Piri-piri Sauce)

for 2 servings:

I will now give you a chicken dish which was prepared for me many years ago in a small seaside restaurant on the Portuguese coast. The cook was young but very good. The place was Ericeira, the cook's name was Pedro. It was indeed a chicken with "prescription," as Pedro had told me in advance. It is a highly spiced dish, hotter than hot but very tasty. I have, however, adapted it a little to conform more to our northern taste and hope that you will try it, for it is certainly worth while.

With this chicken you serve dry, cooked rice, which is the only side-dish which goes with this pimento chicken. And the rice should be unsalted, thus admirably partnering this very hot dish.

1 small tender roaster

A spice blend made of

*2 fresh or dried red or green
Spanish peppers, the size
of which is very small—
about ½ inch. Slice the
peppers lengthwise open
and take out all the seeds,
for they give the very
pungent, hot flavour to a
dish. Chop these peppers
and blend them with*

*1 pinch tarragon
1 pinch thyme
1 pinch basil
1 pinch marjoram
½ crushed bay leaf
2 tablespoons pre-scalded
raisins
¼ cup olive oil
3 tablespoons lemon juice*

We prepare this piri-piri mixture two days in advance, put it in a covered bowl, and keep it in the refrigerator. The evening we are going to cook this chicken dish we divide the bird in two, as was explained for the Italian chicken Diavolo, and flatten it out in the same way (p. 82). At the end of an hour the chicken has become quite flat, and we rub it inside and outside with the piri-piri mixture. And now everything is quite simple. We preheat the grill and put the piri-piri chicken in the immediate vicinity of the heat. It should brown as quickly as possible; then we reduce the heat a little and baste the chicken well and frequently with the remaining piri-piri. This is very important as it gives to this chicken its authentic flavour. We must allow the piri-piri to penetrate the chicken meat as much as possible. There is the danger that we may grill the chicken in too high a heat and by doing so let it dry out too much. To guard against this baste repeatedly. A young tender roaster is done in about 15–20 minutes.

Serve it garnished with parsley and slices of lemon and with the dry-cooked rice. If you cannot do without a gravy of some description then melted butter is the only thing you can serve with this hot chicken. Blend it with lemon juice.

As in Spain so in Portugal, cooks are very fond of the combination of chicken and fresh green peas. Here is a dish with this combination.

Frango com Ervilhas (Chicken with Green Peas)
for 4 servings:

There exists a similar Spanish chicken dish. I have tried both and came to the conclusion that the Portuguese is the more interesting of the two. In Spain this chicken is served with little or no sauce, and in Portugal it is prepared rather as a ragout or stew. The sauce is delicious. I have therefore chosen the Portuguese version.

1 tender roaster divided into four	1 bay leaf
3 onions sliced thinly	2 cloves
1 generous handful of carrots also sliced	1 pinch thyme
½ lettuce cut up in julienne	1 pinch marjoram
1 pound fresh peas (weight shelled)	1 pinch cayenne pepper
	1 pinch black pepper
	salt to taste
	¼ cup olive oil

Heat the oil in a casserole and in it brown the pieces of chicken on all sides. Add all the vegetables, the herbs, and the spices, with the salt and pepper to taste. Bring to the boil and put the lid on the pan. Reduce the heat and allow 20 minutes for the chicken to be done. In this period of time the chicken will not be overdone nor will the vegetables be over-cooked. The peas chosen should be fresh and not too small, and the carrots sliced less thinly than the onions. This is required so that all the ingredients may be done at the same time.

The julienne of lettuce should disappear completely. Its purpose is to act as a vegetable base for the sauce. If lettuce leaves are simmered for some time they turn into a purée.

Before serving taste to see that there is enough salt and pepper in it. Add as an extra two tablespoons of coarsely chopped parsley and/or celeriac leaves or chervil. A special flavour is added to this dish by adding chopped fresh dill, mint, or tarragon leaves.

Since there is plenty of sauce we can serve boiled potatoes or spaghetti with this dish. What makes such a ragout particularly attractive is the fact that it hardly ever fails. The moisture from washed vegetables provides so much liquid that burning or sticking to the pan is impossible.

Frango en Croûte (Chicken in Pie-crust)

for 4 servings:

1 roaster divided into 4 pieces	4 tablespoons white wine or 1 tablespoon brandy with 3 tablespoons water
½ pound lean boiled ham	salt to taste
4 tablespoons coarsely chopped fat bacon	1 pinch black pepper
2 tablespoons butter	1 pinch thyme
1 garnished onion	1 pinch dill or oregano

FOR THE CRUST

¼ pound flour	1 pinch salt
1 egg of good size	water

Cut half of the bacon in thin strips without the rind and fry in butter until brown. Brown in it the pieces of chicken and add the garnished onion with all the herbs and salt and pepper to taste. Stir this mixture with a fork, and only then add the white wine or the brandy and water. Bring to the boil and turn off the heat. Turn on the oven to high. An hour before doing this we should have prepared the crust by working the egg and the flour thoroughly together, adding just enough water to obtain a rather elastic dough. Do not forget a pinch of salt. This dough should rest for about 1 hour in a basin and covered with a damp cloth. We then roll it out into a piece of crust about the thickness of a little finger. We mould it to the shape of the pie-dish we are going to use for the chicken so as to cover it completely. The chicken with its gravy is then put into the dish. The dough is now put in place to cover the top as closely as possible. Let the dough come over the edges, using water, or still better beaten egg-white mixed with a teaspoon of oil, to make it stick.

Put the fireproof dish into the hot oven. At the end of 10 minutes we look to see if the gravy boils. With a glass fireproof dish this is easy to see. In any other type of dish we must listen in order to hear the gravy boiling.

If the gravy does boil then we must reduce the heat a little and allow at least 1 hour for the chicken to be well done. During this time the gravy should continue to boil slowly. After an hour we remove the dish from the oven and baste the top of the crust with an egg-yolk, mixed with a teaspoon of oil. Raise the heat in the oven, place the dish as high as possible in it, and let the top of the crust brown very quickly.

With this rather unusual chicken dish we serve stewed dried fruit such as prunes, apricots, apples, peaches, or a mixture of them. They are stewed in a little water with lemon peel, some demerara sugar, and a piece of cinnamon.

Leaving Portugal, we now continue our tour and visit the northern part of Europe, Scandinavia.

SCANDINAVIA

Since we are following Gallina round the world we cannot possibly leave Scandinavia out of our itinerary, for this area of Europe is not only important but also most attractive to visitors. At the same time I must confess that it is difficult to tell you much about authentically Scandinavian chicken dishes. Denmark, Norway, Sweden, and Finland are better known for their ways with fish. This is perfectly understandable when one considers the geography of these countries, with their long coastline and innumerable fjords. Anyone who has visited Scandinavia will surely remember with pleasure the cunning manner in which both housewives and professional cooks prepare shell and fish dishes. What delicious lobster is served in Sweden and how unforgettable is the sophisticated "Parisian fish dish" for which Denmark is so justly famous! Indeed, there is a restaurant in Copenhagen which prepares this speciality so perfectly that you will think up innumerable reasons why you should return there for more.

Have you, for instance, seen anything more charming than the manner in which shrimps and prawns are served in Scandinavia, laid neatly on an open sandwich and colourfully garnished. One cannot help wondering how all those busy cooks and housewives can find the time to align each shrimp with so much care, achieving the most picturesque of compositions. A garnish of mayonnaise and hard-boiled eggs is commonplace, but what do you think of using instead scrambled eggs with different sweet-sour salads? I can only describe it as daring.

We all know how important the herring is in the Scandinavian cuisine, but do we fully appreciate the interest of herring salad with a sweet-sour dressing? The use of sugar with fish strikes one forcibly on first acquaintance, and I must admit that this typically Scandinavian combination does take getting used to.

Still stranger is the Norwegian herring soup in which thick fresh cream is an important ingredient. From which it will be seen that Scandinavian cooks are not afraid to use their imaginations when dealing with sea fruit and can prepare dishes worthy of the most exacting gourmet.

The Scandinavians have many interesting and excellent meat recipes also, those for pork being the most important. In Norway I fell for roast pork garnished with cooked apples and prunes. Goose and turkey are also great favourites, while the abundance and variety of cheeses, especially in Denmark, is overwhelming. And how cleverly all these ingredients are used in their sandwiches, both open and closed, known as smørre-brød! I cannot end this introduction without mentioning rød-grød med fløde, a fruit jelly with cream which is the national dessert. Wherever you may order it, in the humblest snack-bar, in a picturesque back-street, or in an internationally famous restaurant, you can be sure that it will be perfectly prepared.

Beer and Snaps, by which I mean aquavit, the Scandinavian spirit, are the usual beverages. Wine is reserved for very special occasions as it is expensive in Scandinavian countries.

But what about the chicken, you will rightly ask me? Alas, she does not hold the place I should like in these countries. On the other hand, the egg is justly prized. You will therefore find in this chapter, together with chicken dishes, recipes for egg snacks and novelties.

Before giving you the recipes I must admit that of all the Scandinavian countries the one I know best and which has quite stolen my heart is Denmark. Copenhagen is a delightful city, while where else in the world would you find in the very centre of a large town a resort like Tivoli with its many restaurants, music halls, and dance floors? There are restaurants everywhere, particularly in the neighbourhood of the harbour, and it is there in many a humble little eating-place that I have encountered many of the open sandwiches which I shall describe to you later in this chapter.

Throughout Scandinavia the smørrebrød and smörgåser are to be found in infinite variety, and a whole book could be filled with recipes, but as our business is mainly with Gallina it is to her that my first recipe is dedicated.

Hønse Suppe (Chicken Soup)

for 5 servings:

as many chicken giblets as possible	2 tablespoons vinegar
1 leek	1 generous tablespoon farina
6 carrots	6 cups water
2 slices celeriac	1 bunch pot-herbs
2 sour apples	1 garnished onion
¼ pound dried prunes (soaked overnight)	sugar, salt, and pepper to taste

Wash the giblets well and bring them to the boil in 6 cups of water with the pot-herbs (parsley and celeriac stalks and the green part of the leek) and the garnished onion. Add salt and pepper to taste. When the liquid boils skim it off and reduce the heat to allow the giblets to simmer in the covered pan for about 1½ hours.

In the meantime scrape the washed carrots and slice them

thinly. Do likewise with the celeriac and the white of the leek. Stone the soaked prunes and allow them to simmer in the water in which they were soaked together with the cored, peeled, and quartered apples for about 10–15 minutes. Take the pan from the stove and add some vinegar and sugar. Taste. This mixture should have a very pronounced sweet-sour flavour. If possible use cane sugar.

Sieve the chicken stock. Take out the giblets and cut off as much meat as possible. This meat we then mix with the fruit compote. Skim the fat from the stock and let it come to the boil again.

We now add the slices of carrots, celeriac, and white of the leek and allow 15 minutes for them to become tender. Finally we add to this stock the fruit mixture and taste once more to see that the chicken soup is well salted and peppered. The main point in this recipe is to add enough vinegar and sugar to the apples and prunes to give the soup the required sophisticated flavour.

After this introductory Scandinavian chicken soup comes the

Aegog høns (Egg with Chicken)

for 4 servings:

4 hard-boiled eggs
¼ pound chopped chicken livers
4 tablespoons chopped cooked chicken meat (boiled or roasted)
about 3 tablespoons butter

3 tablespoons cream blended with ½ tablespoon lemon juice
salt and pepper to taste
1 pinch curry powder
4 tablespoons grated cheese

Cut the hard-boiled eggs lengthwise and take out the egg-yolks, leaving the whites unbroken. Make a creamy mixture with the boiled chopped livers, the chicken meat cut up in julienne or diced, the crushed egg-yolks, and the boiling liquid in which the livers were cooked. Add one tablespoon of creamy butter and add salt to taste with the pepper and the curry powder. Check to see whether the mixture is sufficiently savoury. Have a fireproof dish ready, butter it, and put in it the half-sections of hard-boiled egg-whites. Fill these generously with the mixture. This should fill the whole dish, not only the eggs, and should be covered with breadcrumbs. Make a blend with the lemon juice, the grated cheese, and the melted butter as a final covering. Let this dish gratinate in the pre-heated oven. The correct colour is golden brown. When the cheese has melted we are ready to serve.

This dish has the great advantage that it can be prepared beforehand. We breadcrumb and gratinate it only shortly before serving it with buttered toast.

For our next recipe I give you a cold chicken dish.

Höns ock pepparrodsås (Chicken with Horseradish Sauce)

for 4 servings:

¾ pound boiled chicken meat cut up in julienne

2 thin slices celeriac cut up in julienne

2 large sour apples cut up in julienne

about ½ cup mayonnaise

2 tablespoons fresh horseradish, grated finely or *the same amount ready-made horseradish (bottled)*

½ tablespoon French mustard

1 tablespoon sugar

2 tablespoons lightly beaten cream

some lemon juice to taste

FOR THE FINISHING TOUCH

½ very fresh and crisp lettuce

canned mushrooms, as much as you like

whole and chopped parsley leaves

diced ham

The chicken meat should not be overdone. We mix the julienne of chicken with the pre-boiled celeriac julienne (parboil a few minutes only) and add a few drops of lemon juice in order to keep the chicken and the celeriac from darkening. Then we add the julienne of apples and as much mayonnaise as is needed to make a creamy blend. Place on a dish, generously lined with crisp, washed, and dried lettuce leaves. Cover with some more mayonnaise and garnish according to your own artistic talents with the mushrooms, diced ham, chopped and whole parsley leaves.

That we should serve hot toast and butter with this dish is obvious, though I personally prefer buttered rye bread with it.

Now two more egg dishes.

Smørrebrød med æg og cavia (Æg-cavia Snack)

This is a snack especially recommended for a festive occasion. Use small buttered rounds of toast covered with a slice of tomato. Upon these we put a layer of sliced hard-boiled eggs, topped with a 'cloud' of black caviar. Few ingredients, as you observe, but all of them excellent.

Instead of the expensive black or grey caviar we can also use some red caviar. It is less extravagant but less delicately flavoured. Serve with a slice of lemon.

SMORREBROD:

(1) Cover slice of buttered rye bread with: liver paste, chopped sweet-sour gherkins, onions and meat jelly.

(2) Cover slice of buttered white bread with: lettuce leaves, then with slices of cured beef, grated horseradish and pickles.

(3) Cover one half slice of buttered bread with: slices of hard-boiled egg, the other half with slices of tomato. Garnish

(4) Cover slice of buttered white bread with a slice of ham with chopped chives and cress.

and cold scrambled eggs. Garnish with chopped parsley or chives and tomato ketchup.

(5) Cover slice of buttered rye bread with: red beetroot salad, mayonnaise and slices of hard-boiled egg with anchovy.

(6) Cover slice of buttered white bread with: slice of cheese, slices of tomato and some lettuce leaves. Garnish with parsley.

(7) Cover slice of buttered white bread with: sautéed mushrooms. Cover with slice of cheese and butter. Bake in the oven.

(8) Cover slice of buttered white bread with: salt herring, cream cheese and chives.

Fyldte Aeg (Stuffed Eggs)

As every cook has enough imagination to stuff eggs, I am giving you only a few random tips.

With *liver paste*. Blend a creamy mixture of hard-boiled eggs, liver paste (to be bought in most delicatessens), chopped stuffed olives, thick fresh cream, and sherry. Check to see if salt and pepper should be added. Decorate the stuffed eggs with half a filled olive.

With *cheese*. Make a creamy mixture with cream or cottage cheese, chopped radishes, mustard, a pinch of sugar, and unsweetened ruby port. Top with thin slices of radish.

With *shrimps*. Mix thoroughly hard-boiled egg-yolks, mayonnaise, chopped shrimps, some lemon juice, and paprika powder. Decorate these stuffed eggs with a shrimp.

With *chicken livers*. Make a creamy mixture with chopped boiled chicken livers, chopped ham, chopped parsley, a little cream, and a generous amount of fresh chopped dill (or coarsely dried dill if the fresh is not available). Sprinkle with dill.

Before filling the eggs taste the stuffing and make sure that you have the right amount of pepper and salt in it.

And now another chicken dish.

Høne i Tomatsovs (Chicken with Tomato Sauce)

for 6 servings:

1 lean boiling fowl (see that
all the fat is removed)
1 small can tomato purée
6 peeled tomatoes
juice of 1 lemon
1 teaspoon sugar, mixed with
2 crushed cloves
2–2½ cups water, just
enough to cover the fowl

salt and pepper to taste
1½ tablespoons farina,
blended with
1 tablespoon chopped fresh
dill or 1 teaspoon dried dill
a little cream
4 tablespoons oil

Divide the broiler, from which all the fat has been removed, into 6 pieces. Flour lightly, remembering to flavour the flour with the dill and a little of the salt and cream. Brown the pieces of chicken in a pan in the hot oil. Dark brown is the required colour. Add some more salt and pepper, together with the peeled tomatoes cut up in slices, the tomato purée blended with the lemon juice, and the sugar with the crushed cloves. You can also add, if you care for it, 1 slice of onion and 1 bay leaf. Now add the water, but only just enough to cover the pieces of chicken. Bring to the boil, cover the pan, and simmer slowly for about 1½ hours.

Check to see that the chicken meat is tender. The sauce should be a faint pink. To thicken it we blend the farina with some tablespoons of cooled-off sauce. Then only do we add it to the sauce in the pan. Stir with a wooden spoon and let it thicken in about 5 minutes. See if some more salt or pepper is needed and serve in the pan in which you have cooked the chicken.

The sauce is not supposed to be a really thick one, but only slightly thickened. With this dish we serve boiled potatoes.

Høne i peberrodsauce (Chicken in Horseradish Sauce)

for 6 servings:

Here is another chicken dish, prepared with horseradish, which is available in almost all European countries. When you buy it see that the black root is fresh. It should be very brittle, breaking like glass at the slightest touch. Only then can we grate the peeled and washed roots without any difficulty.

With this recipe we work as follows:

1 *small boiling fowl, from*
which the fat has been
removed
4 *tablespoons butter*
2 *generous tablespoons flour*
3–4 *tablespoons dried raisins*
1 *tablespoon lemon juice* or
vinegar
2 *tablespoons cream*

1 *teaspoon sugar*
4 *tablespoons fresh grated*
horseradish or *5 tablespoons*
of the bottled variety
salt and pepper to taste
1 *bunch herbs (parsley and*
dill, if available)
1 *garnished onion*
water

Remove all fat and let the fowl come to the boil in just enough water to cook it thoroughly. Add the bunch of herbs, the garnished onion, and salt and pepper to taste.

When the chicken is done—but not overdone—take it out of the stock, skim, and cut into 6 pieces with scissors.

Prepare a white sauce with the butter, the flour, and as much stock as you need to make a creamy sauce, which must not be too thick. Blend this with the pre-boiled and drained raisins, the lemon juice, the vinegar, the sugar, the horseradish, and the cream.

Taste whether more salt and pepper are needed. Put the pieces of boiled chicken into a nice dish and pour part of this sauce upon it. Serve the rest in a sauce-boat. Serve with boiled potatoes and slices of celeriac, deep fried. A raw thin slice of celeriac needs only about 2 minutes' cooking in hot oil or lard.

Here is a third horseradish recipe.

Hönssalad med pepparrodsås (Chicken Salad with Horseradish Sauce)

for 4 servings:

½ cooked boiling fowl
5 hard-boiled eggs
lettuce leaves

FOR THE SAUCE

3 tablespoons grated horseradish	salt and pepper to taste
4 tablespoons cream or condensed milk	1 tablespoon chopped parsley and the same amount of fresh dill, if available
2 tablespoons vinegar or lemon juice	1 generous pinch of sugar

Skin, bone, and remove the fat from the chicken. Cut the meat up in julienne and add the coarsely broken eggs. Mix all the ingredients given for the sauce and add to them the chicken-egg mixture. Taste to see if there is enough salt and pepper. Put the chicken salad on a dish lined with dry lettuce leaves. Garnish with slices of sweet-sour gherkins and onions.

Cucumber Salad. Blend thin slices of cucumber with a mixture consisting of ⅓ of wine vinegar and ⅔ of oil. Then add mustard, pepper, salt, and chopped parsley to taste. As a finishing touch you can add a generous pinch of sugar. With this salad serve buttered toast and a glass of aquavit or Scandinavian beer.

While I was staying in Copenhagen at the Royal Hotel, Mr. A. Kappenberger gave me a typical Danish chicken.

Dansk høne á la Royal (Danish Chicken Royal)

for 4 servings:

1 big roaster	salt and pepper to taste
3 tablespoons coarsely	3 tablespoons butter
chopped parsley	¼ pound butter extra

Mix the chopped parsley with the 3 tablespoons of butter. Stuff the roaster with it, having first salted the inside of the chicken. Fasten the chicken with skewers and put it in the roasting-pan which you have buttered and to which you added a garnished onion with the browned ¼ pound of butter. When the oven is very hot put in the chicken and roast it for about 30–40 minutes.

Baste and, if necessary, add some water. When the bird is done we take it out of the pan. We carve it, but must make sure not to lose the butter-parsley sauce, which will run out from the inside of the chicken, for this is the best gravy we can ever make. The butter in which we roasted the chicken is blended with the parsley-butter and we serve this gravy in a sauce-boat. With this Danish chicken we should serve a cucumber salad (but, of course, without shrimps), fruit compote, and small round potatoes, roasted in butter and sprinkled with chopped parsley.

Finally, here is another Danish chicken recipe, kindly given to me by Mr. Folke Hildestrand, president of the SAS catering establishment at Copenhagen.

Kylling med Kødfars (Chicken stuffed with Meat)

for 4 servings:

2 boned spring chickens, larded by the poulterer

2 slices of pâté (you buy the kind you care for)

1 truffle (optional)
½ cup cream
1 glass white wine
½ cup butter

FOR THE STUFFING

1¼ cups finely minced veal
1½ tablespoons breadcrumbs
1 egg
salt and pepper to taste

½ teaspoon mixed herbs (quatre épices)
1 tablespoon brandy
1 tablespoon madeira

Mix all the stuffing ingredients with the minced veal to a smooth mixture and add salt and pepper to taste.

Divide the stuffing in two equal parts and put in the middle of each some pâté and half a truffle if you use it. Fill each of the boned chickens with the stuffing and sew up or fasten with skewers. Let the butter brown in a pan and roast the two chickens in it to a good brown colour. Allow 40–50 minutes for this. In the meantime add the white wine, reduce the heat, and cover the pan with the lid aslant.

When the spring chickens are done remove them from the butter. Take the pan from the stove and add any left-over cream which you may have, blended with some pâté. Personally I blend the cream with a coffee-spoonful of cornflour and add some paprika powder. This thickens the gravy a little and, moreover, gives it a rich colour. Taste to see if the chicken gravy is well salted and add some extra pepper. Serve with roasted potatoes and compote.

Now we go with Gallina to Germany.

GERMANY, AUSTRIA, HUNGARY, SWITZERLAND

THIS tour covers four countries, and three of them—Germany, Austria, and Hungary—are difficult to separate gastronomically.

Which, for instance, was the first to prepare Nudelsuppe mit Huhn (chicken noodle soup)? Was it Austria or Germany, or more properly Bavaria, where it was first invented? And is a paprika chicken an Austrian or a Hungarian dish? You could easily precipitate a war by asking an Austrian and a Bavarian cook who was the first to invent the delicious Apfelstrudel. Without the slightest hesitation both would claim the honour.

But if you want to start a really serious culinary argument just ask as innocently as possible where Sauerkraut comes from and whether it is to be considered an Austrian, a Hungarian, or a German national dish.

I myself, having travelled through all those countries, still do not know the correct answer to these culinary questions. All I know is that in Germany Sauerkraut mit Knödel (with dumplings), in Hungary Gefülltes Sauerkraut (stuffed sauerkraut), and in Austria Sauerkrautsuppe (soup) are equally well prepared, while I am aware also that in France, particularly in my native Alsace, sauerkraut forms part of the national cuisine.

I have gone into so much detail here because in this chapter we are going to prepare sauerkraut. Serve it with goulash and you will discover the perfect marriage.

GERMANY

HERE is the first recipe from Germany.

Hühnersuppe (Chicken Soup)

for 6 servings:

the giblets and 1 boiler of which all the fat is taken off	2 tablespoons butter
	½ cauliflower divided into little 'bouquets'
9 cups water	½ can soup-asparagus
salt and pepper to taste	⅓ pound noodles
2 tablespoons flour	

The lean fowl with the giblets (not the liver) are put in the pan and covered with boiling water and salt to taste. Allow this to boil well, then reduce the heat and give it 2 hours of slow boiling. When the meat is tender but not overdone take out the fowl and the giblets. The stock will be clear because we have not boiled the liver, which would make it cloudy. Let the stock come to the boil again, add the cauliflower divided in small 'bouquets' and the noodles. They will be done in about 10 minutes. Only then add the canned soup-asparagus and in a few minutes they will be warmed through.

In the meantime we have skinned and boned the fowl and cut the meat into strips. Add the giblets. Blend the melted butter with the flour and let it turn golden. Dilute it with some of the stock. This thin sauce we add to the chicken stock with the chicken and giblets. In a few minutes we can serve this soup.

In Bavaria, where my mother was born, this soup is considered to be a meal in itself. But if we were very hungry then the soup was followed by a delicious and substantial pancake. As this pancake goes so admirably with this chicken soup I must give you the original recipe.

Eierkuchen mit Speck (Pancake with Bacon)

for 4 servings:

¾ cup flour
4 eggs
1 cup milk
less than 1 cup water
¾ cup home-made
   breadcrumbs

1 tablespoon chopped parsley
¼ pound bacon cut up in
   strips
pinch of salt

Home-made Breadcrumbs. Cook some white bread or rolls in a slow oven until they acquire the brittle consistency of glass. When ready break up the bread with a rolling-pin, having first placed it in a folded cloth so that you can keep the crumbs under control.

Using an electric beater or wire whisk, make a batter with the eggs, flour, breadcrumbs, water, milk, and a pinch of salt. Use two frying (omelet)-pans of equal size and in each fry half the bacon strips. When the bacon is brown and crisp pour half the batter into each pan. Cook until the underside is a light brown, then turn the pancake with a pancake spatula and let it become brown on the other side. Reduce the heat and allow a further 5–8 minutes for the pancake to be cooked.

Main points to remember in order to succeed with these pancakes are:

(1) The bacon fat should be very hot when the batter is added to the frying-pan.

(2) While cooking one side lift up the edges of the pancake with the spatula, tilting up the pan, and let the uncooked batter drip along the edge and go underneath. By doing this the batter becomes brown and the upper side gets dry. We can also turn the pancake over more easily.

(3) When turning the pancake we shuffle it on to a lid of a pan which is the size of the pancake. Into the empty pan we now put some more strips of bacon. When it is hot we put back the pancake with the unbrowned side downwards and let it brown. By this method we shall succeed in serving a nice golden-brown pancake. Instead of bacon, butter or margarine can be used or any other shortening.

In Bavaria special plates are used for serving these pancakes. They are much larger and are the size of the pancakes, which are topped with a lump of butter, chopped parsley, and some lemon juice.

If you prefer a sweet pancake cover with demerara sugar, golden syrup, treacle, or whipped cream mixed with sugar and lemon juice. Many varieties are possible with this type of pancake, which is quite different from the thin pancakes served as a sweet.

Tiroler Knödel (Tiroler Dumplings), which are cooked in boiling water or stock and served with salad.

We need:

¼ pound lean smoked bacon	1 pinch pepper
⅓ pound boiled or roasted left-over chicken meat	1 pinch basil
	3 eggs
about 5 rolls, at least one day old	6 tablespoons flour
	about 1 cup milk
3 tablespoons coarsely chopped parsley	4 cups water or stock, both salted to taste
1 finely chopped onion, not too small	

Dice or cut up in thin slices the rolls, the chicken meat, and the bacon. Fry the bacon in a pan and when crisp and golden add the chicken with the chopped onion. Let these become pale yellow and then add pepper, basil, and the diced or sliced rolls. When all these ingredients have coloured we pour in the milk. Now we take the pan from the stove and let the contents cool off a little. Then we add as much flour as is necessary to obtain an elastic dough which will hold its shape easily. Not all varieties of flour have the same thickening power. You must discover the best flour for yourself, and how much is needed to obtain the right consistency. The dough when kneaded into dumplings should feel like a flexible rubber ball and not like a lump of concrete!

The size and shape should be that of a tennis-ball. Let the salted water or stock come to the boil and add the dumplings one after the other. The water or stock should simmer, but must not be allowed to boil. When the dumplings come to the surface they are ready. Serve them immediately.

They are eaten with sauerkraut or a mixed salad, and taste particularly well when coated with a spicy tomato or curry sauce.

Instead of using chicken meat for these dumplings you can use pork or veal and even fish, shrimps, or crab.

Sauerkraut

The secret of a well-prepared sauerkraut lies in sautéing it first to a golden colour with some sliced onions. For sautéing use lard. For liquid we can use white wine mixed with water if preferred. Watered sherry is also delicious. Sauerkraut is at its most succulent if you:

(1) use more lard than is usual in other dishes;
(2) simmer the sauerkraut slowly and long on a low heat in a covered pan with just enough liquid to keep it from burning or sticking to the pan;
(3) add some tablespoons of juniper berries and some sugar;
(4) add some caraway seeds to the sliced onions;
(5) enjoy a sweet-sour flavour, in which case add, when sautéing the sauerkraut, some peeled, cored, and quartered apples.

If you prepare sauerkraut in this way success and compliments will be yours.

The dumplings mentioned earlier (p. 119) can replace meat and potatoes. But if you use meat then salted smoked pork ribs or knuckles, smoked bacon, Frankfurters and pork chops are excellent with the sauerkraut.

A goulash too is perfect with sauerkraut. I sometimes serve pork chops with sauerkraut, coated with sour cream sauce. Strange though this may sound, my family and guests always seem to think that this is the most sophisticated sauerkraut combination.

So much for our digression on sauerkraut.

Here comes a little hors d'oeuvre dish.

Hühnermayonaise (Chicken Mayonnaise)

for 6 servings:

1 small boiler or ½ big boiler
about 1 cup mayonnaise
3 tablespoons sweet-sour
  gherkins, shredded
1 bottle capers (about 3
  tablespoons)

1 can lobster
some lettuce leaves (the
  larger ones)

Skin the cooled cooked boiler, which should not be overdone; the meat must still be firm, and we bone it with a very sharp knife, in order not to damage the meat. Divide this boned boiler into about 6–8 pieces.

These pieces we put in a marinade in a covered dish. Use a generous pinch of sugar and cayenne pepper to taste, ¼ cup of oil, and 3 tablespoons of wine vinegar. Allow 2 hours in this marinade.

Cover a serving dish with the washed and dried lettuce leaves and arrange the pieces of chicken on them (without the marinade). Cover generously with mayonnaise mixed with chopped green herbs and the shredded gherkins. Garnish with the drained canned lobster, some extra gherkins, and the capers. If you have handy some slices of red radishes, use them to add colour to this dish. Serve with hot toast and butter.

And as we are in Germany try a glass of Rhine or Moselle wine. Since this is no everyday chicken dish why not make it an occasion?

Feines Ragoût von Hähnchen (Delicate Ragout of Spring Chickens, called 'squabs' in America)

for 6 servings:

3 *spring chickens*
½ *cup butter*
1½ *tablespoons cornflour* or *farina*
1 *unpeeled lemon, cut up in slices*
pepper and salt to taste
2 *crushed cloves*

1 *pinch dill*
1 *small bay leaf*
½ *cup stock* or *water with cube (but then, be careful with the salt)*
½ *pound mushrooms, preferably fresh*
½ *pound sausage meat*

We divide each of the three spring chickens in half. We brown the butter in a saucepan and sauté the six chicken halves a golden brown. We then add salt to taste, bearing in mind that if we use water with a cube we add less salt than with unsalted stock.

Add to the chicken the slices of lemon and then the liquid. Let it come to the boil, cover the pan, and reduce the heat. Allow about 15–20 minutes for the chicken to be done. Being so young and tender, they are quickly cooked. Remove them from the liquid with the slices of lemon. Make a smooth paste with the cornflour or farina, the crushed cloves, the bay leaf, and the dill. Add this to the chicken broth with the well-washed and drained whole mushrooms and the chicken halves. Simmer on a low heat. In the meantime you will have prepared small force-meat balls from the sausage meat, which you add to the chicken ragout. Allow 10 minutes for the forcemeat to be done. Add pepper and some chopped green herbs. Check on salt and then serve.

The pieces of chicken with the mushrooms and forcemeat you put in a warm dish and the gravy is served in a sauce-boat.

With it are served German home-made or shop-bought noodles. Boiled potatoes can also be served. When using noodles do not over-cook. Allow about 6–10 minutes in boiling water. Drain then, and rinse with cold water to make them firm again. Re-heat in butter before serving.

Hühn mit Sardellensausze (Chicken in Anchovy Sauce)

for 4–6 servings:

1 large boiler from which all the fat has been removed	½ bottle capers
½ small jar anchovies	1 finely chopped onion
	1 small can mushrooms

FOR THE SAUCE

about 3 tablespoons flour	salt and pepper to taste
2 cups chicken stock	1 egg-yolk (optional)
5 tablespoons butter	

The directions for boiling a chicken have already been given (see Belgian chicken salad, p. 54), and the only point to stress here is that the chicken should not be over-cooked and, moreover, care should be taken not to use too much salt because of the anchovies and capers. All the fat should be skimmed from the chicken stock.

We divide the skinned and cooked chicken into 6 pieces. The anchovies are taken out of the jar, drained, and allowed to soak for about 1 hour in plenty of milk. This we do to remove as much of the salt as possible. The capers are also drained. Chop the anchovies and mix them in a cup with the chopped onion, the coarsely chopped mushrooms, and the drained capers.

Heat the butter in a saucepan and let it turn golden brown. We then brown in it the mixture of mushrooms and anchovies, stirring with a fork until everything is a light brown. Now add the flour and mix it with the rest and dilute with the chicken stock so as to obtain a thickened sauce. Bring this sauce to the boil and allow 5–10 minutes of gentle boiling in an uncovered pan. It should be a creamy but not too thick sauce.

Stir occasionally and then take from the stove. Add the egg-yolk diluted with some cold water or, if you prefer, with cream, stirring with a wire whisk and adding pepper and salt as necessary.

Keep this sauce warm in a double boiler and allow the egg-yolk to thicken the sauce.

Add the pieces of chicken to it and allow them to warm through again. Take the chicken out of the sauce, put it on a warm plate, and coat with some of the sauce. The remainder goes in a sauce-boat. Surround the chicken with boiled potatoes or rice, both sprinkled with chopped parsley.

To end this visit to the German kitchen I will give you a somewhat difficult but delicious chicken dish. It is difficult because its preparation involves a fair amount of work. However, it is such a typically German dish that I must not leave it out.

Backhuhn in Bierteig (Roast Chicken in Beer-batter)

for 4 servings:

FOR THE BATTER

¼ pound flour	1 pinch salt
1 egg	1 tender roaster
1 tablespoon melted butter or	1 pan which will
1½ tablespoon oil	accommodate about
about 1 glass beer	1½ inches high of olive oil

Make a smooth mixture of the flour with the egg and the melted butter or oil. Then add as much beer as is necessary to obtain a smooth, not too thin yet not too thick, white cover. The batter should have a non-drip consistency. Finally add the pinch of salt and let the mixture rest for 30 minutes.

Having divided the roaster into 4 equal pieces, we coat each with the batter. While doing this allow the olive oil in the sauce-pan to become hot. Fry the pieces of chicken golden brown in the oil, reduce the heat and allow about 10–15 minutes for the roaster to be done. Take the pieces out of the oil and drain on absorbent paper.

We need to use a rather large amount of oil because the pieces of chicken should brown on both sides at once. Do not turn them. Let the pieces drain a few moments and serve them with slices of lemon and fried parsley leaves. Warm slices of long French loaves are particularly good. So are fried potatoes with a well-dressed lettuce salad.

Now let us see what Austria has to offer.

AUSTRIA

AUSTRIA is a very beautiful country particularly famous for its gaiety and charm. Austrian wines, popular with young and old, contribute not a little to the warm and friendly atmosphere, and nowhere is this more evident than in its restaurants, cafés, and country inns.

Vienna, Austria's wonderful capital, so rich in its many traditions, is a magic place, and nothing can be more agreeable than to wander through the elegant and historic streets. It is a city where something can always be found to satisfy every taste. Those who love the arts not only can visit the city's many art galleries but can go to its splendid theatres, where internationally famous actors appear regularly, and also to the superb Opera House. For those who love horses, a visit to the Spanische Reitschule (Spanish Riding School) is a must, for there, to be seen in all its perfection, is horsemanship and horses of quality.

Shopping in Vienna is a sheer delight, while wherever you may go in this enchanting country it is an education in itself to walk and observe the people and their surroundings.

Gastronomically speaking, Austria is equally interesting. Austrian cuisine can best be described as refined, being neither extravagant nor complicated or heavy. Nevertheless the Austrians adore rich desserts and puddings. Austrian cooks are past-masters in the art of making torten and many different types of pastry as well as rolls and bread. They love to use fresh cream, usually whipped. Their cream cakes, marvellous confections of meringue and whipped cream, may be compared with the masterpieces of baroque art scattered all over the country. There are the whirls and the rosettes which are equally at home on the façade of a church or palace as they are on an open tart or a deliciously light cake.

Austrians enjoy eating and do so often. They also enjoy drinking coffee, and I was fascinated by the number and variety of their crowded coffee-houses. Equally varied are the names under which coffee is served: with or without cream; white coffee, which implies more milk than coffee, served in large or in small cups; coffee with whipped cream or just 'cream'; strong black or medium coffee; and so on. The mutations seem to be endless.

And do not be too openly astonished if towards midnight your Austrian host should ask you to share a goulash or sauerkraut with him. For he considers both these dishes have a sobering effect after liberal tastings of the Austrian wines, particularly the new "Heurigen" wines. If an inn has these for sale a green bush hangs above the entrance advertising the good news to all and sundry. This in spite of the proverb "A good wine needs no bush."

Although the chicken does not play the most important part in the Austrians' menu, it is a well-loved dish, often served in a variety of ways. Here is my first recipe.

Klare Hühnersuppe (Clear Chicken Soup)

for 6 servings:

This clear soup is ideal for a dinner-party. It is deliciously light and will act as an appetizer for your guests.

1 *boiler from which all the*	1 *large carrot*
fat has been removed	8 *cups water*
a small bunch washed parsley	*salt to taste*
and celeriac stalks	1 *generous pinch pepper*
1 *small leek*	

Divide the chicken into four pieces from which all the fat has been removed. Put it into a soup-pan with the giblets, the coarsely chopped leek and carrot, and the bunch of green stalks without the leaves. The leaves we cut up later and add to the soup just before serving.

Pour in the water and let it come to the boil, adding salt and pepper to taste. After boiling for several minutes, remove any scum and simmer slowly for about 1½ hours in a covered pan. Reduce the heat still further, but the water should go on boiling very gently.

When the pieces of chicken and the giblets are done drain the stock through a sieve. Take out the chicken, the giblets, and the bunch of greens. Skin, bone, and cut the meat in tiny slices.

Put the stock back in the pan and remove any fat that may have been left. Add the chicken meat and salt and pepper to taste. When adding the chopped celery and parsley include freshly ground black pepper. Serve very hot.

As we are discussing chicken soup I would like to give you some varieties of the basic recipe.

Ökonomische Hühnersuppe (Economical Chicken Soup)

for 6 servings:

¼ boiler with giblets   *pepper and salt to taste*
1 veal knuckle, not split open   *8 cups water*

Put all the ingredients with water and salt to taste in a stock pot and let it come to the boil. Remove the scum, then reduce the heat and simmer in the covered pan. Allow about 1 hour for the chicken giblets, and then take them out with a skimmer and leave the veal knuckle to simmer on for about 2 more hours.

Drain the soup and let it cool. Remove all the fat from the surface and bring the stock to the boil again. Skin and bone the pieces of chicken and the giblets. Cut the meat into little pieces and add to the chicken stock. Check on salt and pepper. Those who care for a highly seasoned stock may add some soy sauce, tomato ketchup, or Worcester Sauce. Serve with slices of warm bread.

If you want this soup as a complete meal you can add rice and/or noodles, vermicelli or macaroni and a fair amount of soup vegetables cut up coarsely. Make your selection from beans, peas, cauliflower, and diced celery, which are the most suitable for this soup. You can also use finely cut celeriac, carrots (either the smaller-sized variety or the big winter carrot), leeks, and cabbage.

Meatballs and slices of mushroom can also be added to advantage to this soup.

Now here is a chicken soup which is very easy to make.

Billige Hühnersuppe (Cheap Chicken Soup)

for 4 servings:

the giblets of a boiler
6 cups water
1 packet or can chicken soup

Put the giblets in the pan with water. Bring to the boil and simmer for about an hour. Cover the pan. Strain the liquid and take out the giblets. Cut the meat, dilute the contents of the packet or can of chicken soup with the stock, and boil for 10 minutes. Return the meat of the giblets to the pan and check the salt and pepper. Probably you won't need any salt, as prepared soups are all provided with salt, pepper, herbs, and spices.

Before serving add some freshly chopped parsley or other green herbs.

This is a very simple yet excellent chicken soup.

We continue our tour through Austria and have a look at the

Hühnercroquette (Chicken Croquettes)

for 6 servings:

about ½ pound boiled or
  roasted left-over chicken
  meat from which the bones
  have been removed
1 small can mushrooms

A BÉCHAMEL SAUCE, MADE FROM
  4 tablespoons butter
  about 6 tablespoons flour
  about 2¼ cups milk

And then

fresh breadcrumbs or
  crushed cornflakes
flour
2 eggs

½ tablespoon oil
a deep-frying pan with oil or
  lard

A croquette is always a very welcome and agreeable snack. It should be well browned and very crisp outside, while the inside must be soft and creamy. Make the mixture for the croquettes the day before. The sauce we use for it should be much thicker than a coating sauce.

For this recipe we use left-over chicken meat, but all kinds of meat or even fish and shell-fish can be used in a croquette. Sometimes Dutch housewives even make croquettes with left-over rice or spaghetti. To these they add spices, herbs, and other flavours. We make a croquette with egg and breadcrumbs in the usual manner, frying it in a deep-frying pan.

For this recipe we lightly brown the butter in a saucepan and add the flour. Stir to make a thick light golden mixture, which afterwards is diluted with the scalded milk. Bring it to the boil, stirring all the time with a wire whisk, then simmer in an uncovered pan for about 5 minutes. Only then do we put in the tiny pieces of chicken (they should be cut up very finely) with the coarsely chopped and well-drained mushrooms. Add salt and pepper to taste and a pinch of nutmeg. Personally I add to this mixture, which should be rather thick, some Worcester Sauce and 1 tablespoon of cream, blended with 1 egg-yolk.

The consistency of the warm mixture you have prepared is a guide to the consistency of the croquettes. If, therefore, the mixture when warm is rather liquid the croquettes will not hold their shape. With a mixture of the correct consistency you spread it out in a layer of about ½-inch thick upon a flat plate. Let it cool and keep it for one night in the refrigerator.

Next day make thick, finger-shaped rolls from the cold mixture. First roll them through flour, then through the beaten egg, to which we have added half a tablespoon of oil, and finally through the breadcrumbs. To ensure that each croquette is well coated it is wise to repeat this process a second time. In the meantime the oil or lard in the deep-frying pan has become hot. We put the croquettes—not all at one time—into the wire basket belonging to the pan and put the basket into the oil. These croquettes brown immediately, but we must allow them to remain for a few minutes to let the insides become hot.

Drain and serve on a napkin on a warm dish. Add some fried parsley. In Holland we serve these croquettes on a slice of buttered bread garnished with a slice of lemon or mustard and dried parsley.

Instead of shaping the croquette mixture into the familiar

long rolls we can usefully employ it for cocktail parties by shaping it into little balls. These are also fried in oil and served on wooden sticks with mustard served separately, if required. If you have to keep these croquettes warm because your guests are late, put on your oven for about 10 minutes, reduce the heat, leave the oven door open, and place the wire basket with the croquettes in it on a fireproof dish. The croquettes will then keep warm and crisp.

In Austria they often serve a green pea purée with these chicken croquettes. The day before you need it cook some soaked dried green peas in as little water as possible. Add to the boiling water 1 garnished onion (1 bay leaf and 2 cloves), a bunch of green herbs, salt and pepper to taste, and 1 teaspoon of caraway seeds.

Allow to boil slowly in a covered pan for about 1 hour for the peas to be done. Sieve through a Chinese strainer, keeping the boiling liquid, and finish this purée in the following manner. Fry a generous amount of finely chopped onion in a lump of butter or lard and add to it a pinch of dill and savory with a little more mixed spices. Blend these fried onions with the green pea purée and add as much of the boiling liquid as is needed to obtain a creamy purée. Taste to see if salt and pepper are needed.

This pea purée is also delicious with roasted pork chops and a lettuce salad.

If fresh dill and savory are not available then use the coarsely dried specimens.

Omelet mit Hühnerleber (Chicken-liver Omelet)

for 3 servings:

½ pound chicken livers
5 tablespoons butter
1 chopped onion
5 eggs

about 2 tablespoons water or
milk
1 tablespoon madeira
pepper and salt to taste

Beat the eggs with the milk or the water to a smooth mixture, add salt and pepper to taste. Let it stand a while.

Wash the chicken livers in plenty of water, drain well, and cut them into small pieces, the size of a domino cut in two. In a heavy iron pan brown 2 tablespoons of butter and sauté in it the pieces of liver and the chopped onion until light brown. The heat is turned up, and we allow about 10 minutes for the chicken livers to be done and the liquid to evaporate. Only then do we add salt and pepper to taste. Be careful the eggs are also salted. We stir with a fork, as a wooden spoon would harm the livers and mash them up.

Reduce the heat, put an asbestos mat under the pan, and now prepare the omelet. In another heavy iron pan melt the remaining butter and let it become hot without colouring. Beat the eggs just once and pour this mixture into the pan. Shake the pan and allow the omelet to set, but not to lose its fluffy consistency. Then add the chicken livers, blended with the madeira, putting them in the middle of the omelet. Glide on to a warm dish and fold in two. Top with some chopped parsley, chives, or celeriac leaves, whatever is available.

The surface of a perfectly cooked omelet should look like a fluffy cloud; only the underneath part should be firmly set, yet not too dark a brown colour—light brown is the correct colour.

Should the omelet stick to the pan, do not panic. Just add a piece of butter and let it slide under the omelet. Shake the pan once again, and the omelet will come off easily.

If the chicken liver omelet is to be the main dish serve it with roast potatoes and mixed salad.

Bratkartoffel (Roast Potatoes). Many roads lead to Rome, and many are the ways in which to roast potatoes.

Raw Potatoes. Slice the peeled raw potatoes and dry them in a cloth. We allow some lard to become hot in a heavy iron pan. Let the sliced potatoes become golden brown. Do not put all the slices in at once, but only a few at a time. Every time a layer has turned brown we move it to the side of the pan and add another layer to brown lightly.

When they all have had their turn we reduce the heat and allow about 10 minutes for the potatoes to be well done. Add salt and pepper to taste and some paprika powder if you care for it. This will add a glamorous pink colour to the potatoes!

Boiled Potatoes. Boil 2 pounds of unpeeled potatoes. Preferably use a steaming-pan or a pressure cooker. The skins must remain whole. Peel the potatoes as hot as you can stand and slice them. While they are still lukewarm mix the potato slices in a bowl with one finely sliced onion, salt and pepper to taste, and ½ tablespoon of paprika powder.

Let these cool in a covered bowl and have a heavy iron pan ready. Lard the pan and add the potato slices to it. They will brown quickly and afterwards should only get warm. Serve with chopped parsley or, even better, with chives.

These potatoes should be crisp, well browned, and pinkish owing to the paprika powder. It is important that every roasted potato dish should be served immediately. Keeping them warm for latecomers makes them soggy and unpalatable.

Gratinierte Hühnerleber (Gratinated Chicken Livers)

for 4 servings:

¾ *pound chicken livers*
2 *finely chopped onions*
4 *peeled tomatoes*
1 *pinch thyme and dill*

1 *teaspoon paprika powder*
4 *tablespoons butter or lard*
salt and pepper to taste

CREAMY MASHED POTATOES, MADE FROM

2 *pounds potatoes*
1–2 *eggs*

2 *tablespoons butter*
scalded milk

FOR THE GARNISH

⅓ *cup grated Gruyère or*
Parmesan cheese
1 *tablespoon butter*

Wash the chicken livers well and take off all the fibres and membranes. Cut them into small, but not too small, pieces, sauté quickly to a golden-brown colour in the 4 tablespoons of butter or lard. Then add the chopped onions, the peeled tomatoes finely sliced, with the herbs, the paprika powder, and salt and pepper to taste. Stir with a fork and allow 10 minutes cooking in an uncovered pan. Have ready a well-greased fireproof dish covered with breadcrumbs. The oven should be pre-heated for about 10 minutes.

We have already prepared the potato purée and now put an abundant layer of it in the fireproof dish. On it we spread out the chicken livers with the gravy and cover with the rest of the potato purée. Spread the grated cheese and melted butter on top of the purée and put this dish as high in the hot oven as possible. Of course, for this a grill is ideal. This dish should be gratinated in as short a time as possible in order not to dry it out. Golden brown is the correct colour.

With this dish try a good glass of Austrian white wine. I can particularly recommend the Gumpoldskirchner.

Hühnerbrot (Chicken Sandwich)

for 4 servings:

½ boiled fowl (the other half we use for a chicken consommé)	juice of ½ lemon
	some lettuce leaves
	1 fresh paprika
4 slices white bread	about ⅓ cup mayonnaise
1½ tablespoons chopped chives	butter

Cut the skinned, boned, and previously well-boiled chicken into julienne. Mix with ¼ cup of the mayonnaise and the lemon juice. Add as extra flavour some tomato ketchup and Worcester Sauce, but be sparing with these.

Have the slices of bread buttered and cover each with a washed and well-dried lettuce leaf. Put the chicken mixture on this and cover with a criss-cross of paprika cut up in julienne, after having been boiled, allowed to cook, and drained. Garnish with some more mayonnaise and chopped chives.

A simple yet sophisticated hors d'oeuvre.

Here is another exquisite Viennese speciality.

Wiener Backhendl (Deep-fried Viennese Spring Chicken)

for 4 servings:

2 *spring chickens, each*
divided in half
home-made breadcrumbs
2 *eggs*
½ *coffee-spoon oil*

flour
2 *lemons*
1 *deep-frying pan with oil* or
lard
salt and pepper to taste

Combine the beaten eggs with the oil. Breadcrumb each half-chicken twice. Let the oil or lard in the pan become hot. Fry the pieces of chicken in it to a golden colour and allow 10–15 more minutes on a reduced heat to get done. A spring chicken needs no longer if the frying oil or fat is adequate and quite hot.

Remove with a skimmer from the pan and sprinkle salt and pepper to taste on the chicken halves. Put them upon a dish which is covered with a napkin. It takes the abundance of oil. Garnish with slices of lemon and serve it with potato chips, French-fried, or roasted potatoes. The choice is up to you. In any case, top the potatoes with chopped parsley.

A mixed salad goes admirably with this chicken dish. If you want to spoil your guest ask the poulterer to bone the chicken for you. This makes the eating both easy and more agreeable.

Wiener Schnitzel (Viennese Schnitzel—collop of veal)

We now have become so familiar with the Viennese way of double-breadcrumbing that we might as well try to prepare this famous speciality, although Gallina has little interest in it. In order to succeed satisfactorily with a Wiener Schnitzel the following points are essential. For one person we order a collop of about ¼ pound beaten into a long, thin slice. Then we make breadcrumbs from old white rolls—a really important point. Further, it is a necessity that we twice breadcrumb each veal collop and add salt to the breadcrumbs.

Last but not least important is that we fry the collops in a heavy iron pan in which there is a half-inch of hot lard. Each collop should brown at once on both the sides. If insufficient lard is used and the meat has to be turned the bread coating will become moist and fall off. Never cover the pan.

By working according to these rules our collops will be served crisp, brown, and well done as required for a Viennese Schnitzel. A thin collop fried in lard needs about 10–15 minutes for cooking, not more.

Garnish with half a hard-boiled egg on a slice of lemon and a rolled-up anchovy sprinkled with chopped parsley.

Roast potatoes, green peas, or a well-dressed green lettuce salad are the correct accompaniment of a Wiener Schnitzel if we wish to follow the Viennese tradition.

Personally I prefer French bread and a lettuce salad with a veal collop instead of the roast potatoes and green peas. A glass of white Austrian wine or beer is to be recommended.

Hühnersulze (Chicken in Aspic)

for 6 servings:

1 small lean boiling fowl	1 pinch thyme
1 veal knuckle (a big one)	1 pinch marjoram
2 cups water	1 teaspoon peppercorns
½ cup vinegar	salt to taste
1 garnished onion	about 2 tablespoons gelatine
1 bunch green stalks (make	powder
your own choice)	1 glass madeira
1 pinch dill	

Let the veal knuckle come to the boil in a pressure cooker with the 2 cups of water and then allow 2 hours' simmering. Drain and cool. Skim off the fat from the stock. Remove all the yellow fat and divide the chicken into 4 pieces. Put them in a suitable pot with the stock from the knuckle and add the vinegar, all the spices, the herbs, salt to taste, the peppercorns, the garnished onion, and the bunch of greens. Bring to the boil, cover the pot, reduce the heat, and allow 1–1½ hours for the chicken to be done. Do not over-cook. An important point is to see that no steam can escape from the pot, and so we put a tightly rolled cloth round the rim of the lid. When the chicken meat is done pour the liquid through a sieve. Allow it to cool and skim off the fat. Skin and bone the pieces of chicken and cut them up into not too small pieces.

Put these chicken pieces into a glass bowl and garnish with slices of sweet-sour gherkins, onions, and quartered tomatoes from which the liquid has been removed. See that the stock is well salted and has a sharp, vinegary taste. Be sure you have taken off all the fat, for this must be a very lean stock. Make a mixture of the gelatine powder and the glass of madeira. Bring the stock to the boil again and blend it with the gelatine-madeira mixture. Stir with a wire whisk and allow to cool. When it starts setting and ceases to 'run' pour the mixture over the chicken in the bowl. Allow this chicken in aspic to stand for one whole night in the refrigerator so that it can set and become firm.

Garnish a glass bowl with lettuce leaves and turn the chicken in aspic on to it. Should it refuse to come out of the bowl easily, put the bowl for a second in boiling water. The chicken in aspic will now come away without further trouble.

Cut the aspic into slices, using a very sharp knife, and each time you cut dip the knife first in boiling water to make the cutting easier.

If you feel like garnishing this aspic lavishly then you can use smoked beef tongue cut in julienne, hard-boiled eggs cut into quarters, radishes cut up in slices, and lean ham cut in julienne.

Serve bread with it or, better still, fresh toast and butter. A glass of dry sherry is a perfect accompaniment.

And here is another Viennese favourite of mine.

Marholt Gebratenes Huhn (Marholt Roast Chicken)
for 2 servings:

1 *spring chicken*	*red currant jelly with some*
2 *sweet apples which will not*	*sugar*
mash while cooking	*boiled potatoes and green*
about ½ cup butter	*peas*
salt to taste	

Allow ⅔ of the butter to turn brown and hot in a pan. Roast a young, tender spring chicken in it, letting it brown on all sides. Add salt to taste and put the cover aslant on the pan. Reduce the heat and allow the steam to escape. Check occasionally to see that the roasting goes on progressively. It should take about 30 minutes for this chicken to be done.

Should the gravy reduce too much add a very little boiling water or stock from time to time. In an oven such a chicken would need only about 20 minutes to be cooked. Have a heavy iron pan ready and brown the remaining butter in it. Roast the peeled, cored, and sliced apples to a golden brown. This should be done rather quickly.

When the chicken is nicely cooked cut it up into two halves. Put them upon a pre-heated shallow dish and cover each half with the roasted apple slices, topped with the currant jelly you have mixed with the sugar. And if you like it add some lemon juice.

With this dish we serve large boiled potatoes scooped out and made into small balls, and the green peas. Everything is served on one dish except the gravy, which goes into a sauce-boat.

Frische Erbsen (Fresh Green Peas)

for 3 servings:

about 1½ pound green peas
   (weight shelled)
5 outer lettuce leaves
1 small chopped spring
   onion

2 teaspoons salt
1 tablespoon sugar
some boiling water
2 tablespoons butter

Wash the lettuce leaves and drain well. Cup up into julienne and brown lightly in the hot butter in a pan. Add to it the chopped onion, salt to taste, and the sugar. Stir. When this turns a golden brown, and only then, put in the shelled and washed fresh green peas. Bring to the boil and add some water if required. We need only the bottom of the pot covered very sparingly.

Cover the pot and reduce the heat. Allow only 15 minutes for young peas and even less if they are prime peas. Older peas, of course, need a longer time. Peas require from 8–25 minutes according to age and quality.

If you have done everything correctly you will discover that the finely chopped spring onion, the julienne of lettuce leaves, and the water have completely lost their identity.

The lettuce thickens the peas; moreover, they add a wonderful flavour to this dish.

Now it is time for us to leave Austria and follow Gallina on her tour through Hungary.

HUNGARY

It is a long time since I was in Hungary. I am lucky, however, in that I know a number of Hungarian restaurateurs and chefs, thanks to whose kindness I have been made familiar with contemporary Hungarian cooking. During the last few years I have been often to Austria and have had an opportunity to sample innumerable Hungarian dishes in the many Hungarian restaurants of Vienna. Beware, however, of ever telling a Hungarian cook that you have tasted "somewhere in Austria" the dish he has just prepared for you. He would be mortally offended, as I suggested earlier on.

Every one knows that paprika is the distinctive flavour of such Hungarian dishes as their incomparable goulash, yet it was not in Hungary that these peppers, either fresh or dried and ground into a powder, were first used.

The paprika known and used throughout Europe is the sweet variety first cultivated in Hungary. In the East, as in Africa and even in Spain and Portugal, there are other sharper, hotter varieties. It might be thought that since paprika is so widely used in Hungarian cooking other spices and herbs are neglected. Nothing could be less true, for Hungarian cooks most skilfully marry paprika with caraway seeds, dill, marjoram, or thyme. Equally successful is the combination of paprika, tomato purée, and onions, blended with sour cream, basil or marjoram, and garlic. Indeed, it would be no exaggeration to say that the cooks in Hungary use a generous pinch of this exotic powder in every dish.

A word here about butter. Hungarians consider it is suitable only for invalid diets. For normal purposes they use lard, goose or chicken fat, and some oil. If used sparingly these fats are just right for this type of cuisine. Spring chicken, sucking pig (Spanfarkl), pancakes, onion and mushroom fritters, and many other sweet or savoury items can be roasted or fried a golden brown in lard. I therefore strongly recommend the use of lard for the following recipe. You may be interested to know that it is believed that the tasty soups of meat, vegetables, herbs, and spices, which are a staple food of gypsy diet, are the origin of Hungary's national dish, the goulash soup.

Here is the first recipe, given to me by the Von Hollay couple, who have a pleasant eating-house in Amsterdam.

Ujhazileves (Chicken Soup)

for 6 servings:

1 lean boiling fowl from
which all fat has been
removed
7 cups water
3 big carrots, well cleaned
and coarsely sliced
1 parsnip, peeled, coarsely
sliced

2–3 turnips, peeled,
coarsely sliced
2 tomatoes, peeled, sliced
1 thick slice celeriac
salt to taste
1 teaspoon peppercorns

FOR THE NOODLE-DOUGH
1 cup flour
2 egg-yolks
some water

Wash the boiler and divide into 6 pieces. Put in a pan and
pour the water on it. Let this come to the boil and skim off
thoroughly. After 1½ hours we add all the coarsely cut-up vegetables with salt to taste and the peppercorns. Let the soup come
to the boil again, skim off once more, and allow 30–40 more
minutes for the chicken to be done. Reduce the heat. Check to
see if it is tender but not over-cooked and then pass the soup
through a sieve. Take out the pieces of chicken and keep the
vegetables apart on a plate. Skin and bone the chicken, cut into
dice or strips, and put with the vegetables. Make a dough of the
flour with the egg-yolk, a pinch of salt, and as much water as is
necessary to obtain an easily worked elastic dough.

Roll this out as thin as a penny, and again roll it up and cut
into ribbons. Shake these out in order not to let them stick together.

Let the broth come to the boil again and put the ribbons of
dough in it. When they rise to the surface they are done. Now
add the pieces of chicken with the vegetables and make every-

thing warm again. Taste to see if there is enough salt and pepper in the soup and then serve.

The same couple gave me the following recipe.

Paprikásburgonya (Paprika Potatoes)

for 4 servings:

2 pounds potatoes
about 4 tablespoons lard
2 thinly sliced onions

1 tablespoon tomato purée
salt and pepper to taste

If available

2 tomatoes, peeled and sliced
1 fresh paprika, cut up in
thin strips
½ tablespoon Hungarian
sweet paprika powder

Brown the onions in the hot lard, add the thinly sliced raw potatoes with salt and pepper to taste and the tablespoon of paprika powder. Now pour over just enough water so that the potatoes are not covered completely. Bring to the boil, cover the pan, reduce the heat, and allow about 20 minutes for the potatoes to become soft and creamy. The water should evaporate in the meantime. If paprikas are available add them 10 minutes before serving this dish, well drained and cut into slices. Add too the peeled and sliced tomatoes (if available) from which some of the liquid has been pressed out. Remember to take the seeds out of the paprika or the flavour will be too hot. Finally add the tomato purée. Stir and serve.

Magyaros Csirkesaláta (Hungarian Chicken Salad)

   for 8 servings:

1 small roaster	1 boiled beetroot
1 leek, cut up in strips	2 hard-boiled eggs
1 garnished onion	rather less than 1½ cups
salt and pepper to taste	mayonnaise
1 pinch crushed caraway seeds	½ cup cream
4 cups water	1 tablespoon fresh chopped tar-
6 deep-freeze prawns	ragon or ¼ tablespoon dried
4 tomatoes	tarragon
1 lettuce	½ tablespoon gelatine powder

Boil the chicken in the water, together with salt and pepper to taste, the leek, the garnished onion, and the tarragon. For a young roaster allow about 20–30 minutes. The meat should be tender but not over-cooked.

Put the chicken with the stock in a sieve. Take out the roaster and skin, bone, and cut it into 4 pieces. Put aside the two breast pieces; the rest (the dark meat) we cut up in small strips or dice.

Boil the frozen prawns in 2 cups of stock. When they rise to the surface they are done. Peel and allow to cool off.

Wash the lettuce, take off the outer leaves, and put them in a dry cloth. Cut up the tender lettuce heart in julienne and mix with the pieces of dark chicken meat. Have a pretty bowl ready and garnish with the outer lettuce leaves. They should be completely dry. Put the chicken-julienne mixture on them, blended with as much mayonnaise as is necessary to make a creamy salad.

The shrimps and the pieces of white breast meat we now cut up in long strips and mix with some mayonnaise. Place this on the chicken salad and garnish with sliced tomatoes, hard-boiled eggs cut in quarters, diced beetroot, the whole topped with chopped parsley.

Prepare the mayonnaise in the following manner.

Mayonaise Collée (see p. 57). Make less than 1½ cups of mayonnaise according to your usual recipe or make a blend with ready-made mayonnaise and salad sauce. Dilute the gelatine with the lemon juice and 1 coffee-spoon of boiling chicken-stock. Add to the mayonnaise some Worcester Sauce and cayenne pepper. Allow this mixture to cool a little, and only then blend it with the mayonnaise. Let this stand for about 2 hours in order to set and thicken. We now add the mayonnaise to the chicken salad.

This mayonnaise will have a firm consistency, and thus make it easier to dress the chicken salad as we would wish it.

Serve with hot toast and butter.

Another, somewhat similar, tasty chicken salad is the

Jercesaláta Csaki (Hungarian Chicken Salad Csaki)

for 4 servings:

¾ *pound boiled chicken meat, preferably the white meat*

6 *tablespoons diced, well-boiled potatoes*

1 *lettuce heart cut up in julienne*

1 *generous teaspoon paprika powder*

2 *hard-boiled eggs*

½ *green paprika*

mayonnaise, with which we blend lemon juice and black pepper, with salt to taste

1–2 *sweet-sour gherkins*

Mix all the ingredients except the hard-boiled eggs. Lay a foundation of washed and dried lettuce leaves in a salad-bowl. Place the salad on the lettuce leaves. Top with an extra layer of mayonnaise sprinkled with some more paprika powder. Garnish with the eggs cut up in quarters, and strips of green pimento and sweet-sour gherkins also cut up in strips.

A Hungarian friend in London, Mr. Paul Weisz, a restaurant owner, gave me the following two recipes.

Vagdalt Csirkemaj (Chopped Chicken Liver Pâté)

for 6 servings:

1½ pounds fresh chicken livers

4 tablespoons rendered down chicken fat

2 tablespoons lard

3 not too big chopped onions

salt and pepper to taste

½ clove of crushed garlic

2 hard-boiled eggs

chopped parsley

Wash the livers and take off all the membranes and other attached fibres. Sauté to a golden brown in the hot lard with the chopped onions and the garlic. Let simmer for about 10–15 minutes in an open pan. Stir and add salt and pepper to taste. When the livers are done take off the stove and chop. Now mix with the chicken fat and add to it as much as is needed to obtain a smooth pâté. Taste once more for salt and pepper. Put in a glass bowl, press it well, allow it to cool and set. Prepare this pâté the day before in order to allow it to get set well. Top with the chopped hard-boiled eggs and the parsley. Serve with rye bread or, if available, Hungarian black bread. Try it with a glass of Tokay (Hungarian wine) or some Slivovitz (a heady spirit made from plums).

Csirkepaprikás (Paprika Chicken)

for 4 servings:

2 spring chickens
about ½ cup lard
1 pound onions
1½ tablespoons paprika
  powder

salt to taste
½ cup sour cream
1 coffee-spoon cornflour
1 clove of garlic
2 tablespoons tomato purée

If available

1 fresh green paprika
3 peeled tomatoes

Let the lard get hot at full heat and fry the sliced onions a golden brown. Reduce the heat to simmering point and add the paprika powder, the clove of garlic with the tomato purée, and the salt. Let simmer, but do not cover the pan. When the water has partly evaporated, and not before, add the sliced paprika and the peeled cut-up tomatoes with the cut-up chickens.

Cover the pan, reduce the heat, and let the chickens simmer slowly for about 30 minutes. They should be very tender.

Blend 1 coffee-spoon of cornflour with the sour cream (if you have no sour cream but only thick fresh cream, add some lemon juice to it). When the chickens are tender take them out of the pan. Stirring all the time, blend the cream-flour to the sauce and put the chickens back in the pan. Turn the pieces over in the thickened creamy sauce in order to coat them well. In Hungary this paprika chicken is served with tarhonya, noodles, boiled potatoes, or gnocchis, called galuska in Hungary.

Some Hungarian cooks declare that this dish is at its best when prepared with fresh cream; others insist that a paprika dish is only authentic when made with sour cream. It is up to you to decide which you prefer. Personally I prepare it with sour cream, but I assure you that this is entirely a matter of taste. I also add a little cayenne pepper as I think it gives such a hot, exotic flavour to the chicken. When I intend to prepare a chicken or veal paprika recipe I order the cream well in advance. This cream is not kept in the refrigerator. Instead, the bottle or carton is kept in a warm corner of the kitchen, uncovered. If, however, you have to prepare this recipe at short notice, we work, as explained before, with lemon juice. If the meat used is beef we do not add cream, but provide as extra a generous pinch of crushed caraway seeds and much more onion. Allow roughly half the weight of onion for the total weight of the meat. For 2 pounds of beef we shall therefore need 1 pound of onions.

Here is the recipe for the gnocchi.

Galuska

2 cups flour
3 eggs
salt and water

Blend the flour with the eggs and add just enough water to make a thick, creamy batter. Add salt. Stop working this dough when it begins to bubble. Have a large pan of boiling water ready. Using two coffee-spoons take small portions of dough, the size and shape of large cherries, and drop them into the boiling water. They will rise immediately and are then ready. Take out with a skimmer.

In Hungary this is done far more efficiently, for they use a sieve with holes the size of cherries. The batter is worked through the sieve, and the tiny balls drop into the water.

When the galuska are done, pour cold water over them. They then become firm once more while at the same time cooling off. Before serving we sauté them in hot butter. That is all.

Mr. Weisz told me that he remembers quite well how, when he was a child and one of a large family, his mother used to make *tarhonya* every Saturday. And a lot of work it is. A dough is prepared from 1¼ cups flour and 6 eggs with salt to taste. It should be a soft, creamy dough which, when well worked, is put through a sieve with tiny holes in order to obtain long strings of dough, which, after being cooked, must be allowed to dry. We then break them into little pieces as small as rice-grains, and when quite dry we sauté them in lard to a golden brown and serve them with the paprika dish. They look like sautéed rice, but the taste is quite different, delicate and unusual. I agree that making tarhonya involves a lot of work, but it is worth while.

Like the Austrians, the Hungarians love deep-fried chicken. It is not necessary to describe the recipe here, for we have given it in the chapter on Austria. Instead you might like to know how the Hungarians prepare mashed potatoes and a cucumber salad. Both these dishes are served with fried chicken.

Burgonya Fözelèk (Mashed Potatoes)

Bake 2 pounds potatoes in their jackets. It is important that the potatoes should all be more or less equal in size. Before baking, wash well and dry. Turn each potato in a bowl in which there is some oil. Each potato should be well coated with oil. The baking pan is also oiled. Pre-heat the oven for about 15 minutes. Put the potatoes on the baking-pan and let them bake in the hot oven for about 30–45 minutes. When they are done, take them out and cut open the skins on one side. Scoop out the potato with a small spoon and put it in a bowl. Add salt and pepper to taste. Sauté a finely chopped, not too small onion to a golden brown in 4 tablespoons of lard and add it to the potatoes in the bowl. Blend thoroughly.

Butter a fireproof dish and add breadcrumbs to it. Top the potato mixture with breadcrumbs and pour a little melted butter over it. Bake to a golden brown either in the oven or, for preference, under a hot grill, where it will then brown more rapidly.

Ugorkasaláta (Cucumber Salad)

Peel a big, firm cucumber and slice or shred finely. Put in a glass bowl and sprinkle liberally with salt. Allow it to stand for

1 hour and then squeeze out the cucumber to remove the salt and the liquid. Put the dry cucumber back into the bowl. Stir in a mixture of wine vinegar to taste, a fair amount of sugar, 1 crushed and chopped clove of garlic, a generous pinch of red paprika powder, and some freshly ground pepper. Top with crushed cummin seeds and chopped parsley. A deliciously fresh and cunningly flavoured salad.

We ought now to leave Hungary in order to have a look at Switzerland, but first I should like to give you the vegetable rice dish so often served with a fried chicken.

Zöldség és Rizs (Vegetable Rice Dish)

for 6 servings:

1½ cups rice	1 chopped onion
½ pound young carrots	2 tablespoons butter
¼ can mixed vegetables	salt to taste

You will need two pans—one with a lid for the rice and one without a lid for the vegetable mixture. In one pan we sauté the chopped onion in 1 tablespoon of butter to a light yellow brown. We add the unwashed rice and stir with a fork. Then we pour the required amount of water upon it to cook a dry rice. The rice is not supposed to turn either light or dark brown. It should be yellow in colour. Allow 17 minutes for the rice to be cooked. For this cover the pan and reduce the heat to a minimum.

In the other pan we let the remaining 1 tablespoon of butter turn light brown; then we add the washed, scraped, and shredded carrots and simmer in an uncovered pan for 8–10 minutes, when the carrots should be done. Then we add the drained canned vegetables with salt to taste and some freshly ground pepper. Do not cover the pan, for the liquid coming from the vegetables should be allowed to evaporate.

When the rice is well cooked and dry we add the vegetable

mixture to it and stir with a fork in order not to mash up the rice grains.

Taste to see whether more salt or pepper is needed. Serve with a deep-fried chicken and sprinkle the rice with chopped parsley. Garnish with slices of lemon.

To finish the chapter here is a last recipe.

Bableves (Bean Soup)

for 6 servings:

about 1 pound beef bones	3 tablespoons lard
1 pig's trotter	3 tablespoons flour
½ pound dried haricot beans	1–2 crushed cloves of garlic
½ pound dried white beans, soaked in about 4 cups water	2 fresh pimentos, a red and a green one
1 cup mixed vegetables	½ cup fresh cream
2 large onions	⅓ pound Hungarian sausage (called Kolbasz)
salt and pepper to taste	½ cup noodles
6 cups water	

The day before we propose to use make a stock with the beef bones, the pig's trotter, 6 cups of water, and salt and pepper to taste. Allow at least 2½ hours for simmering. Skim once in a while. At the end of 2½ hours pour the soup through a sieve and let the stock cool. Remove all fat. The brown and white beans, well washed, have been soaked overnight, and we now add them to the stock with the 4 cups of water in which they were soaked. Bring to the boil and then reduce the heat, allowing a further hour for the beans to be well done and tender. We now add the soup vegetables, cut up in slices with a coarsely chopped onion. Cook for another 15 minutes.

In the meantime heat the lard and let it turn light brown. Add the pimentos cut in strips and the crushed garlic. Let these brown and add the flour, which should also brown. Dilute with some cups of the hot soup. Add about 3 cups and bring to the boil. We cook the noodles in this liquid, allowing only 10 minutes.

Add this mixture to the soup, together with the sausage cut up in slices, and the cream. The soup should not come to the boil again.

Taste before serving to see if it is well salted, and eventually add some more pepper. Served with French bread this soup is really a complete meal.

We can now follow Gallina to Switzerland.

SWITZERLAND

HAVING spent the greater part of my life on the borders of Switzerland and Alsace and, moreover, worked for two years in a Lausanne cookery school, Switzerland holds few secrets from me. As a country it is unique, offering the tourist pleasures that range from strenuous mountaineering to the delight of the table.

Though small in size, Switzerland is infinite in variety, divided as it is into twenty-two cantons, or districts, each one proudly offering the visitor a special highly individualized cuisine.

Some of these dishes naturally resemble one another basically, but there are subtle differences between those of the various regions, the Italian Swiss, the French Swiss, and the German Swiss displaying marked variety.

On the shores of Lake Geneva you will be served deliciously prepared fish dishes such as the Omble Chevalier (golden trout), a fish very similar to a salmon-trout.

A Berner Platte as served in Berne is a combination of sauerkraut with innumerable sausages, meats, and bacon. Cooked with a great deal of imagination, this is a delicacy well worth considering. And how could one possibly overlook the innumerable ways in which chicken is cooked, recipes in which, not unnaturally, cheese, cream, and eggs play outstanding parts?

Delicious food is served in most if not all the country's hotels. How could this be otherwise in a country which boasts one of the best hotel-schools in the world? And the pupils who leave it are rightly proud of the certificate which enables them to enter the hotel-restaurant business.

Every time I return to Switzerland I am amazed and delighted all over again at the skill and ingenuity of Swiss cooks. Always there seem to be new dishes to enjoy. The very art with which they display their chocolates and pastries, the variety of their cakes and desserts, thrill me, and a good pastry-cook or confectioner's counter reminds me of a wonderful still-life.

But I should stop talking in general and concentrate on giving you the first of my Swiss recipes.

Fricassé de Volaille Stöckli (Fricassee of Chicken)

for 4 servings:

1 roaster, boned
5 tablespoons butter
2 onions, thinly sliced
¼ cup de-greased meat gravy (use left-overs)
¼ cup stock, or water with a cube

½ cup thinly sliced vegetables, whatever is available
1 pound raw potatoes, diced
1 tablespoon tarragon mustard
¼ cup cream
1 teaspoon mixed spices
salt to taste

Ask the poulterer to bone the roaster and carve it into 6 pieces. Brown the butter in a pan and sauté the pieces of chicken a golden brown. Add salt to taste and an extra 1 teaspoon of mixed spices and the sliced onion. When these also have turned to a golden brown add the coarsely chopped vegetables, which should include carrots, diced celeriac, and, of course, some peeled and sliced tomatoes. Stir once more, and when all the ingredients are nicely browned add the gravy with the stock or stock substitute. Bring to the boil, then reduce the heat and put the lid on the pan. We allow the pieces of chicken about 10 minutes' braising and then add the diced raw potatoes. Allow a further 20 minutes for the potatoes to cook. The chicken will be ready at the same time. Check to see if this is so and add the tarragon mustard mixed with the cream. Stir with a fork and turn down the heat to very low. Taste if enough salt and pepper have been added to the gravy and serve.

Serve the chicken pieces with their gravy in a pre-warmed shallow dish.

Here is a second chicken speciality.

Poulet Casanova (Chicken Casanova)

for 4 servings:

1 big roaster divided in 4
   pieces
salt and pepper to taste
less than ¼ cup olive oil
1 teaspoon paprika powder
2 sliced onions

2 teaspoons flour
1 cup tomato sauce, not too
   thick, to which is added
   eventually a generous
   tablespoon mango chutney
3 tablespoons cream

GARNISH

1 pound tagliatelli (thin flat
   noodles)
4 fresh roasted pimentos

2 thick slices of ham
1 small can pineapple

Heat the olive oil in a pan and sauté the 4 pieces of roaster till golden brown. Add the onions, not too finely sliced, and let them also brown. Stir in the flour with salt and pepper to taste and the paprika powder. Only then do we add the tomato sauce, but not the mango chutney, which comes later. Put the lid on the pan, reduce the heat, and allow the chicken to become tender in about 25–30 minutes.

In the meantime we cook the tagliatelli in plenty of boiling water and salt to taste. Allow about 7 minutes. Put in a colander and let cold water run over it. Drain well. Before serving, sauté the tagliatelli in hot butter as they should become quite hot again. The pimentos are washed and cleaned and cut in halves, all seeds and membranes having been removed. Dry the halved pimentos and let them rest. Dice the ham and brown in an ounce of butter. Add the pimento halves. Brown and allow about 10 minutes to be done. Now add the slices of pineapple, and we are ready. Before putting the chicken sauté in a warm dish we must add the mango chutney to it with the cream and stir. Now put the tagliatelli also in a warm dish and cover them with the ham-pimento-pineapple mixture. Taste to see that everything has enough salt. Have ready on the table a bowl with grated cheese, preferably Gruyère.

Cherubin de Volaille Neuchâteloise (Cherubin Chicken from Neuchâtel).

for 4 servings:

1 *boned roaster*	*breadcrumbs*
1 *egg*	*grated cheese*
1 *teaspoon oil*	1 *cup butter* or *margarine*

GARNISH

2 *pounds potatoes*	1 *pound fresh garden peas*
½ *cup butter* or *frying fat*	*(weight shelled) or 1*
2 *tablespoons mixed fresh*	*pound canned peas, not*
green herbs	*too small*
salt to taste	*some lettuce leaves*

Cut the boned roaster in halves and egg and breadcrumb as usual, but with the difference that we mix the breadcrumbs with ⅓ of their weight of grated cheese. This addition gives a wonderful taste to the chicken. Dip twice into the breadcrumbs in order to be sure that they are well coated.

Allow the butter to brown nicely and then brown the chicken in it. If frying in a pan cook for 25–30 minutes. If you want to use a cover put the lid aslant on the pan in order to let the steam escape. With the lid aslant the cooking will be done quickly. If you prefer you can also cook this chicken in a deep-frying pan. It will then need only about 15 minutes.

Pommes Parisiennes (Parisian Potatoes). In the meantime we have peeled and dried the potatoes. With a potato-borer we scoop out small round balls. These we fry in hot butter or fat or deep-fry in the frying-pan to a golden brown. In an omelet-pan this will take about 18 minutes, and in the deep-frying pan we allow a bare 5–7 minutes. When done we put them in a hot deep dish, sprinkling the chopped green herbs over them and adding a little salt. For the green herbs we might make a choice from fresh parsley, celery leaves, chives, marjoram, and dill.

The *peas* are shelled and washed. Cut some of the outer lettuce leaves in a coarse julienne and braise in butter. Add salt and a little sugar. Then add the fresh peas and bring to the boil. Cover the pan and reduce the heat. If the peas are young only 10 minutes are needed. When dealing with older peas we allow 15–20 minutes. Young peas need no water. The washed lettuce leaves will give enough moisture, but older peas need a little water. The point here is that if the peas are properly cooked we need not drain them. That is the secret of this way of preparing peas. Moreover, the lettuce leaves disappear completely while cooking, binding the peas and thickening the butter.

With this cherubin chicken, roasted tomatoes—the smaller kind—are also excellent. We wash the tomatoes, but do not peel. We fry them for about 5 minutes in an omelet-pan in hot brown butter or oil until they are a golden brown. The main point is not to allow the small tomatoes to become overdone and lose their firmness. They should be light brown outside and hot inside, no more.

Crèpes de Volaille Mornay (Chicken Pancakes Mornay)

for 4 servings:

½ cooked small boiling fowl without any fat	chopped parsley
¼ pound mushrooms	1½ cups mornay sauce
1 can peas	4 pancakes

Skin and bone the fowl and cut in small pieces. Add to them the sliced mushrooms, which we have already sautéed, and let this mixture get hot in very little butter. Taste to see whether it needs salt and pepper.

Now prepare a creamy, not too thick white sauce with butter, flour, a mixture of half milk and half water with a meat cube, or some stock, which is more tasty. When the correct consistency is reached add a generous amount of grated cheese, the choice of which is up to you.

Leave the saucepan with the mornay sauce on a very moderate heat and prepare meanwhile the 4 pancakes according to your favourite method. Fill each pancake with some of the chicken-mushroom mixture, roll them up, and put them in a buttered fireproof dish. Pour the mornay sauce over it and gratinate the top in a pre-heated oven or under the grill.

The correct colour is light golden. Meanwhile heat the peas and add chopped parsley. When using canned peas I always drain them well and then heat them in a lump of hot butter which should not turn brown. Never stir canned peas, just shake the pan—they are so easily mashed. Serve the peas separately, and if you fancy it serve also a glass of Swiss white wine.

And here is another very tasty Swiss chicken recipe.

Emincé de Volaille Fellman (Chicken Ragout)

for 6 servings:

1 boiling fowl completely
de-greased
water with salt to taste

¾ PINT SUPREME SAUCE MADE WITH

1 pinch caraway seeds
1 ample pinch dried tarragon
or 1 tablespoon fresh
tarragon
⅓ pound fresh mushrooms,
sliced, or 1 can mushrooms

1 small can tomato purée
3 tablespoons butter
2 tablespoons flour
about 2 cups chicken stock
¼ cup cream

Remove all the yellow fat from the boiling fowl and cut in half. Put in a pan with a bunch made from parsley and celery stalks, 1 slice of onion with 1 bay leaf, 2 cloves, and 1 piece of mace stuck to it. Tie all these ingredients together or put them in a piece of muslin. Pour as much water on the chicken as is necessary to cover the two halves. Bring the water to the boil, put the lid on the pan, and reduce the heat. Allow this fowl to become tender, yet not overdone. When the fowl is cooked take it out of the water and pour the stock through a strainer.

With this chicken stock we prepare the

Suprème Sauce. Heat the butter in a pan and then add the caraway seeds and the tarragon with the tomato purée mixed with the flour. Stir and add as much of the chicken stock as is required to obtain a creamy, not too thick sauce. Add salt and pepper to taste. Then add the sliced mushrooms to the sauce and let them become cooked in it.

To serve this chicken we bone the two chicken halves completely and divide the meat in pieces. These pieces we put in a deep dish and pour over them the suprème sauce—with the cream added. With this we serve cooked dry rice or well-prepared mashed potatoes with peas or asparagus. French beans, too, go well with this dish.

The last Swiss recipe is the

Poulet Belle Époque (Edwardian Chicken)

for 4 servings:

1 roaster	⅓ pound mushrooms
½ cup butter	1 cup cheese sauce
salt to taste	1 can asparagus
1 glass white wine	

This recipe is not difficult to prepare, and the result is an excellent dish. Divide the roaster into 4–6 pieces and sauté them until golden brown in the butter. Every single piece should be nicely golden but not darker. Add salt to taste and pour the wine over it. Allow these pieces of chicken to cook in a covered pan for about 25–30 minutes. With a strainer remove them from the wine-butter sauce.

Mix 2 tablespoons of hot butter and the same amount of flour. Dilute this mixture with the wine sauce from the chicken and add the fresh whole mushrooms. Let the sauce come to the boil, reduce the heat, and allow the mushrooms 5 minutes' cooking time. The sauce should be allowed only to simmer. Put the pieces of chicken into a fireproof dish, add the very well-drained asparagus, and pour over it the sauce with the mushrooms, to which we have added about 3–4 tablespoons of grated cheese.

Gratinate the dish in a very hot oven or under the grill to a nice golden colour. If we put the dish in immediate contact with the heat only 3–5 minutes are needed.

We must now follow Gallina to Poland.

POLAND

THANKS to the helpful kindness of a number of Polish house-wives and chefs in hotels and restaurants, I have been able to gather a number of recipes for this book. For life in Poland—as I was able to observe during my stay there in 1962—has changed considerably since the Second World War. The population has suffered much, and one cannot help feeling even to-day that normality has not yet returned.

The visitor from abroad cannot help realizing how hard and difficult life is for the Poles. But how else could they have re-built Warsaw so admirably unless innumerable sacrifices had been made and a very strong hand demanded that these sacrifices be shared by all? Inevitably all these happenings have made their impact on Polish cookery. This is easily understood when comparing to-day's meals with those enjoyed by visitors who went to Poland before 1939, while comparison with the days before 1918 shows an even more striking difference. At the same time I must admit that in Warsaw's principal restaurants one can eat very well indeed. I came across a number of dishes well worth including in this chapter.

Vodka, the national drink, always plays an important part in Polish life, and many glasses of it are drunk at luncheon and dinner, and it is often served to you in its bottle in a bucket of ice.

Polish beer is good and the price reasonable, but the same cannot be said for wine. Wine is imported, and the prices asked for a bottle are ludicrously high and no one can afford it. This is probably one of the reasons why so many different types of vodka and beer, all of them excellent, are sold. As well as clear vodka, which is rather strong, there is egg-vodka (smooth and creamy) and wisniowka, which is red in colour and not unlike cherry-brandy in flavour. Other favourites are cacao and coffee vodkas, while the varieties of clear vodka are innumerable for all tastes and purses.

Now let us take a look at the ingredients that are available most of the time in Poland and notice at once the prevalence of vegetables. Foremost among these is the beetroot and many varieties of cabbage, cauliflowers, cucumbers, mushrooms, and fruit such as apples, pears, and plums in season. When available they figure daily on the menu of the Polish housewife.

Meat is always well cooked in the restaurants of the leading Polish hotels, and the chicken has always been highly regarded and very elegantly served. But for most households the chicken to-day is looked upon as a luxury, too expensive for the daily round. Considering the prices asked for chicken in a restaurant this is easily understood. Mushrooms, on the other hand, are a commonplace; both fresh and dried, they are used in innumerable recipes, with fish, meat, in soups, and as appetizers. Since the import of food into Poland is severely restricted one rarely sees oranges or lemons. On the other hand, the Poles are skilful in the preparation of dishes using apples or cranberries as their base, while the horseradish is much appreciated and served either as a sauce or in typical dishes.

The Polish cook is particularly clever with potatoes. Their mashed potatoes, as well as roasted and fried potato dishes, are wonderful. The same can be said for their meat, mushroom, or fish stuffings used with famous meat, fish, and poultry recipes. And we should not forget to mention their stuffed cabbages, tomatoes, and pastries. Chocolate is a great favourite in Poland and extensively eaten. Its quality is good, and the same can be said of all their confectionery. Ices are prepared with great skill and imagination. The baking of cakes, tarts, and biscuits, including many chocolate varieties, is one of the daily tasks of the Polish cook. That is, if the required ingredients are available.

Whipped cream is one of the most favoured items on the Polish menu, and it is indeed used generously, although much less than in earlier days. As a whole food has become more sober than before, and the same can, in fact, be said of the whole country's way of living.

I will now start by giving you a typical Polish speciality, although it has nothing to do with chicken.

Barszes z Pasztecikiem (Bortsch with Stuffed Savoury Pastries)

for 4–5 servings:

at least 1 pound raw beetroots peeled and diced

1 pound lean beef with or without a bone. If you use half the amount of meat have a bone extra

½ pound vegetables among which are carrots, celeriac, leek, red cabbage, parsley

1 bay leaf

1 pinch cayenne pepper

salt to taste

1 onion with 1 clove of garlic

5 cups water

FOR THE COLOURING

4 peeled beetroots to be boiled in 1 cup water and the juice of 1 lemon

First we cook the pound of raw diced beetroots in 2 cups of water. In what is left—about 3 cups of water—we bring the meat or the meat and the bone to the boil. Let simmer for at least 2 hours, taking care that the water does not evaporate. When the beetroots are done pour the ruby-coloured water through a sieve. In this liquid we now boil all the vegetables cut up coarsely, together with the bay leaf and the crushed clove of garlic. When done we also pour it through a sieve. The onion is cut up finely, and we sauté it in 1 tablespoon of butter. Mix together with the red liquid and the strained stock and add salt to taste with cayenne pepper. There remains the deep red liquid which we must prepare the day before. To do this we grate the 4 peeled beetroots and cook them quite a long time in 1 cup of water. This liquid should be very dark red. We work it through a wire strainer in order to have a dark-red vegetable stock. To this we add the lemon juice, and finally we pour it into the beetroot soup we have already prepared. Let the bortsch come to the boil again and serve this soup without any garnish in it. It is served in cups.

The *pastries* served with this bortsch are unique. Sometimes they look like baby ears; then they are very small and sparsely stuffed. For them we must use puff-pastry. To prepare it well is both tedious and difficult. Therefore it is simpler to use ready-made puff-pastry. The tiny rolls having the shape of an ear are called *uszka*; the other kind, oblong in shape and rolled up, are called *pieroski*. In Poland they use several kinds of stuffing. Personally I liked the mushroom filling best. I cannot give you an exact amount for the ingredients, as this will depend on how many pastries you are going to fill and what size they are. But I shall describe the method of making them.

Roll out the pastry and cut the desired shapes, either small ear or long oblong rolls. Fill with a small amount of stuffing, seal, and deep-fry golden brown. As soon as they come to the surface and float in the deep-frying oil or fat they are ready. They should be served at once, two per person.

To give you some idea of the proportions here is a mushroom filling:

Half-pound of well-washed, dried, and finely chopped mushrooms, 1 finely chopped small onion, 2½ tablespoons of butter, about 6 tablespoons of breadcrumbs preferably made with old white bread, salt and pepper to taste. We mix all the ingredients well, and we then have a small amount of filling. We do not use more than 1 tablespoon for one uszka and just a bit more for the pieroski.

If you serve the clear bortsch soup there should be something to accompany it besides these tiny filled pastries. In Poland they also serve with it cooked white beans topped with chopped parsley or creamy mashed potatoes.

Here is a chicken recipe given to me by a teacher in a Warsaw cookery school.

Kurczeta po Polsku (Polish Roasted Chicken)

for 6 servings:

3 spring chickens

FOR ROASTING
3 tablespoons butter
3 tablespoons lard

FOR THE STUFFING
3 rolls soaked in milk and squeezed afterwards
4 tablespoons butter
2–3 eggs—the more the better
the chopped liver and heart of 3 chickens

2 tablespoons breadcrumbs
4 tablespoons chopped fresh dill or 1½ teaspoons dried dill
pepper and salt to taste

First we prepare the stuffing, and for this we separate the egg-yolks from the whites. Whip the whites, squeeze the rolls well, and mix them with the chopped livers and hearts, pepper and salt to taste, the butter (which should be soft), the egg-yolks, breadcrumbs, and dill. For preference fresh dill should be used as it is tastier. To end with we add the well-beaten egg-white and check if this mixture has the correct consistency. It should be like a creamy omelet. If it is too creamy add more breadcrumbs. Divide in three parts and stuff each spring chicken with it. Fasten with skewers or sew with thread.

Turn the oven full on, and in the meantime put a saucepan with the butter and the lard on the stove. Let this brown. When the oven is very hot put the chickens in a roasting-pan in the oven, but first pour the browned butter and lard over the chickens. Let the chickens brown in the hot oven as quickly as possible. Then reduce the heat a little and allow about 30 minutes of roasting. In order to have a savoury gravy which does not burn we add some cut-up leek (the white as well as the green) tied in a bunch with some parsley stalks to the roasting-pan. Baste the chickens now and then with this gravy.

Serve on hot plates; each guest has a half-chicken with some of the exquisite stuffing next to it. With it they serve in Poland a cucumber salad.

Mizeria ze Smietana (Cucumber Salad)

Make a creamy mixture with cream, finely chopped onions, salt, pepper, and sugar. Shred the cucumber coarsely and over it pour the creamy mixture, to which has been added a fair amount of lemon juice. This salad should have a sweet-sour taste.

With these chickens we eat boiled potatoes also well sprinkled with fresh chopped dill. If lacking the dill, parsley will do.

Kotlet de Wolaj (Chicken Cutlets)

for 2 servings:

2 boned skinned raw breast-pieces of a roaster
½ cup butter

2 tablespoons chopped parsley
pepper and salt to taste

about ½ cup home-made
breadcrumbs
1–2 eggs
1 tablespoon melted butter
or oil

a deep-frying pan with oil or
fat

Let the butter get soft, but not by heating it on the stove. Leave it somewhere in the kitchen in a warm place for some time before you need it.

Chop the parsley, washed and well dried beforehand. Put the deep-frying pan filled with oil or fat on a low heat without the lid. Have a wooden board ready and covered with breadcrumbs, a soup-plate with 2 beaten eggs mixed with a tablespoon of melted butter or oil, salt to taste, and some cayenne pepper. Flatten the two boned breast-pieces as much as possible with a meat chopper. Then with a very sharp knife make a long incision in the middle, but in such a way that the meat is not cut right through. Mix the soft butter with the chopped parsley and salt and pepper it to taste. Fill each incision of these two pieces of white chicken meat with half the green butter mixture. Roll up the chicken meat and sew it up with thread. Egg and bread-crumbs these two chicken rolls according to the standard rules. Breadcrumb the pieces twice over in order to have them well covered. Now we deep-fry them in the fat or oil which by now should be quite hot. We must reduce the heat under the deep-frying pan when the two chicken rolls are well browned and allow a little less than 15 minutes for them to be nicely cooked. Serve them on a warm plate with slices of lemon. With this dish we serve mashed or French-fried potatoes and a macedoine of vegetables including green peas, asparagus, and slices of car-rots. If we do not feel like preparing fresh vegetables we can buy a can of vegetable macedoine or use frozen vegetables. We heat both kinds in butter, add salt and pepper to taste and some chopped parsley. A point to remember in eating these chicken cutlets is that when cutting them on the dish we must be careful not to spill the butter which comes out, for the butter-parsley mixture has become hot while deep-frying and will serve as the perfect gravy.

Another way of preparing chicken cutlets in Poland is as follows:

Kotlet po Polsku (Polish Chicken Cutlets)

for 4 servings:

½ boiled or roasted fowl	2 tablespoons chopped fresh
3 white bread rolls soaked	dill
in milk and squeezed	salt and pepper to taste
afterwards	1 tablespoon breadcrumbs
⅓ pound mushrooms	½ cup butter or lard
3 tablespoons butter	some lettuce leaves

Skin and bone the chicken, chop up the meat and the washed and well-dried mushrooms. Using a fork, add and mix to it the well-squeezed bread rolls, the 3 tablespoons of soft butter, the tablespoon of breadcrumbs, and the fresh dill with salt and pepper to taste. Should fresh dill not be available use chopped parsley, celery, and ¼ teaspoon of dried dill coarsely chopped. After mixing the chicken meat with all the other ingredients we should have obtained a mixture of good consistency. It should not be too creamy, but should be sufficiently firm to shape into cutlets. Flour or breadcrumb these cutlets according to your taste. A breaded cutlet looks much nicer and is tastier than a cutlet which is only floured. The floured cutlets are roasted in hot butter in an omelet-pan, the breaded ones are deep-fried.

In both cases they have only to brown, as they are already cooked. When hot, serve them sprinkled with chopped parsley and placed on a lettuce leaf. Roasted potatoes and a red beet-root salad go well with these cutlets.

Swikla z Chrzanem (Red Beetroot Salad with Horseradish)
for 4 servings:

1 pound boiled red beetroots

FOR THE SAUCE

*the juice of 1 big lemon or
the same amount of
vinegar
3 tablespoons grated fresh or
prepared horseradish
1 lettuce
½ cup cream*

*1 tablespoon chopped dill or
a pinch dried dill
2 tablespoons chopped onion
or shallot
pepper, salt, and sugar to
taste*

Cut the beetroot in thin slices. Do not shred them, for they then get too soggy. Cover a salad bowl with the washed and well-dried lettuce leaves. Put on the slices of beetroot and pour the sauce over it. This sauce is very easy to prepare. Mix the finely chopped onion or shallot with the vinegar or the lemon juice, add salt, pepper, and sugar to taste. Be generous with the sugar; this is important. Add the grated horseradish and the cream. If you wish you can use condensed milk with half of the ½ cup of cream only. As a finishing touch we add the dill—for preference fresh dill as its flavour is so much better.

If we have to use dried dill it is advisable to mix in with it some fresh green flavours such as chives, chervil, or parsley. Marjoram tastes well in this salad.

How to deal with horseradish root will be found in the Scandinavian chapter on page 112.

Here is a very savoury chicken soup.

Zupa z Kury (Clear Chicken Soup)

for 6 servings:

½ boiling fowl
2 large carrots
½ cup noodles
pepper and salt to taste
¾ cup coarsely cut-up
vegetables

2 tablespoons chopped
parsley, chives, and the like
7 cups water

Remove all the fat and bring the chicken to the boil in the water, together with the coarsely chopped soup vegetables. When the water boils thoroughly reduce the heat and put the lid on the pan. Allow about 1½ hours for the bird to be done, but we must see that it is not overdone. Add salt and pepper to taste. In the meantime cut the two peeled and washed carrots into julienne. When the chicken is cooked pour the stock through a sieve. Let this broth come to the boil again and add the julienne of carrots and the noodles. Reduce the heat and allow only 10 minutes for the carrot julienne and the noodles to be done. While this is happening we must skin and bone the chicken and cut the meat into small pieces. These we will add to the soup a few minutes before serving. See that it is well salted and peppered and add some chopped green. This makes a very simple yet excellently nutritious soup with which we should serve very small squares of bread and put paprika powder and tomato ketchup on the table for those who like them.

Another chicken soup tasted in a Polish-Jewish restaurant was also a zupa z kury (chicken soup) prepared in the same way but with the difference that soaked white beans were cooked in the strained chicken broth (that is, when the chicken had been taken out) and the noodles added later. This chicken soup is flavoured with fresh green herbs and some paprika powder. It is a more complete meal than the other version.

This is about the last of my Polish chicken recipes!

Kurczeta Duszone z Warzywami (Braised Chicken with Vegetables)

for 6 servings:

1 big boiling fowl divided in 6–8 pieces

½ pound vegetables, including green peas or dried green peas (soaked), little pieces of cauliflower, parts of onions, diced celeriac, leek cut up very coarsely, runner beans, if available fresh asparagus, small carrots

3 tablespoons lard
2 tablespoons flour
2 tablespoons butter
2 tablespoons chopped parsley or dill
salt and pepper to taste

Brown the lard well in a pan and sauté the pieces of chicken with all the coarsely cut up vegetables until nicely browned. If canned vegetables are used, however, add them only a few minutes before serving. Do try to have some fresh vegetables in this dish, for it will taste so much better. When all these ingredients are a deep golden colour add salt and pepper to taste, pour just enough water on to cover, and put the lid on the pan. Reduce the heat and allow about 1½ hours for the pieces of chicken to be cooked. Put a dishcloth wrung out in water round the lid to ensure that no steam can escape.

When the chicken is done we finish the dish by stirring the melted butter and the flour into a smooth mixture in a little saucepan. Dilute this mixture with some of the chicken stock and then add this thick sauce to the chicken. Stir with a fork and boil for about 10 minutes in an uncovered pan. Check for salt and pepper, finish with the chopped parsley and/or dill and serve. Boiled rice or potatoes go well with this dish.

Before leaving Poland I should like to give you a speciality I particularly enjoyed and which in former days was a favourite with hunters.

Bigos (Sauerkraut)

for 4–6 servings:

2 pounds sauerkraut
1 pound white cabbage finely shredded
¾ pound fat pork cut up in dice
¾ pound lean pork diced
4 tablespoons butter, margarine, or lard
2–3 sliced onions
2½ tablespoons flour
salt and pepper to taste

2 bay leaves (not too large)
8 cardamom seeds (a ginger flavour)
2 cloves of garlic
15 soaked dried prunes
¾ pound Polish sausages (if not available we can use the Hungarian kind called kolbasz or some English smoked sausage)

For this recipe we work with two pans. In one we prepare the sauerkraut and in the other we cook the white cabbage.

Sauerkraut. Lightly brown the diced fat pork in half the butter, lard, or margarine, and then add the sliced onions with the diced lean pork, the cardamom seeds, and the bay leaves. When all the ingredients are a golden colour we add the sauerkraut and as much water as is needed to let the sauerkraut cook for about 2 hours without allowing it to stick to the pan. This is very important.

Start by adding only a little water, and then, when the sauerkraut has boiled for about 10 minutes, check to see if it has enough liquid, adding some more water if it is required. Allow the sauerkraut to simmer for at least 2 hours in a covered pan on reduced heat.

White Cabbage. Using the other pan, we let the remaining butter turn golden and sauté the shredded white cabbage in it until it is also a golden colour. Now add the cloves of garlic with the soaked drained prunes and pepper and salt to taste. But remember that the sauerkraut is already salted, and so do not overdo the additional salt. Bring the cabbage to the boil, pouring in ⅓ pint of liquid in which the prunes were soaked. Cover the pan, reduce the heat, and allow about 30 minutes' cooking time.

The cabbage must be tender and the prunes stoned after cooking. During the cooking process shake the pan from time to time so as to mix the prunes well with the white cabbage. When both the sauerkraut and the cabbage are done mix them together.

If we have a lot of liquid left over—which should not really happen—we use only about 1 cup of it and stir in the flour. Bring the sauce to the boil and finally stir it into the bigos. In the meantime we must cut the sausages in slices and fry them in hot oil to a golden brown. We put them next to the prunes. The bigos is a wonderful dish, and a little of the white sauce makes it so creamy.

We serve this speciality in a warm deep dish. But we take care to have the prunes and the sausage on top of the bigos, as they make the dish look so much more appetizing.

In Poland it is not usual to serve potatoes with this dish.

And here is just one more Polish speciality.

Omlet z Lososiem Wedzonya (Omelet with Smoked Salmon)

It is not necessary to instruct you in the making of an omelet. Every cook prepares an omelet in her own way. However, I should like to mention that we can only succeed in preparing a perfect omelet when we limit its size and make it for, say, 3 servings. For this use 5–6 eggs beaten with 3 tablespoons of water or beer, ½ tablespoon of tomato ketchup, and a few drops of tabasco sauce, pepper and salt to taste. This is indeed a wonderful omelet mixture. It is best to prepare two light creamy omelets at a time. When done put a slice of smoked salmon in the middle of each. Fold the omelets and serve immediately.

Serve toast and butter with it. This will make a very light and attractive warm first course.

Now for England.

ENGLAND

WITHOUT any justification people abroad have often been heard to say that one cannot get a good meal in England. I have never agreed with this, and the more I know England the more am I convinced that the English are good cooks and well versed in the culinary arts. Unfortunately, a visitor to England may be bitterly disappointed with what he is served in the restaurants and hotels in the smaller places. This is true of many other countries, but it is equally true that France proves the exception to the rule, for there in every wayside inn and in every restaurant, even in the smallest village, one is served with perfect food. But then, as I have said before, the French are born cooks.

I consider that the English housewife is at her best when roasting joints of prime meat. The Dutch housewife, on the contrary, is clumsy and inexperienced as regards oven roasting, and so only too often she roasts her joints and chickens on top of the stove. The English housewife never has the slightest difficulty with her oven. She is indeed a *rôtisseuse de naissance*. Whether she prepares a big or small joint of meat or a big or small roasting chicken in the oven it always comes out perfectly cooked. Where else in the world does one see such beautifully roasted joints such as a saddle of mutton or lamb, beef, pork, or veal, or those handsome fillet steaks? Roasting time and method seem to present no problems to the English cook.

The English are born gardeners, and where they have a garden there is usually a border for herbs of various kinds. With their widespread Commonwealth connexions they are familiar with many spices imported into the country and sold widely in shops and stores. When walking through London's Soho you will come across many shops stocking imported herbs and spices and other exotic ingredients such as dried fish in many shapes and sizes, dried vegetables from innumerable countries, and many other ingredients from all over the world.

The chicken has always taken a most important place in English cookery. It is prepared in many ways, but as with meats perhaps the English excell most in grilling and roasting.

But if I am to talk to you about real English chicken recipes I should prefer to give you some very original, very old-fashioned recipes that I have discovered in old English cookery books.

First comes a chicken recipe from Florence White's cookery book. In this book many women, and men too, describe the way they prepared their dishes. I have chosen a typical English chicken dish for you.

Chicken Pudding

for 4 servings:

THE CRUST

1 pound flour
¾ cup beef suet finely minced
½ teaspoon salt
about ½ cup water with
    3–4 tablespoons flour or the
    yolks of 4 eggs and a little
    water

THE STUFFING

1 cut-up chicken, floured
some slices of ham cut into
    strips about ¼ inch long
chopped parsley leaves

some button mushrooms
pepper and salt to taste
a thin slice of veal or fresh
    pork

You will also need a closely woven cloth wrung out in hot water. Put this inside a colander with the edges hanging well over and see that the cloth is well floured. Prepare the crust, roll it out, and then place it in the cloth, so providing a space ready to be packed with the chicken mixture. Put in the pieces of chicken (they should not be too big). Scatter over this the ham, the parsley, and the mushrooms, with pepper and salt to taste. Cover with the thin slice of veal or pork. Pour a teacup of water over it and then seal the top with suet crust moulded with side crust by pinching the edges together. Cover with a piece of buttered paper, then bring up the edges of the cloth and tie them tightly with string so that water cannot get in during boiling. Put in a greased basin and let cook in water for about 3 hours. The water must be kept well on the boil and hot water added if necessary. Keep the lid on.

And here is another chicken recipe.

Chicken Croquettes

for 4 servings:

¾ cup chopped white cooked chicken meat
½ cup smoked tongue (bought ready)
¼ chopped mushrooms
1 tablespoon chopped parsley
pepper, salt, and nutmeg to taste

2 cups Béchamel sauce (rather thick white sauce), made from 3 tablespoons butter, 5–6 tablespoons flour, and rather less than 2 cups milk

BREADCRUMBING
1 or 2 egg-yolks
2 teaspoons oil

pepper and salt to taste
breadcrumbs

FOR GARNISHING
fried parsley
2 cups tomato or curry sauce

a frying-pan with oil or vegetable fat

Mix the chopped chicken, the finely diced tongue, the chopped parsley, and the chopped mushrooms with the thick hot Béchamel sauce. Add salt, pepper, and nutmeg to taste, and let this all come to the boil in a saucepan. Check the consistency of the mixture; it should not be runny but creamy and rather thick. Spread on a large plate; let it cool and become firm.

For the breadcrumbing: mix egg-yolks with oil, pepper, and salt to taste in a not too small bowl. Spread out a generous amount of breadcrumbs on a wooden board. When the mixture has completely cooled shape it into finger-long sausages. Next flour them lightly; then roll them in the egg-yolks and finally in the breadcrumbs. Repeat this process once more.

A double breadcrumbing of this sort makes the croquettes indeed *croquant* (crunchy). The oil or fat in the deep-frying pan has in the meantime become quite hot. Deep-fry the croquettes a golden-brown colour and let them get heated through and through. Take them out with a skimmer and drain off the oil or fat.

Serve with fried parsley and tomato or curry sauce.

Now we will prepare a special soup for invalids.

Invalid Chicken Broth

for 4 servings:

1 boiling chicken	some flavours (herbs or spices
6 cups water	if allowed)
pepper and salt to taste (if allowed)	

Skin the chicken and take off all fat. Chop all the giblets very finely. Put the chicken meat, divided in four parts, with the chopped giblets in a pan. If the patient is allowed it add 1 slice of celeriac, 1 tiny piece of mace, a bunch of green herbs, and 1 small onion. Pour on the water and bring to the boil. Reduce the heat and allow about 2 hours' cooking in a well-covered pan. Pour the broth through a sieve and let cool. The fat which has come to the surface should be skimmed off completely. If this is not forbidden we can add salt and pepper to taste when the broth has come to the boil again, and also the chicken, now boned and divided into small pieces.

If you would rather serve the broth without the chicken garnish you can use the chicken meat for a stew, prepared as follows:

Brown Chicken Fricassee

for 4 servings:

1 cooked boned chicken divided in not too small pieces	1 bunch green herbs (parsley, celery, or chive stalks)
	1 bay leaf
5 carrots cut in slices	2 cloves
10 peeled shallots or 2 onions	2 slices of fat bacon

Cut the bacon in small pieces and let them fry in a baking-pan. When they are brown add the onions and the carrots with the herbs to it. Allow about 15 minutes' simmering in a closed pan.

After having tasted the carrots to see if these are done add the pieces of chicken with the bay leaf and the cloves. In 10 minutes it should be ready. The pieces of chicken are already cooked and should not be overdone.

Taste to see if the fricassee has enough salt. Should you wish to add a special flavour then you can put a tablespoon of brandy or whisky into it.

Serve this fricassee with boiled potatoes and a well-prepared vegetable dish. This fricassee is served in its gravy with the bay leaf, the bunch of herbs, and the cloves removed.

French beans are delicious with this dish, but personally I prefer cauliflower without white sauce.

From the Dominions I got the following recipe.

Chicken Casserole

for 4 servings:

1 roaster divided in 4–6 pieces	5 slices fat bacon
salt to taste	3 slices lean bacon
1 ample pinch of pepper	flour and water
2 finely chopped onions	2 tablespoons chopped herbs
¾ pound peas (fresh and weighed shelled)	(parsley, chives, and/or celery)

Fry the lean and the fat bacon a golden-brown colour and flour the pieces of roaster. Roast them in the browned lard a golden brown and add salt to taste. Now add the shelled and washed fresh peas (not too small) with the chopped onions. Let both vegetables turn golden. Add one more tablespoon of flour and stir the flour through the gravy with a fork. Put the lid on the pan and reduce the heat. In about 25 minutes the pieces of roaster are done if the bird is not tough.

At the end of the first 10 minutes we look to see that the sauce has not become too thick. If it has, then add 2 or 3 table-spoons of water or stock. I am assuming that no water has been used as the washed peas should supply sufficient moisture.

When the roaster and the peas are done we add some pepper and check to see if there is enough salt.

Serve with celery (red) braised in butter after having first boiled it in water and salt. Remember that celery must never be over-cooked. To handle fresh celery cut off the top stalks with the green leaves. These leaves can be added to the chicken fricassee. The top stalks themselves are peeled thinly, but only if necessary. With very young celery this peeling is not usually re-quired, and all we need to do is to wash them well. Serve the thin stalks as an appetizer with cocktails.

The lower part must be well washed and peeled with a vege-table peeler. We then cut the stalks in halves lengthwise and boil in water and salt. And, as already said, we braise them in butter or, if you prefer, in lard.

Boiled potatoes or rice go well with this fricassee. If we use rice we can garnish with roasted tomatoes cut in halves.

Serve this chicken in its sauce with the garnish in it.

And how about trying the following chicken soup?

Chicken Minute Soup

for 4 servings:

½ a small-sized boiling fowl   bunch green herbs
6 cups water
1 packet curry or mushroom
   soup or 1 can curry or
   mushroom soup

Boil the chicken in the 6 cups of water with a bunch of green herbs (to which some tarragon should be added), 1 garnished onion, but no salt. We have, of course, removed all the fat beforehand.

We should not salt this stock because the packets or cans of soup are already salted. As we want to prepare a minute broth we prepare it in a pressure cooker. We allow only about 20 minutes for the cooking. Strain the broth and let it cool a little and then add the contents of the packet or the can and bring to the boil again. Stir with a wire whisk.

When the soup boils we reduce the heat and allow about 10 minutes before serving. In the meanwhile we have skinned and boned the half-chicken and cut the meat in strips. These strips we add to the soup 5 minutes before serving with, if needed, some salt or pepper.

Some cream added to this chicken soup will further improve the flavour.

Sauté Chicken Livers

for 2 servings:

¼ pound chicken livers	salt and pepper to taste
5 slices bacon	2 tablespoons sherry
¼ cup mushrooms	

Fry and brown the bacon in an omelet-pan. Wash the livers thoroughly in order to let them become a browny-yellow without any red threads remaining. Dry them well and flour. Sauté them in the hot bacon to a golden colour and add salt and pepper to taste. Now sauté the sliced mushrooms with them and allow to simmer in an open pan for about 10 minutes. The livers are now done. We remove the pan from the fire and add the sherry. This dish we serve either on a slice of freshly made toast or on cooked rice. Personally I always add some Worcester Sauce.

How does an English cook prepare a chicken for the oven? This is the recipe I was given as answer to this question.

Roast Chicken with Sausage-meat Stuffing

for 4 servings:

1 roaster
½ cup cooking fat
pepper and salt to taste

FOR THE STUFFING

½ pound pork sausage meat   2 tablespoons breadcrumbs
pinch mixed herbs and spices   1 egg or some stock or water
the grated rind of ¼ lemon   pepper and salt to taste

We first prepare the stuffing by mixing all the given ingredients. An egg will always improve this stuffing. If we do not use an egg, we must add some stock or water in order to prepare a smooth stuffing.

We stuff the breast of the chicken with the mixture, using our fingers to ease the skin of the breast from the meat, being careful not to tear it. The stuffing is pushed evenly under the skin of the breast, which is then sewn up with thread or fastened with skewers.

Turn on the oven to reach a medium heat and let the fat in the roasting-pan get brown. This roasting-pan should be neither too large nor too small. When the fat is brown place the roaster in it and baste before putting the pan back into the hot oven. When the roaster has turned brown all over we add salt to taste.

For a tender roaster allow about 15 minutes for each pound weight and 15 minutes over. Now and then we can baste the bird with the gravy. If you do not wish to remain in the kitchen for the basting cover the chicken with some aluminium foil or wax-paper. Butter or margarine can be used instead of cooking-fat. Fat bacon placed on top of the chicken is an excellent basting medium.

With this roast chicken we serve a bread sauce prepared as follows.

Bread Sauce. Use about 6 tablespoons of breadcrumbs made with very old dry rolls crushed on a bread-board with a rolling-pin. Personally I use an electric meat grinder for this kind of work. We also need 1 small onion to which 1 bay leaf is fastened with 2 cloves, pepper and salt to taste, and about 2 cups of milk with ¼ cup butter or margarine.

Mix the breadcrumbs with the whole onion and pepper and salt to taste in a saucepan. Pour the milk over it and put this pan, well covered, in the oven about 30 minutes before the chicken is to be served. Having removed the garnished onion from the bread sauce, stir the butter or margarine into it with a wire whisk. This sauce is served with the roast chicken. We can, of course, also prepare the sauce on the stove, but it is easier to cook in the oven.

With it go roast potatoes and new turnips.

New Turnips

for 4 servings:

about 2 pounds turnips
salt and pepper to taste
1 cup water
the juice of 1 lemon

2 tablespoons butter or margarine
1 tablespoon chopped parsley

Peel the turnips thinly and cut them in not too thin slices. Bring the water with the lemon juice to the boil and then add the sliced turnips with salt to taste. In a covered pan on reduced heat allow about 6–10 minutes' cooking. They should never be over-cooked, for then they lose some of their flavour. Drain and then sauté them in the hot butter or margarine. Taste to see if they are well salted; add some pepper and the chopped parsley just before serving. You can also prepare a white sauce with the boiling liquid, butter, and flour, adding to it some fresh lemon juice for extra flavour.

Having given you some English chicken recipes, I cannot end this chapter without having a recipe from Mrs. Beeton's *Book of Household Management.*

As I work there lies beside my typewriter a copy of one of the very first editions, with its wonderful red-leather binding and luscious illustrations. Since first published this book has often been revised. Personally I like the original edition best of all.

Mrs. Beeton—I don't know if she really cared for cooking or was just an inspired gastronome—knew what the art of cooking meant. The book covers so wide a field that one cannot help feeling that Mrs. Beeton enjoyed good food and loved cooking it.

Here is her

Chicken Pilaff

for 4 servings:

1 *roaster or tender young boiling fowl*	2 *Spanish onions*
6 *cups water with 2 pounds of scrag or neck of mutton or just 6 cups ordinary stock*	2 *small onions*
	1 *tablespoon curry powder or paste*
	1 *carrot*
¾ *cup rice*	1 *blade mace (small)*
½ *cup butter*	6 *black peppercorns*
	salt and pepper to taste

Divide the chicken into pieces convenient to serve; skin and bone them. Put the backbone, neck, giblets, and bones in the water with the mutton or use the stock and add the outside of the Spanish onions, the carrot, mace, and peppercorns. Gently boil for about 2–2½ hours. Then strain. Heat ¼ cup of butter in a stewing-pan; dice the Spanish onions and fry them to a light brown. Add the rice with 3 cups of stock, season with salt and pepper, and cook gently. We melt the remaining butter and fry the pieces of chicken nicely brown and then let them simmer. When the rice has absorbed the greater part of the stock, we take out the chicken and add the curry powder or paste and mix well with the rice. Continue cooking until the rice and the chicken are perfectly tender, adding some more stock if necessary.

A few minutes before serving re-heat the butter in which the chicken was fried, cut the 2 onions into slices, and fry them brown. Place the pilaff in the centre of a hot dish, scatter on the slices of fried onions, and serve.

And with this last chicken recipe we say good-bye to England and follow Gallina to Greece and Turkey.

SECOND TOUR:
Greece and Turkey

I CONSIDER it perfectly logical to deal in one chapter with these two countries, Greece and Turkey, because of the great similarity in their methods of cooking. Indeed, sometimes it is almost impossible to tell by either its flavour or its appearance to which country a particular dish belongs.

GREECE

I VISITED Greece a few years ago and was much impressed by the exquisite simplicity of Greek cooking, reflecting a sobriety which is to be found in many other aspects of Greek life. They make inspired use of their native fruits, the sweet oranges, the peaches, lemons and limes, seedless raisins, a delicious melon remarkable for its pale yellow flesh, and a whole variety of vegetables, sweet peppers, egg-plants (aubergines), cabbage, beans, and vine leaves. Mutton and lamb are greatly appreciated, but chicken, although equally popular, is still looked upon as a luxury.

Fish and all kinds of shellfish, on the other hand, are a commonplace. Fish in particular is beautifully prepared and eaten with pleasure by all classes. You will ask in what way Greek cooking differs from others. This is a difficult question to answer. As I said, Greek cooking closely resembles that of its neighbours, which leads me to say that it is at times reminiscent of the Levant and even the Far East.

Equally evident in the Greek kitchen is the influence of all the different peoples who at one time or another made an impact on Greece. Byzantines, Armenians, Rumanians, Albanians, the Jews, even the Kurds, all left their mark, the Jews bringing with them recipes based on the precepts of the Talmud and wholly eschewing pork. It is probably because of religious taboos that so little pork is eaten in these countries, though grilled bacon and pork cooked and served on skewers is popular everywhere, particularly in Greece. That there should be little meat available, with the exception of mutton and goat, is not entirely surprising in a country as lacking in good pasture as Greece, and it is therefore natural that the principal national dishes should be based on mutton, lamb, goat, or kid, with ghee (clarified goat-milk butter) used as the cooking-fat. This ghee is similarly used in Turkey, as well as in the Near and the Far East. The Greeks too have always been famous for the cunning way in which they use herbs, particularly fresh green ones, and spices, while they are also clever at grilling, which after all was one of the earliest beginnings of cooking. Even to-day no restaurant is complete without its panoply of huge skewers on which are grilled the most heterogeneous morsels. For grilling the best quality olive oil is used, and this applies equally to Turkey. Needless to say, olives, both black and green, are among the most popular and constant appetizers in this country of olive groves.

Whoever goes to Athens must not omit a visit to the port of Piraeus, or to the many restaurants along the coast. They offer a wide variety of local specialities, and chief among these are the deep-fried shrimps and small lobsters and the succulent, never-to-be-forgotten fish-soups. In every dish you will find quantities of garlic and olives . . . lots and lots of them.

If savoury dishes are popular with the Greeks this does not mean that they do not also have a sweet tooth. Indeed, the quantities of sweet confections they can eat from morning till night is almost unbelievable, and all washed down by innumerable cups of Greek or rather Turkish coffee. The many wayside inns, coffee-shops, and restaurants small and large are crowded all day long, and the men, smoking their Turkish pipes, give one an impression of *dolce far niente* or deep and true relaxation.

Incidentally, for those of my readers eager to hear all about Turkish coffee I have given the recipe in the second part of this chapter. For now we must turn to the Greek cuisine, which will include chicken and national dishes.

Here is the first of the recipes given to me by a young Greek cook who works in a Greek restaurant in Rotterdam. He knows how to outline Greek recipes in such a way that they can easily be prepared by a non-Greek, and I am sure you will like the food. Here is his chicken soup.

Soupa Avgolemono (Chicken Soup with Lemon)

for 6 servings:

1 lean boiling fowl with giblets, wings, and neck	2 large eggs
about 2 tablespoons rice	8 cups boiling water
1 juicy lemon	salt and pepper to taste

Put the cut-up chicken with the giblets, neck, and wings in a stock-pot and pour the 8 cups of boiling water over it. Add salt to taste and let the water come to the boil again. Allow the chicken to simmer gently for about 1½–2 hours, or less if it is a tender fowl, as it should not be overdone.

Try it now and then to see if it is done. This is important, as later on we need the boiled fowl for a main dish. When it is done, take all the pieces of chicken out of the stock and put them on a dish. Cover and allow to cool.

The stock must be brought to the boil again, and we cook the rice in it for about 20 minutes. Meanwhile we beat the eggs with the lemon juice. When the rice is done we add pepper to taste and check to see if the soup is salted enough.

Now with a wire whisk we beat the egg and lemon juice into the soup. Beat energetically in order to obtain a wonderful golden froth at the top of the stock.

Pour the soup into the soup-plates and see that every guest has an equal share of this golden egg-froth.

We serve the boiled fowl with a Domates sauce (tomatoes) and risi (rice).

For this sauce heat about ½ cup of olive oil in a saucepan and fry till golden 2 sliced onions, 1–2 cloves of garlic (crushed), a tablespoon fresh marjoram or oregano (if dried only 1 teaspoon). Add salt to taste and cayenne pepper. Now we peel a pound of small tomatoes and add them to this mixture with 1 good tablespoon of tomato purée, 2 tablespoons cornflour diluted with about ¼ cup of chicken stock or water with a meat cube. Remember that when using a cube less salt is needed. Let this sauce simmer gently in an open pan for about 30 minutes, by which time it should have thickened as some of the liquid has evaporated. Then we work it through a sieve and finish it with ½ cup of Bulgarian yoghurt blended with some sugar. Before serving try for salt and pepper. If you do not care for yoghurt you can use cream instead.

To prepare the risi for 6 servings we heat 1 tablespoon of olive oil in a pan, but do not let it get too hot. We add 1 pound of rice, washed at least 4 times. Let this drain well before adding it to the oil. Pour on as much water as is required to cook the rice dry, and allow 17 minutes for it to be finished.

In the meantime we have rubbed some old coffee-cups with oil, and each cup we fill with the cooked rice, pressing it well down. Then we turn them over on to a hot dish. You have now prepared nice cup-shaped little moulds.

The cooked, warm chicken is divided in pieces. Arrange these round the rice moulds and pour part of the tomato sauce over them. Serve the rest in a sauce-boat. This chicken can also be served cold.

Salata Kremilia (Greek Salad *à la Clem*)

for 6 servings:

a cooked chicken
4 not too small onions finely
    sliced
6 big, firm peeled tomatoes,
    divided in small parts
3 tablespoons pickles (*pot*)
1½ tablespoons black-stoned
    halved olives
1½ tablespoons green-stoned
    halved olives

6 tablespoons olive oil
3–4 tablespoons lemon juice
pinch cayenne pepper
some salt
if available 1 egg-plant and
    1 pimento, both raw and
    cut up in julienne

Mix all these ingredients except the fowl and allow about 3 hours for the salad to marinate in a covered bowl. For the sake of colourfulness you should use an egg-plant (aubergine) and, if you like them, one green and one red pimento (paprika). The more pimentos, the better does this salad taste.

We divide the chicken in pieces, not too big, but skinned and boned. Put them in a circle on the salad or if you prefer in a separate bowl, on a bed of lettuce leaves. Serve with bread and butter.

And here is a Greek barbecue version for chicken.

Kotopoulo kotta Stofvarno (Barbecue Chicken)

for 4 servings:

1 tender roaster
¼ cup butter
salt and pepper to taste

1 small lemon, unpeeled
and sliced

Dry the outside of the chicken and stuff the inside with the slices of lemon. Sew or fasten with skewers. Butter or oil the whole outside of the bird and add salt to taste. The oven or grill should be full on for about 10 minutes before we put the chicken in to brown as quickly as possible. Only then do we reduce the heat. Allow 20 minutes' cooking time, but here again much will depend both on the tenderness of the chicken and the heat of the grill or oven. Now and then we baste with olive oil or butter to keep the chicken from drying out or turning too brown.

In the meantime we prepare the tomato sauce as described on page 192, while the potatoes have been prepared in the morning.

Patates (Potatoes in the Greek Way)

for 4 servings:

2 pounds potatoes
the juice of 2 lemons
salt and pepper to taste
¼ cup olive oil

1 tablespoon oregano (wild
marjoram) or ½ teaspoon
of the dried variety

Butter a fireproof dish or use olive oil. Peel the potatoes and cut them lengthwise in thin slices. Put these slices in the fireproof dish in layers and add salt and pepper to taste, together with the oregano. We pour the lemon juice over the top layer and as much olive oil as we think necessary to prepare a creamy potato dish. I use at least ¼ cup, but a Greek cook would use even more. The oven has been turned on for 10 minutes already, and we put this dish in it. Let the contents come to the boil and then reduce the heat and allow at least 45–60 minutes for the potatoes to become done and creamy. This dish looks just as fluffy and creamy as a well-prepared omelet. The potatoes with the combined flavours of oregano, lemon juice, and olive oil are absolutely delicious to eat. There is, however, one point to bear in mind. While the potatoes are baking in the oven watch to see that they do not dry out. To prevent this cover them with aluminium foil if they begin to look dry. The oil does the cooking for you. Prepare this dish in the morning as it is served cold. According to my Greek friend, these potatoes are well prepared only if a spoon put into the mixture gives the impression that you are stirring thickly whipped cream.

Divide the chicken into 4 pieces and add some pepper. Put them on a dish and pour the tomato sauce over them and serve with the cold potatoes.

And now I will give you some completely different recipes that have nothing to do with the chicken but are very typical and, moreover, so easy to prepare.

Here is a Greek fish soup.

Psarosoupe (Fish Soup)

for 6 servings:

at least 2–3 pounds sea fish
(gurnard, John Dory,
tunafish, or red mullet)
½ celeriac
1 leek
4 tomatoes
5 carrots
1 garnished onion
1 bunch green stalks

2 tablespoons rice
2 tablespoons tomato purée
2 tablespoons olive oil
1 lemon
about 8 cups water
salt and cayenne pepper to
taste (but be careful with
salt)

Wash and clean the vegetables, cut the celeriac into not too thin slices and dice them. The carrots as well as the leek and the peeled tomatoes we cut up in not too small pieces.

Put the fish into a stock-pot with all the vegetables, the garnished onion, and the bunch of green stalks. Reserve the rice and the tomato purée. Pour the boiling water over this mixture and add a little salt and bring to the boil again. The water will have come off the boil because of all the cold ingredients added to it. Simmer for about 10–15 minutes, then the whole fish should be done. This will depend on size, so please check. Take the fish out with a skimmer, but leave the vegetables in the fish stock. Bone and skin the fish and put it between two plates. Have a saucepan ready in which to heat the olive oil. Fry the rice in this till golden brown and then add the tomato purée. This mixture we add to the fish soup and cook the rice gently for about 20 minutes.

We are now almost ready. Take the garnished onions with the green bunch out of the soup and add to it the medium-sized pieces of fish. Coarsely chop the leaves of the green stalks, take the pan off the stove, and add them to the soup. Taste to see if it is salted enough and add cayenne pepper with the lemon juice.

Serve this soup very hot and with pieces of warm bread, fried in hot oil. We put some of these pieces in each soup-plate and pour the soup over it.

Here as a diversion is another Greek speciality.

Taskembab Pakataridis (Mutton Ragout)

for 4 servings:

1 pound or a little more mutton or lamb
¼ cup olive oil
2 onions
1 clove of garlic
1 bay leaf
2 tablespoons chopped parsley or dill
1 can tomato purée
3–4 tablespoons water
salt and pepper to taste

Prepare a mixture of the finely chopped onions, the bay leaf, the chopped clove of garlic, and the olive oil. Cut the meat into medium-sized pieces. Add them to the oil mixture in a bowl and cover. Allow these to marinate for an hour. Then pour this mixture in a pan and cover with the water, which is blended with the tomato purée and salt and pepper to taste. Bring to the boil in a covered pan and allow 1–1½ hours of gentle stewing. The time will depend on the meat we use. Mutton will, of course, take longer than lamb.

Serve in a deep dish and add the chopped parsley or dill or both, which is best. With it we serve cooked rice. Before leaving for Turkey I will give you one more very typical Greek dish.

Fakasoupa (Lentil Soup)

for 5 servings:

As in so many other exotic countries, there is in Greece a wide variety of lentils. In Greece for this soup they use the light-yellow kind. If there are not available then use the well-known brown lentils. Work as follows:

1 *pound lentils well washed and soaked for about 3 hours in about 5 cups of water*	2 *tiny cloves of garlic*
	the juice of 1 lemon
	1 *bay leaf*
	2 *cloves*
⅓ *pound soup vegetables, among which mainly celeriac, onion, and green dill stalks play an important part*	*pinch oregano* or *marjoram*
	pinch thyme
	salt and pepper to taste

Let the lentils come to the boil in the liquid in which they were soaked. Reduce the heat and allow about 1 hour's cooking time.

In the meantime cook the cut-up vegetables with herbs and spices in 1 cup of boiling water. Do not put them in cold water and then bring to the boil. Put them directly in boiling water. Boil for 20 minutes. When the lentils are done we sieve them with the cooking liquid through a Chinese strainer, and to this purée we add the cooked vegetables with their liquid. We shall then have all in all about 7 cups of liquid. Now we add salt and pepper to taste and, off the stove, the lemon juice.

This is a comparatively simple yet delicious soup. While they are cooking I usually add to the vegetables very small pieces of mutton or lamb. They give a particularly fine flavour to the soup.

And now let us take a look at Turkey.

TURKEY

TURKEY has for me an irresistible attraction, and I am willing to return to it as often as possible. From the first I was enchanted by all those beautiful mosques and palaces. How could I ever possibly forget the Aya Sofia? Equally impossible to forget is Sultan Achmed's Blue Mosque. The mosques are places of rest and tranquillity where the Turks crouch, rapt in prayer. I can never hear without a tightening of the throat the call to prayer, as from the top of the minaret the muezzin summons the faithful to worship.

Four times the call is repeated as the muezzin sends out his voice to the four corners of the world. Beautifully situated on the Golden Horn and the Bosphorus, Istanbul is surely unique among the lovely cities of the world.

Equally fascinating, if simpler in character, are the smaller Turkish towns such as Izmir, once called Smyrna and principally known to Europeans as the source of raisins and currants. Izmir indeed lives on these dried fruits which are a source of trade and prosperity.

But now to Turkish cuisine—and how superbly the Turks, both men and women, can cook! They are past-masters in the handling of ingredients and flavours, principal among which is yoghurt, used in both sweet and savoury recipes. On my very first walk through Istanbul I was fascinated by hundreds and hundreds of jars containing yoghurt to be seen in practically every shop-window. In restaurants, pastry-cooks', bakeries, groceries, dairies, there were to be seen the yoghurt itself and attractive dishes in which yoghurt is the chief ingredient. There would seem to be no end to Turkish ingenuity where cooking with yoghurt is concerned.

Another Turkish peculiarity is the variety of barbecues they use for cooking both in restaurants and out of doors, where at almost every street corner the most luscious smells rise in the air. These grills can be either horizontal or vertical and are equipped with huge, sword-like skewers. On these they cook small pieces of mutton or lamb, aubergines, marshmallows, pimentos, tomatoes, with bay leaves and onions. Fish, either whole or in pieces, combined with vegetables, spices, and herbs, also are grilled, and a favourite is swordfish. I was particularly impressed by what I can only describe as 'vertical' roasting. The dish prepared on it is called Doner Kebab. For this the Turkish cook uses layers of fat and lean lamb stuffed with a mixture of onions, herbs, and spices, pressed into a long, roll-like joint. This was my favourite dish, but alas! it cannot be reproduced in Europe as we do not have the necessary 'vertical' grill. In the large hotels and restaurants these grills, which have to be in constant movement, are turned mechanically. The street-corner cook, however, has to turn his by hand, which he does very smoothly and with little effort. When the outer layer is cooked brown it is pared off with a huge knife and served to the client on a hot plate, together with cooked rice or dried beans, while the meat itself is garnished with a spoonful of yoghurt and chopped dill or mint.

I could write a great deal more about Turkish cuisine in general, but we must now look at some of their recipes. I must, however, pay tribute to the art of Pandeli (former cook to Kemal Ataturk), whose restaurant is famous in a country where cooks are quite outstanding.

And here is the first of my recipes, all of which were given to me by a Turkish cook.

Yoghurt Corbasi (Yoghurt Soup)

for 6 servings:

7 cups stock made with mutton or bones if you want to economize
2 generous tablespoons flour
2 tablespoons butter

½ cup thick, creamy yoghurt
1½–2 tablespoons mint, chopped
not too much salt

We prepare the stock the day before, adding to the water soup vegetables according to taste. (Carrots, onions, parsley, or dill are essential.) I sometimes make this stock with half a small boiling fowl as well as mutton. The result is a wonderfully tasty stock. I often have to use a boiling fowl, as regrettably mutton or lamb is not always available in Holland.

When the stock has cooled skim off the fat. The meat is used later in making kofta, which is tiny meatballs fried in a pan or grilled (see p. 314 in the chapter on Egypt). We put the yoghurt in a bowl with some salt. If it is rather thin then drain it through muslin in order to get rid of the water. Melt the butter in a pan and blend in the flour. We must stir this mixture into the stock, which in the meantime has been brought to the boil again. Reduce the heat and let this flour-butter mixture thicken the soup a little. Only then do we add the blend of yoghurt and salt. The soup should not boil any more. Check to see if there is enough salt in it and serve in cups. Some people add lemon juice as a final touch.

Tavuk Corbasi (Turkish Chicken Soup)

for 4 servings:

5 cups chicken stock,
prepared with 1 boiling
fowl used later for a
ragout, with the exception
of one breast piece
2 generous tablespoons flour
2 tablespoons butter

2 tablespoons chives or a
mixture of fresh parsley
and dill
2 tablespoons chopped mint
1 cup thick yoghurt
2 tablespoons uncooked rice
a pinch of turmeric

Prepare the chicken stock in the usual manner, then drain
and skim off the fat, and bring it to the boil again. Add the rice
and allow 20 minutes for cooking. In the meantime we prepare
a creamy sauce with the butter, the flour, and the yoghurt. We
cook it very gently and while stirring add the turmeric. This
sauce we blend into the chicken stock to thicken it. The rice is
now cooked, and we taste to see if there is salt and pepper
enough in this soup. With the pan off the stove we add the
chopped fresh herbs. I add a little lemon juice to this soup. Skin
and bone the meat of the one breast piece and cut it into small
pieces. Add them 5 minutes before serving the soup.

Cherkes Tavagu (Chicken with Walnut Sauce)

for 4 servings:

1 small boiling fowl, from
which all the fat has been
removed
1 large carrot
½ pound walnuts
1 tablespoon paprika powder

2 onions
salt to taste
pepper to taste
1 bunch parsley
3 thin slices rye-bread

Boil the fowl in as much water as is needed to cover it completely and add salt to taste, the carrot, only 1 onion, and the

bunch of parsley stalks. Skim regularly and see that the water only boils slowly.

Allow about 1–1½ hours for a small fowl. It should not be overdone. Let the fowl cool in its stock.

Grind the walnuts until very fine and then mix with the finely chopped onion and the three slices of bread. This bread must first be soaked in some of the chicken stock after the fat has been skimmed off and then squeezed out. Add the paprika powder and a little salt to taste.

This mixture is finally strained through muslin, and should give us about one teacup full of oil and liquid. The oil comes from the walnuts and the liquid from the bread.

Blend the mixture remaining in the muslin with 1 cup of lean chicken stock. Its result is a kind of a thick nut-bread dough.

We have taken out the chicken from the stock and skinned and boned it. The meat is divided into very small pieces. Half of the thick bread-walnut dough is put in a greased dish. The rest of it is used as a top cover for the chicken mixture.

The walnut liquid from our teacup is now poured over the chicken meat mixture. This oil blend should be a reddish colour owing to the paprika powder. Serve cold with bread and cucumber or tomato salad.

Piliç Dolmasi (Roasted Stuffed Chicken)

for 4 servings:

1 tender roaster	½ cup butter
½ cup rice (uncooked)	salt to taste
¼ cup raisins (if available	1 cup water
Smyrna dried raisins)	
¼ cup pignolia nuts (if not	
available use ¼ cup	
unsalted peanuts)	

Soak the peeled nuts for about 4 hours in boiling water. They become very tender, but keep them covered in order that the water should remain hot as long as possible. Add the raisins at the end of the third hour. Chop the chicken giblets finely. When the soaking time is over brown the butter in a pan and sauté the well-drained peanuts and raisins with the chopped giblets and rice until they turn a golden colour. Be careful not to over-cook. Add salt and pepper to taste and then pour in the cup of water. Bring to the boil in a covered pan and cook for about 27 minutes. Now take the lid from the pan and allow a few more minutes' cooking on a low heat so that the rice may become quite dry and shiny.

Stuff the chicken with the rice-giblet mixture and fasten the skin with a skewer or sew it. Now we must butter it lavishly all over, put it in the roasting-pan, and pour the remaining browned butter over it. Do not try to economize on butter as it will form part of your gravy afterwards.

Sprinkle with salt to taste and let the chicken brown in the pre-heated oven. Reduce the heat and allow about 30–40 minutes for it to be done. Remember to baste regularly and reduce the heat further if necessary.

When the chicken has browned we add a leek and some carrots, cut lengthwise, to the gravy. They furnish the liquid and keep the gravy from becoming too dark. Since one cannot prepare this recipe without adding some water, I prefer to use vegetable liquid.

Serve this chicken with the rice stuffing only. If, however, you want to serve it with an original Turkish salad proceed as follows:

Caçik (Cucumber-yoghurt Salad)

for 4 servings:

2 cucumbers
1 teaspoon salt
a generous pinch sugar
pinch dried dill or 1
    tablespoon chopped fresh
    dill
1½ cups yoghurt
1 crushed clove of garlic

about 4 tablespoons olive oil
1½–2 tablespoons wine
    vinegar or the same
    amount lemon juice
1 tablespoon chopped fresh
    mint or ½ teaspoon dried
    mint

Peel the cucumbers and cut lengthwise. Take out the seeds and cut in crescent-shaped slices—not too thick nor yet too thin. Put them in a bowl and add salt with all the other well-blended ingredients with the exception of the olive oil, the dill, and mint (if used fresh).

We now have a very creamy cucumber salad. Let it stand for about 15 minutes and just before serving add the herbs with the oil.

Taste to see if it is salted enough and add some freshly ground pepper. I usually serve some slices of white bread with this salad, and for preference French bread.

Here is another chicken recipe given to me by Mr. Egrem Yegen, maître cuisinier in Istanbul, manager of the Istanbul cookery school, and author of many cookery books.

Tavugu Dolmasi (Stuffed Chicken)

for 6 servings:

1 big boiling fowl without
any fat on it

FOR THE STUFFING

about ¼ pound calf liver
with the giblets
½ cup rice (uncooked)
2 tablespoons butter

pinch dried marjoram
1 teaspoon turmeric powder
salt and pepper to taste

FOR THE BOILING OF THE FOWL

9 cups water
1 big carrot cut lengthwise or
4 smaller carrots, whole
1 bay leaf

2 cloves
1 thin leek, cut twice
lengthwise

Chop the liver and the giblets, but not too finely. They should be small coarse pieces. Chop the onion and prepare the stuffing.

Brown the butter in a pan and sauté the chopped liver with the marjoram and the turmeric powder. Stir and add the unwashed rice. Keep stirring to let the turmeric turn these ingredients yellow. Now pour on as much water as is required to dry-cook the rice. Cook in a covered pan on a reduced heat, allowing about 17 minutes or rather less, as the rice will go on cooking when used as stuffing in the fowl.

Stuff the fowl, from which the fat has been removed, and sew or use skewers to fasten the skin.

Have ready 9 cups of boiling water and the prescribed vegetables in a pan with a lid. Add salt and pepper to taste, place in the boiling fowl, salted inside only, and let the water come to the boil again. Then cover immediately and reduce the heat. Seal off the sides of the lid of the pan with a strip of dough made from flour and water. But make it fairly thick as the heat will reduce it. Let the water boil gently but constantly for about 2 hours. This, of course, again depends on the tenderness—or, should I say, the age—of the fowl. If you want to make sure that the water boils listen with your ear close to the pan.

Thanks to the dough the water will not evaporate and will continue to cover the boiling fowl, keeping all the flavour inside.

Serve this chicken skinned and cut up in rather big pieces. With each piece serve some of the stuffing and a cup of the stock, which you will have checked first for salt and pepper.

We have now come to the end of our Turkish chicken recipes, but before we leave Turkey I must tell you how to prepare stuffed aubergines and Turkish coffee.

Patlican Imambayildi (Stuffed Aubergines)

for 4 servings:

4 aubergines
5 onions
5 very big, peeled tomatoes
1 crushed clove of garlic
1 bunch parsley (fine pieces
  of the stalks with the
  leaves are coarsely
  chopped)

1 tablespoon sugar
salt and pepper to taste
olive oil

Wash the aubergines and cut them lengthwise. Scoop out the meat with a spoon but do not damage the outer peel. Cut up the onions in thin slices and the peeled tomatoes in tiny pieces. Put these ingredients in a bowl. Add the crushed garlic clove, with the meat scooped out of the aubergines, the coarsely chopped parsley, and salt to taste. Blend well and set the bowl aside. Now rub a fireproof dish with oil, using a round one for preference, and sprinkle with breadcrumbs. Put in the aubergine halves. Add 3–4 tablespoons of olive oil and the sugar to the mixture in the bowl. It should be quite a smooth blend by now.

Fill the aubergine halves with the mixture and cover the dish with a piece of aluminium foil or wax-paper. Cook gently in the pre-heated oven for about 1½–1¾ hours and then take out the dish and let cool. Add pepper and serve in the fireproof dish with pieces of warm French bread.

A glass of the wonderful raki, the typical drink of the country, prepared from raisins strongly flavoured with aniseed is an excellent accompaniment. I suggest, however, that you first try raki mixed with iced water.

Turkish Coffee

for 2 servings:

less than 1 cup water
2 tablespoons sugar or more
if you like sweet coffee

2 generous teaspoons very
finely ground coffee
1 Turkish coffee-pot with
handle

Turkish coffee-pots are called 'cezve' and have the amount of cups that can be prepared in them inscribed on the bottom. They are really little pans with a long handle made from aluminium, copper, or even from silver or gold.

Turkish housewives have a special very thin, elongated coffee-mill to grind the coffee to a fine powder. Most of these mills are also made from copper. The coffee-beans are ground to a very, very fine powder, which is an essential secret of success.

Pour cold water in the coffee-pot and add the coffee with the sugar. Stir and bring slowly to the boil on a low heat, stirring again before it does so. When boiling take the pot off the heat and pour only the froth which has developed into the coffee-cups, distributing it equally. Then do the same with the rest of the coffee, including some of the dregs. By pouring the coffee in this rather complicated way into the cups we prevent one cup from getting all the dregs.

Let the coffee cool a little as, of course, it is sizzling hot when served. Drink with care, and the less we stir the liquid the better. We drink only three-quarters of the coffee as the remainder consists mainly of the dregs.

And now we must follow Gallina to the Far East.

THIRD TOUR:
The Far East

It would need a whole book to tell of my experiences in and impressions of the Far East in my search for new chicken recipes. Little did I think that India, Thailand, Cambodia, Viet Nam, Hongkong-Kowloon, and Japan would impress and fascinate me as they did. I came away with unforgettable memories in which are mingled the beauty of the great cities; the fantastic temples; the palaces and mosques of India; the people in their gaudy, brilliant clothes, and those whose friendliness and helpfulness made a profound impression on me.

Wherever I went, even in smaller towns such as Agra and Benares, I found the hotels very comfortable and the service excellent. And where else can one find such fascinating, well-stocked, and tempting shopping galleries?

Wholly different yet equally fascinating was Bangkok, in Thailand, with its splendid Buddhas of gold and jade and its waterways reminiscent of Venice. The hotels in Bangkok are quite remarkable for their comfort and their luxury, and not least among their luxuries are the swimming-pools set amidst exotic flowering shrubs round which the hotels are built. Most of these hotels, too, have roof gardens and restaurants overlooking Bangkok's main river.

Pnom-Penh, the capital of Cambodia, has little of great interest for the tourist or the gourmet. In the near-by Siem Reap, however, the traveller can see the overwhelming beauty of the great temples of Angkor-Vat and Angkor-Thom. They are miracles of construction and carving, dating back to the thirteenth century and built by the Khmers, the early inhabitants of Cambodia. Although in ruins, they are still breathtaking in their size and beauty.

Neighbouring Viet Nam and its capital, Saigon, are quite different. Saigon offers few aesthetic experiences, but the busy life of its overcrowded streets and markets, always filled with an excited, colourful population, is both stimulating and fascinating, while Cholon, the important Chinese quarter, is worth a visit. Hongkong is famous for its beauty and the exotic character of its little fishing ports, the most charming of which is called Aberdeen. Equally fascinating is the Kowloon Peninsula, and to visit both is a unique experience. There is, of course, striking evidence everywhere of Britain's influence. There are excellent places for shopping or window-gazing, and the Chinese quarter would tempt any shopper. There are innumerable hotels in both Hongkong and Kowloon, while the floating restaurants of Aberdeen are world-famous for their exquisite Chinese fish dishes. Chinese food is much simpler, perhaps, than Indian food, but it is exceedingly good and prepared with a great deal of care and imagination. I will write later about Japan when I speak of my stay in Tokyo.

INDIA

A GREAT deal can be learned in this country in the culinary domain, and particularly in the difficult art of using herbs and spices to the best advantage.

While in New Delhi I stayed as a paying guest with the Puri family. Their cook, Manzé, went to a great deal of trouble to teach me just how to prepare a real curry and taught me how to use the various herbs and spices used in Indian cookery. I am grateful to him for his patient tuition. I shall always remember my first visit to the spice market in Old Delhi, where, wanting a good blend of curry powder, I simply asked for curry. To my surprise the man in the market replied: "Madam, if you wish for curry you must go to the restaurant over there, where they will, I know, serve you gladly." Only later did I realize that the original name for a curry dish was 'turcarri,' abbreviated in the course of the years to 'turri.' The British, as so often happens with a foreign word, mispronounced it 'curry' and used it to indicate the dish's dominating ingredient. The Indians, however, use it only for the dish itself that they are serving. So many herbs and spices go into a good curry powder that they do not consider it appropriate to use only one name for the blend as a whole.

In India any meat, with the exception of beef, which is never touched on religious grounds, can be used for a curry dish. Chicken, various kinds of fish and shellfish are all used, but the more usual ingredients are lamb or mutton. Delicious curries can also be made from vegetables and/or potatoes.

Malay Chicken

for 4 servings:

1 medium chicken cut up in pieces	3 small onions sliced
4 medium potatoes peeled cut up in cubes	1 tablespoon curry paste
	1¼ inch cinnamon
1 small coconut grated extract milk	salt and sugar to taste
	5 tablespoons vegetable fat or butter

Heat the fat or butter and brown in it the cubes of potato. Set them aside. Brown then in the same fat the pieces of chicken, add the onions with the curry paste and the cinnamon. Stir, add salt and sugar, some water and the potato cubes. Let come to the boil. Reduce heat, cover the pan well. Allow about 30–40 minutes for the chicken to be done. Stir now in the grated coconut and the milk. But dilute in the milk ½ tablespoon of flour. Allow 5 minutes for the curry sauce to thicken.

Vindaloo (Mutton Curry or Indian Chicken Curry)

for 4 servings:

1¼ pounds mutton cut into squares or 1 roaster divided into 6 pieces	1 tablespoon flour
	2 finely chopped onions
2 tablespoons lime juice	¼ cup butter
	¼ cup cream or yoghurt

FOR THE CURRY-BLEND

1 *chopped clove of garlic*	2 *crushed cloves*
pinch powdered ginger	1 *tiny piece cinnamon*
1 *teaspoon turmeric*	6 *crushed cardamom seeds*
¼ *teaspoon crushed caraway seeds*	*a little salt to taste*
	pinch chili powder

Mix the ingredients well for the curry-blend. If you prefer to do so you can use instead 1 tablespoon of ready-prepared curry paste or powder. It is more fun, however, to do one's own mixing, and since I visited India I do my own blending in a mortar and pestle specially kept for the purpose. Having prepared the curry powder, brown the chopped onions in the hot butter, then add the curry and stir with a fork. This mixture must be brown and not yellow-coloured.

When the correct colour has been obtained add the meat and allow it also to become brown. Only then do we add the flour, which in turn must also brown. Finally add the lime juice with the cream or yoghurt and cover the pan with a lid, which must fit it tightly. Reduce the heat and allow 40 minutes or even longer cooking time.

Now and again check to see whether extra liquid is needed. If so then pour in very small quantities, a tablespoon or so at a time. Before serving check if there is enough salt and add some ground black pepper. Serve with dry, boiled rice and a cauliflower curry dish. Put a jar of mango chutney on the table for your guests to help themselves. In India the housewives prepare their own chutney in huge earthenware jars, and delicious it is too.

Curried Gobhi (Curried Cauliflower)

for 4 servings:

1 firm cauliflower
¼ teaspoon turmeric powder
a little less powdered ginger
1 clove
1 chopped onion
2 tablespoons butter

¼ teaspoon mustard powder
¼ teaspoon crushed caraway
seeds
good pinch black pepper
a dash of cream

Mix all the ingredients together except the cauliflower, which is put alone in a pan, covered with boiling water and kept boiling for 8 minutes, when it is drained and allowed to cool. When cold divide the cauliflower into small clusters the size of a carnation. Brown the remaining ingredients in a pan and when very dark stir the mixture gently with a fork into the pieces of cauliflower, which should absorb the curry sauce and become golden. Add some cream and cover the pan with its lid. Reduce the heat, and cook for about 20 minutes. A wet cloth should be placed round the edge of the lid so that none of the steam can escape. Shake the pan from time to time. When ready serve the rice with the cauliflower and, if liked, sprinkle with chopped celery, mint, or parsley.

If you prefer potatoes to rice with this dish try the following:

Curried Alu Gobhi (Curried Potatoes and Cauliflower)

For four persons peel 4 large potatoes, slicing them not too thinly. Put the sliced potatoes, together with the boiled cauliflower clusters, in the butter and curry mixture, remembering to use more butter in this recipe than was used in the preceding one. Stir with a fork till all the ingredients are golden brown, then add two tablespoons of yoghurt and the juice of half a lemon. Stew in a covered pan until the potatoes are done. Check for salt, bearing in mind that in India they use very little salt for their curried dishes.

Another delicious Indian speciality is:

Mulligatawny Soup

for 6 servings:

There are innumerable recipes for this delicious soup, but the following, in which a boiling fowl is used, seemed to me the best of all.

1 *small boiling fowl from which all the fat has been removed*
5 *cups water*
1 *large chopped onion*
2 *cups coconut milk* or 2 *cups consisting of part milk and part cream or yoghurt*

1 *finely crushed clove of garlic*
2 *tablespoons butter* or *vegetable fat* or *margarine*
salt and pepper to taste
3–4 *tablespoons flour*
1 *tablespoon curry powder*

MY OWN BLEND

½ *teaspoon crushed coriander seeds*
1 *teaspoon powdered turmeric*
generous pinch chili powder
1 *clove (crushed)*
¼ *teaspoon crushed caraway seeds*

tiny bay leaf
pinch mustard seed
generous pinch paprika powder

To make your own curry-blend mix thoroughly all ingredients, pounding them with a pestle in a mortar.

Whatever the liquid used, coconut milk or a mixture of milk and cream or yoghurt, add to it 3 tablespoons of grated coconut. Let it stand for a couple of hours until it has thickened and then work through a fine sieve.

In a deep pan or stock-pot brown the butter or fat and fry in it the chopped onion, together with the curry powder. Remember that if using ready-made powder you must add a bay leaf and a crushed clove of garlic. Stir with a fork until the mixture is a deep brown in colour and only then add the fowl, carved into 6–8 pieces. Let these, too, turn brown, add salt and pepper to taste, and stir in the flour.

When this in its turn has become brown pour the 5 cups of water over it. Bring to the boil, place the lid on the pan, and reduce the heat. Simmer for 1–1¼ hours. The fowl should be tender but not over-cooked. When it is ready remove the joints with a skimmer and place them in a bowl. Now is the moment to use the coconut milk or milk and cream (or yoghurt). First check to see that the flour has sufficiently thickened the soup, which should have the consistency of a smooth Béchamel sauce. If it appears to be too thin add a little cornflour, or vice versa a little coconut milk if it is too thick. Mix well with the soup and bring to the boil again. Reduce the heat and add the chicken joints. Before serving check for salt and pepper.

Should you wish to serve mulligatawny soup as a main dish add rice after removing the chicken and cook before adding the coconut milk.

Mutton Mulligatawny

Prepare precisely as for the preceding recipe, but instead of a boiling fowl use 1 pound of finely chopped mutton. This soup will need cooking for only about 30 minutes.

I had the following delicious dish in one of the simpler restaurants in New Delhi—Wengers'.

Peas Pilaff with Rice (Curried Peas and Rice)

for 4 servings:

¾ pound rice
¾ pound deep-freeze peas or
¾ pound dried peas, soaked
 overnight
2 finely chopped onions
1 clove of garlic
1 tablespoon curry powder
1 tiny bay leaf
2 cloves

2 tablespoons coarsely
 chopped fresh mint or
 celery
1 tablespoon chopped pickles
3 tablespoons butter or
 vegetable fat
water
salt and pepper to taste

Cook the dried peas in the liquid in which they were soaked. They should be tender but firm. If you use frozen peas then first let them thaw out.

Brown the butter or fat in a pan and fry all the ingredients in it with the exception of the peas, the fresh mint, celery, and the pickles. Add the unwashed rice and stir with a fork. Allow to become golden but not brown. Then add as much water as is needed to cook the rice. Give 17 minutes for cooking.

Add the cooked peas to this mixture, stir with a fork, and pour in as much liquid as is needed to obtain a creamy but not soggy consistency.

Taste to see whether more salt is needed and add some freshly ground pepper. Stir again with the fork and finally add the coarsely chopped herbs and the pickles. If you use frozen peas mix them with the rice and give a further 10 minutes' cooking time.

Serve with it:

Egg-molee (Curried Eggs)

for 4 servings:

4 hard-boiled eggs
1 chopped onion
1 tablespoon curry powder
1 crushed clove of garlic
1 tablespoon flour
2 tablespoons butter or
  vegetable fat

2 tablespoons yoghurt
1 tablespoon cream
1 finely sliced fresh red
  pimento
pinch powdered chili

Shell and halve the hard-boiled eggs. Brown the butter or the fat in a pan and fry the chopped onion in it with the crushed clove of garlic until light brown. Then add the sliced pimento with the powdered chili. Let them colour a little, and only then stir in the curry powder. Stir with a fork and finally add flour, salt and pepper to taste. Stir and simmer for a few minutes in an open pan. Now add the yoghurt with the cream in order to thicken the sauce.

The sauce should be very creamy. Taste to see if it needs more salt or pepper and put the egg halves into it. Let them warm through thoroughly. Pour carefully into a pre-heated dish so as not to break the eggs and serve with the peas pilaff with rice.

But besides these curry dishes there are many other Indian recipes well worth trying out.

Aubergine Fritters

for 4 servings:

2 aubergines cut up in finger-
  thick slices
½ teaspoon powdered
  turmeric
2 eggs
½ cup flour
water

1 dessertspoon oil
½ tablespoon powdered
  paprika
salt and pepper to taste
a deep-frying pan with oil or
  fat

Mix the 2 eggs, the flour, the powdered paprika, the powdered turmeric, and a little water into a light pancake batter. Add a pinch of salt and stir in the oil.

Wash the aubergines and cut up in finger-thick slices. These slices are dried between two cloths. Dip some slices—only a few at a time—in the batter. In the meantime let the fat or oil in the deep-frying pan get hot. In it we deep-fry these slices of aubergine, well covered with the batter, to a golden brown. They are done as soon as they are brown and only need a few seconds.

The following delicious 'snack' was served to me at a cocktail party in New Delhi. With it we drank Whisky on the Rocks, a very popular American drink much favoured in India. I cannot leave India without telling you about it.

Kadu-Gurini (Egg and Shrimp Dish)

for 4 servings:

½ pound small shrimps or 8 deep-freeze prawns (the big ones)
1 Spanish pepper, fresh or dried
1 small chopped onion
1 generous teaspoon turmeric powder

1 dessertspoon mustard powder
5 tablespoons grated coconut
1 tablespoon water
3 eggs
salt to taste
4 tablespoons fat or butter

Prepare a blend with the mustard powder, the turmeric, and the chopped onion. Stir in the shrimps or the prawns, cut up in pieces, and the very small Spanish pepper finely sliced but without any seeds. Brown the butter or the fat in a pan and fry this mixture to a golden brown. It must not be either yellow or dark brown.

In the meantime mix together the grated coconut, the water, and the raw eggs, lightly beaten, with salt to taste.

The prawns are now light brown and very hot. Pour this egg mixture on the prawns, increase the heat, and shake the pan energetically. The eggs should set and become incorporated with the other ingredients. Just that and no more is required. Taste to see if the dish is savoury. If it is not then add some extra freshly ground black pepper, or—and this is best—some saffron.

Serve with boiled rice.

I must tell you how I was taught to cook rice in India.

Cooking Rice the Indian Way. Allow at least 8 cups of water for about ¾ pound of rice. The water should continue boiling in the open pan. Stir it once only. Do not allow more than 10–12 minutes for the rice to be done. Take out some grains of rice with a skimmer in order to see if they are cooked. If they are, then pour the contents of the pan in a colander and drain, first letting cold water run over the rice. Turn the oven on high and put the rice on an oven-pan. When the oven is quite hot let the rice dry and get hot through. A few minutes only is required. Serve immediately.

Personally when the rice is cooked and drained I do not use the oven. Instead I sauté a tablespoon of finely chopped onion in 2 tablespoons of butter or oil till golden brown. In this I heat the rice and then serve. The grains are then appetizingly and beautifully separate.

And to end here is a lentil dish.

Dal-Moong (Lentil Dish)

for 4 servings:

about 1 pound lentils soaked
for 2 hours in water
1 large chopped onion
1 tablespoon curry powder
½ bay leaf

2 cloves
2 tablespoons chopped herbs,
including mint
½ tablespoon salt
a pinch of cayenne pepper

FOR THE EXTRA COLOURING
1 teaspoon powdered
turmeric

Further

*4 tablespoons butter or
vegetable fat*

Brown the chopped onion in the butter or the fat and add
the drained lentils to it. Stir and add the cloves, the bay leaf,
the curry powder with the powdered turmeric, salt and pepper
to taste. Now pour over it about ½ cup of the water in which
the lentils were soaked and bring to the boil.

Put the lid on the pan, reduce the heat, and allow about 30
minutes for the lentils to cook. Remove the lid after 20 minutes
and see if the lentils are about done. If they are, then let the
liquid evaporate in the open pan. Before serving add the chopped
herbs. With these lentils we serve hard-boiled eggs. We shell
and halve them and add them to the lentils. If required we can
also serve cooked rice or potatoes with them.

And now we must leave this fascinating and lovely country
and proceed to Thailand.

THAILAND

I HAVE already spoken of the great beauty of this fascinating country where the population lives almost as much in as on the water. Bangkok, the capital, can easily hold its own with Venice, save that it is much less sophisticated.

On the water is the famous floating market which no visitor to Bangkok should miss. True, it is now highly commercialized to attract the tourist, yet even so it is well worth visiting for its gay colourfulness unlike that of any other place I know.

When crossing Bangkok's main river, the Chao Phya, and its tributaries, one can feel the impact of the lively, exotic scene reflected in the rippling waters. I enjoyed too the experience of gliding by boat into the jungle to which the innumerable channels lead. On each bank of the tributaries are long rows of huts built on piles sunk into the water, and every veranda is richly decorated with pots of flowering orchids. Travelling on the rivers in the early morning, you will see the obvious pleasure with which the old and young bath and wash in the river.

The rivers swarm with shipping. Large and small boats carry merchandise to and from the market. The merchants, male and female, are decorative in their gaudy clothes and wide straw hats.

Another note of variegated colour is provided by the goods sold in the floating market and along the river-banks. There are bananas of many shapes and sizes, a great variety of melons, pumpkins, pineapples, coconuts, papayas, cucumbers, avocados, aubergines, and lemons, or rather limes. Besides fruit there are tobacco plants, coconut oil, palm oil, palm leaves, straw hats, and a bewildering selection of straw baskets.

With such a wealth of fruit and vegetables, herbs, and spices the people of Thailand are naturally adept at preparing many highly flavoured and tasteful dishes. Personally I consider their fruit breakfast among their most attractive meals. This breakfast consists of part of a grapefruit as large as a coconut with coarse but tasty flesh; sweet, juicy, sun-ripened pineapples; small, very firm, and delicately flavoured bananas; sweet limes, delicious when eaten like a tangerine or orange; and juicy, red-fleshed water melons.

Unfortunately, in this chapter you will find only two original Thai recipes. As a cookery editor I was offered on arrival a little book filled with Thai recipes, but as every cookery expert visiting the country receives exactly the same book I am afraid I cannot offer you anything very original. I have therefore described here only those few recipes given to me by hotel cooks in Bangkok. Two are strictly Thai, the others have been somewhat adapted to European taste. This, I gather, is quite usual in Bangkok, where European food is becoming increasingly fashionable.

Kai Erawan (Chicken Erawan)

for 4 servings:

1 tender roaster	¼ pound mushrooms
1½ tablespoons soy sauce	1 clove of garlic
1 tablespoon vinegar	5 shallots
2 tablespoons finely chopped onions	pinch crushed coriander seeds
4 tablespoons lard	salt and cayenne pepper to taste
1½ tablespoons chopped dried beforehand soaked ginger (or ginger balls preserved in syrup)	juice of 1 lime or 1 lemon 1 teaspoon demerara sugar pinch monosodium glutamate

Order a tender, boned roaster and remove the skin. Cut the roaster in pieces, in size and shape of a string bean. In Thailand they use black rather gelatinous mushrooms which in most European countries are available only in dried form. I therefore advise you to buy very big fresh mushrooms for this recipe. Wash them well, let dry, and cut them up in slices. Cover them with lemon or lime juice to prevent discolouring.

In Thailand they use both the fresh and the dried ginger root. To prepare it peel a piece of the ginger root and put it in salt water to remove its penetrating flavour. We can also use a small piece of dried ginger, soaking and peeling it before use. Personally I prefer ginger in syrup. It is easier to handle and gives an attractive sweet-spicy flavour to a dish.

Cut up the mushrooms and the sweet ginger finely. Heat the lard in a roasting-pan and brown the tiny slices of chicken; then add the chopped onion, the whole shallots (if you prefer you can use only chopped onions as it makes little difference), the crushed garlic with the slices of mushrooms (remove them with a strainer from the juice), the cut-up ginger, the crushed coriander seeds, and salt with cayenne pepper to taste. Do not reduce the heat until all the ingredients have turned a golden brown. Only then do we allow less heat and cover the pan. Allow not more than 10 minutes for all the ingredients to be done. This will probably be more than enough as the slices of chicken are so small that they will hardly need any cooking time.

We now prepare a blend with the soy sauce, the vinegar, the lemon juice or the lime juice, the pinch of monosodium glutamate, and the teaspoon of demerara sugar. This blend is added to the chicken and brought to the boil again. We can now serve it after having tasted it for salt and cayenne pepper. With it we serve boiled rice.

Bean Sprouts

This is a product very much used in Oriental rice and vermicelli dishes. Although we always talk and read about bean sprouts, we should know that we are dealing with pea sprouts, the Indonesian name of which is Katjang idjoe. They are small shoots coming from very small green peas. When bought the tops of these white sprouts are covered with a tiny green cap, which should be pulled off as much as possible.

In many countries fresh bean sprouts are available; if not we can buy them canned. In either case drain them well for about 10 minutes.

Kai Khun Charoonsri (Chicken Khun Charoonsri)

for 4 servings:

1 pound thick vermicelli or egg-noodles
½ pound bean sprouts
½ pound cooked chicken meat, skinned, boned, and cut up in strips
½ pound raw pork cut up in strips
1 crushed clove of garlic
1 dessertspoon brown sugar
2 tablespoons soy sauce
2 teaspoons Worcester Sauce
pepper and salt to taste
1 finely cut up Spanish pepper, fresh or dried but without seeds
3 generous tablespoons lard or butter

Soak the vermicelli or egg-noodles for about 3 minutes in boiling water, then pour cold water over them and allow to drain well. Wash the bean sprouts in a generous amount of water. Drain thoroughly (this is rather important and I recommend doing this several hours before using).

The chicken meat should be lightly cooked. Brown the lard or butter in a pan and fry the strips of raw pork a golden brown. Do the same with the cut-up cooked chicken. Golden but not dark brown is the correct colour. To these we add the clove of garlic, the small pieces of Spanish pepper (without seeds as they are too hot for this recipe), the brown sugar, and pepper and salt to taste.

Stir with a fork and then add the vermicelli or egg-noodles with the bean sprouts. Use a kitchen fork for the stirring so as not to break up all these ingredients. Let them get golden brown and crisp. Remove the pan from the stove and add the soy sauce with the Worcester Sauce. Serve immediately.

In a real Thai restaurant you could not possibly have a meal with only one single chicken or pork dish, and therefore they serve with these chicken dishes a bowl of dry, cooked rice and the following chicken sauce.

Chicken Sauce. Combine equal parts of cooked chicken (½ pound) cut up in strips and cooked green peas (frozen peas or soaked dried peas not over-cooked). Sauté sliced onions in hot lard or butter till golden brown and add 1 crushed clove of garlic, 1 teaspoon of curry powder blended with 1 crushed clove, a pinch of cayenne pepper, the juice of ½ a lemon, some tablespoons of grated coconut (do not be too sparing), and 1 generous tablespoon of chopped almonds.

Finally add the strips of chicken and the green peas. Dilute this mixture with 1½ cups of boiling stock. Check to see that it is salted enough and well flavoured with the curry powder and the grated coconut. Serve this sauce hot or cold.

Another dish they serve with this chicken is

Prawns-in-the-net

for 1 serving:

*2 fresh or frozen prawns
egg-batter mixed with
  cayenne pepper and soy
  sauce*

For about 12 prawns (6 servings) we need a batter made with about 1 cup of flour, 1 egg-yolk, salt to taste, a tablespoon of soy sauce, a generous pinch of cayenne pepper, the well-beaten egg-white, and as much water as is needed to obtain a good coating batter.

Peel and de-vein the prawns. Dip them in the egg-batter and see that they are well coated. Fry in deep-frying oil or fat till golden brown. When they float up to the surface they are done. These can be served with dry, boiled rice.

Chicken Salinee

for 4 servings:

1 boned roaster
1 cup gado-gado sauce
prepared from ground
peanuts blended with
water (gado-gado sauce is
available in all shops
which supply Oriental
food)

4 tablespoons grated coconut
4 tablespoons breadcrumbs
1 egg
pepper and salt to taste
oil

Divide the boned and skinned chicken meat in dices and stick them on skewers. Prepare a blend with the grated coconut, the raw egg, about 4 tablespoons of breadcrumbs, and ½ cup of oil. Pepper and salt to taste. Roll the skewered chicken meat over in this blend and roast in hot oil or fat till golden brown. Prepare in the meantime the gado-gado sauce with boiling water. It looks like a brown peanut sauce. You can if you wish use instead of gado-gado some peanut butter blended with soy sauce and tomato ketchup. To this mixture we add the boiling water with some brown sugar to taste. The consistency of this sauce should be like a Béchamel sauce.

The chicken and the sauce are both served cold.

A very good dish I was given in Bangkok is:

Rice Belvedère

for 4 servings:

¾ pound rice
2 tablespoons oil
1 chopped onion
1 clove of garlic

½ tablespoon curry powder
  blended with
½ tablespoon paprika powder
1 tablespoon soy sauce

FOR THE GARNISH

½ pound not over-cooked
boned chicken, turkey, or
pork meat
½ pound small shrimps or
cooked fish
4 not too ripe bananas

4 tablespoons butter
juice of 1 sweet lime or 1
small lemon
1½ tablespoons tomato
ketchup
salt and pepper to taste

Heat the oil and sauté the chopped onion with the clove of garlic and the unwashed rice till golden brown. Add the curry and the paprika powder. Stir and then add as much water as is needed to dry-cook the rice. Cook for 17 minutes. In the meantime brown the butter in a deep pan and cook till golden brown the pieces of chicken or the meat you have chosen with the shrimps or the pre-boiled fish. If you care for a rich dish use both shrimps and fish. The fish should not be quite done, and the correct colour is golden. Allow a few minutes' further frying and then reduce the heat.

When the rice is nearly cooked add to the mixture of meat, shrimps and/or fish the peeled whole bananas. They should be allowed only 5 minutes of sautéing and browning.

Finally pour over the lime or lemon juice with the tomato ketchup and add salt and pepper to taste as a finishing touch.

Make a mound of the rice on a warm dish and arrange on it all the other ingredients with some Chinese soy sauce as a final flavouring. The bananas should be placed on top when serving.

With this rich dish I was given a side-dish consisting of slices of sweet-sour gherkins, hard-boiled eggs halved and generously sprinkled with paprika powder which had been blended with chopped Spanish peppers (without seeds), tomato ketchup, and demerara sugar, making a wonderful spice combination for the eggs, cucumber slices blended with tiny pieces of unpeeled lemon, and sweetened with brown sugar. If a sweet line is available we should not need the sugar.

To complete the course there were strips of onions blended

with pepper, salt, sugar, and chutney from a jar. All these ingredients were beautifully arranged on a dish.

The natives of the country drink cold tea, ice-water, or lemonade with this dish. I quenched my thirst with a cool glass of beer, for these spicy dishes make me very thirsty!

Here is a real Thai dish.

Cian (Fried Fish)

for 6 servings:

1 *piece boned fish of about 2 pounds weight*
5 *tablespoons butter* or *lard*

FOR THE SAUCE

1 *tablespoon vinegar*
3 *tablespoons Chinese soy sauce*
a *generous pinch of demerara sugar*
1 *piece tamarind of about ¼ inch, well soaked*
3 *tablespoons stock* or *water*

a *generous pinch of crushed cardamom seeds*
2 *tablespoons chopped onions*
1 *clove of garlic*
pepper and salt to taste
½ *teaspoon turmeric powder*
a *pinch of monosodium glutamate*

Brown the butter or lard and fry the floured fish in it till golden brown. Allow about 5 minutes of frying in an open pan. Remove the fish from the pan and fry the chopped onions in the butter or lard till golden. Now add all the other ingredients except the stock or water, the vinegar, and the soy sauce. Let all the ingredients fry gently for a few minutes and then add the liquids. Bring to the boil and put the fried fish into this sauce. Reduce the heat and allow about 20 minutes' gentle cooking for the fish.

The time, of course, depends on the size of the fish used. Check to see that it is nicely done. We cook in an open pan so as to allow the liquid to be reduced a little. Serve cooked white rice with the fish.

A ham-pineapple dish served to me in the Rama Hotel in Bangkok was so good that, although not of Thai origin, I should like to give you the recipe.

Fried Ham with Pineapple

for 4 servings:

4 slices of cooked ham, each of about ¼ pound
4 slices canned pineapple (in Thailand they use fresh pineapple)

2 tablespoons flour
pepper, salt, and paprika powder to taste
3 tablespoons soy sauce
5 tablespoons butter or fat

Brown the butter or fat in a saucepan and let it get very hot. Prepare in the meantime a smooth mixture with flour, paprika powder, a little salt (the cooked ham is already salted), pepper, and soy sauce to taste. Turn over each slice of ham in this blend. Fry one slice after the other in the hot fat or butter. Let them get brown and very hot and then remove from the pan. Put them in a hot dish and fry the slices of pineapple in the same pan to a golden brown. Sprinkle some extra paprika powder on them. On each plate arrange one slice of ham and cover it with a pineapple slice.

A garnish was added to each plate of some well-cooked whole potatoes sprinkled with chopped mint. Chopped celery and parsley can be substituted for mint if preferred.

A salad was also served which was prepared in the following manner:

Mixed Salad

Make a mixture of ⅓ of shredded cabbage (raw), ⅓ of finely sliced red radishes, and the same amount of onions cut up in strips. The sweet-sour dressing is made with demerara sugar, vinegar or lemon juice, cayenne pepper, and olive oil. This raw salad must marinate for about 30 minutes in this dressing before serving.

Now we leave Thailand and continue our tour via Cambodia and Viet Nam to Hongkong-Kowloon.

CAMBODIA AND VIET NAM

I COULD write reams about Cambodia, or rather about the magnificent temples of Siem Reap, but this is a book devoted to culinary experiences, and, alas, there is little of interest to relate about Cambodia's cuisine. In the few hotels in Pnom Penh, the capital, the rule is European food, indifferently served. There are a number of Chinese restaurants, but here again the meals served do not begin to compare with those in Hongkong's Chinese restaurants, nor in Cholon, Saigon's Chinese quarter. Moreover, Cambodia is an expensive country to stay in. A whisky costs about fifteen shillings, while a bottle of wine will cost anything from three to eight pounds. Room charges are in keeping with these exaggerated figures.

But if one wants to see the magnificent temples at Siem Reap one is forced to spend at least a day in Pnom Penh. The hundreds of superb temples built in Siem Reap by the Khmers in the twelfth century make a visit to Cambodia obligatory to anyone travelling in the Far East, but one is never tempted to tarry long in Pnom Penh. And as soon as possible after the visit to Siem Reap one speeds on to Saigon and from there to Hong-Kong-Kowloon.

Saigon is the capital of South Viet Nam, and a pleasant excursion while there is a visit to Cholon, the Chinese quarter, with its many restaurants, bars, and exotic shops. In one of its most famous restaurants the menu contained no fewer than 440 Chinese dishes, and I had a most perfectly well-prepared Chinese dinner, although it was difficult and embarrassing to make a choice, particularly when all the dishes appeared to be equally splendid. I enjoyed particularly:

Vi Cá Mang Hôp Nau Gach Cua (Shark-fin Soup)

for 4 servings:

¼ pound shark-fins cut up in thin strips (available in the United States and in most European countries, dried or canned

4 cups stock made from 15–20 chicken legs
1 small can asparagus soup
1 small can crab meat soup vegetables

As we cannot always buy fresh or dried shark-fins we can make do with a can of shark-fin soup. It sounds, yet is not, very expensive, but we must obtain 15–20 chicken legs well washed and cleaned with which to prepare the 4 cups of stock. We must add the usual soup vegetables and simmer for a couple of hours. Drain the stock and let it cool. You may be surprised at the jelly-like stock provided by the chicken legs. Skim off the fat, if any, and let the stock come to the boil again. Then add the shark-fins or soup and taste to see if more salt or pepper is needed. Shortly before serving add the canned asparagus soup and crab meat, the latter divided into small pieces. This is a delicious soup to which we can give as a finishing touch some tomato ketchup or Worcester Sauce. A raw egg-white, beaten with a pinch of monosodium glutamate and ½ teaspoon of corn-flour, can also be added. The raw white when well beaten in with a wire whisk changes in the hot soup into long white strips.

Another very tasty dish was the

Vit Hap Táo Yeu (Red Lacquered Duck)

for 4 servings:

1 wild or domestic duck	pepper and salt to taste
1 egg-yolk	½ tablespoon of demerara
5 tablespoons red sauce (a	sugar
Chinese sauce available in	1 generous tablespoon sweet
shops stocking Oriental	paprika
specialities)	a generous pinch of
8 tablespoons oil	monosodium glutamate

Pre-heat the grill as much as possible. In the meantime thoroughly rub the bird with a mixture made from all the listed ingredients. The mixture will be red. Whether we prepare the duck whole or halved, as described in the recipe of the Pollo alla Diavolo (see under Italy, p. 82), will depend on the grill. If necessary we can also prepare the duck in a very hot oven which must not be closed completely during the cooking time. By allowing the steam to escape we obtain a good imitation of grilling.

Place the duck in as close contact as possible with the heat, for we want to grill the outside as quickly as we can. Then we must reduce the heat. From time to time while grilling rub more of the red blend into the duck. A young bird will be done in about 40 minutes, a young wild duck needing a little less time. The result is a red, very shiny duck deliciously flavoured.

The use of an egg-yolk is important. I use 2 egg-yolks as they make the colour brighter and the blend more effective.

If you have no oven or grill you can also roast this duck in a roasting-pan on top of the stove. But if we do this we must rub in the red blend more frequently. In order to brown it quickly use lard or oil. Roast in an open or half-covered pan in order to let all the steam escape.

In preparing the blend for this method the egg-yolk is added only shortly before serving the duck. And we must blend this egg-yolk with a teaspoon of cornflour to make it stick better.

Please take into account the fact that a roaster or a young wild duck needs only about 20–25 minutes of hot-grilling.

With this duck serve vermicelli lightly pre-boiled and well drained.

Mi Xoe (Sautéed Vermicelli)

The thick vermicelli is best for this recipe. When well drained, sauté golden yellow with chopped onions, tiny pieces of ham or shrimps, using lard or oil for the sautéing.

Before dishing up add chopped parsley or mint. As no sauce is served with the duck the sautéed vermicelli is an excellent accompaniment. I often prepare a roasting chicken with this red blend.

In Cholon I was served a red-lacquered domestic duck which was quite perfect.

Leaving Viet Nam, we continue our tour to Hongkong-Kowloon.

HONGKONG-KOWLOON

THESE two cities always remind me of a split-pea, for although they are virtually one settlement, the population is split between the British and the Chinese. They do, in fact, represent two completely different races and civilizations. One could truthfully say two different worlds.

Most of the luxury hotels are run on British lines. In the Palm Courts afternoon tea is elegantly served while a string band plays music.

The licensing hours are fixed, luncheons and dinners are served only between certain strictly observed hours. There are also a number of exclusive British clubs. In every hotel, where, incidentally, the room service is so smoothly operated by the Chinese, there is what amounts to a shopping arcade. One can, in fact, do all one's buying without leaving the hotel, a great advantage to a woman as the hot and humid climate can be very trying. One should not, however, limit oneself to hotel shopping, for nothing could be more amusing than a shopping expedition to Kowloon, that rambling, untidy city on the peninsula which is so unlike the orderly, efficient big-business Hongkong.

In Kowloon shopping becomes obsessive, for there are so many lovely things to hold the attention. Kowloon is a free port, and this means low prices. The result is that tourists buy as much as they possibly can and often run themselves right out of money. The prices are so low that willy-nilly one is tempted to go on and on acquiring jewellery, *objets d'art*, antiques, dresses, coats, shoes, and cameras until all one's money is spent.

Eventually all the purchases are taken to your hotel in a suitcase, thoughtfully lent by an obliging shopkeeper. It is all great fun until one faces the customs officer on the return home.

From the very first moment of entering the widespread Chinese quarter you feel the full impact of Chinese life. The streets, both large and small, are brimful of activity and full of noise and colour. Besides the excellent English and Chinese restaurants to be found here, you will also come across Russian ones. There I have tasted delicious Russian meals. You must not be surprised, therefore, if I end this chapter on Chinese cookery with two Russian recipes.

Here is the first Chinese recipe.

Bong Cai Xao Sauce Cua (Cauliflower with Shrimps)

for 4 servings:

1 cauliflower, divided into little bouquets	1 teaspoon sugar
	1 teaspoon salt
4–8 prawns, shelled and de-veined	5 tablespoons lard
	1 generous pinch turmeric
5 tablespoons stock	powder and monosodium
1 tablespoon cornflour	glutamate
1 chopped onion	1 tablespoon soy sauce

Make a well-blended sauce with all the ingredients except the cauliflower and the lard, and then add the prawns. Brown the lard in a saucepan and fry the floured cauliflower bouquets a golden brown. Add to this mixture the sauce with the prawns in it and let it slowly come to the boil. Then cover the pan and reduce the heat. Allow about 10 minutes for the tiny pieces of cauliflower to be done. This sauce will be somewhat thick owing to the cornflour. Serve in a bowl and add black pepper to taste. Dry-cooked rice is eaten with this dish. In Kowloon this dry-cooked rice is mixed with fried onions and little pieces of chicken, the rice being served as a little package, wrapped up in lotus leaves and looking most attractive.

With these dishes you are also served with small pieces of sirloin steak.

Thit Bo (Beef Dish)

for 2 servings:

¼ pound sirloin steak, divided in portions of about 30 grams each	1½ tablespoons Chinese wine, which can be replaced by dry sherry
3 tablespoons soy sauce	stock
½ teaspoon ginger powder	oil
1 chopped shallot	

I was told by a Chinese cook to leave the steak for at least two days somewhere in the kitchen, but not in a cool place or in the refrigerator. Just a reasonably warm place was recommended.

Mix all the ingredients with the exception of the steak, which is cut up in small, flat pieces. Leave these pieces to macerate for about an hour in the blend. After removing them from this sauce dry them in a cloth and flour lightly. Turn them over in oil. Heat a little oil in an omelet-pan and add the meat. When the oil is smoking hot they will brown quickly and be cooked in about 1–2 minutes. This is understandable when we remember that their weight is only about 30 grams each. Remove the meat from the omelet-pan and pour in the remainder of the sauce. When it is warm serve this sauce, lightened with some stock, in the bowl in which we have already put the meat.

This meat can be eaten very easily with chopsticks. It is so tender that every morsel melts in the mouth.

Dip some rice in the sauce and eat this with chopsticks. In China they bring the bowl very near to the face and with the chopsticks convey small portions of rice into the mouth. It is indeed a most amusing way of eating, but you have to get accustomed to it and it takes a little time. The result is that you taste every little morsel far more thoroughly than when eating it quickly in our own knife and fork fashion.

Chao Fan (Fried Rice)

for 4 servings:

about ¾ cup rice, dry-cooked in the morning	3 eggs
	1 teaspoon salt
½ pound ham or left-over meat cut up in small strips	1 big finely chopped onion
	4 tablespoons oil

The ham or meat is cut up finely. Blend the chopped onion with the beaten eggs and the salt. Let the oil get hot and fry in it the cooked rice till light yellow. With a kitchen fork stir in the onion-egg blend and let it thicken the rice and turn it a golden colour. Then add the ham or meat to it and stir again. Allow 2–3 minutes for the ham or meat to become hot. Serve immediately.

Xuang Heo Xao Mang (Sweet-sour Pork)

for 4 servings:

1 pound lean pork meat without bone, cut up in small dices
¾ cup flour
1 egg-yolk

1 beaten egg-white
generous pinch salt
1 tablespoon soy sauce
1 dessertspoon oil
a deep-frying pan with oil

FOR THE SAUCE WITH GARNISH

6 ginger balls from syrup, sliced
1 small can pineapple
2 tablespoons soy sauce
2 tablespoons pineapple sauce
1 tablespoon demerara sugar
salt and cayenne pepper to taste

3 drops tabasco sauce
1 clove
1 tablespoon sherry
3 tablespoons butter or lard
1 tablespoon cornflour

We first deep-fry the pieces of pork meat, doing this preferably in the morning. Prepare a batter with the beaten egg-yolk, the flour, salt, soy sauce, oil, and as much water as is needed to obtain a thick good-coating batter. This batter should look like porridge. To end with we add the well-beaten egg-white to it. Having already heated the oil in the deep-frying pan, we now put the pieces of pork into the batter. When they are well covered on all sides we remove them from the batter with two forks and drop them in the very hot frying-oil. They brown immediately, and when they come floating to the surface they are done. Allow for these diced pieces of meat about 3–4 minutes only. Remove with a skimmer and let them drain in a colander covered with tissue-paper.

Let the meat cool. About 15–20 minutes before eating we brown the butter or the lard in a fireproof dish. In it we again brown the cooled, diced meat. The butter or lard must be very hot. In the meantime we have prepared a blended sauce with all the ingredients indicated above. The ginger is sliced, the pine-apple diced. Let this simmer in the pan with the pork meat for no longer than 5–8 minutes. Your dish is now ready and should be hot through and through. We do not cover the pan, for we want to let the sauce evaporate a little and so thicken.

With this dish, too, we serve cooked rice.

Another Chinese dish to end with:

Jou Szu Tsai Tang (Meat and Vegetable Soup)

for 4 servings:

½ pound soup vegetables cut up in thin strips of ½ inch
⅓ pound pork meat cut up in the same size
4 cups stock
1 teaspoon salt
generous pinch crushed cardamom seeds
pepper to taste
pinch monosodium glutamate
1 tablespoon sherry

Prepare a good stock with meat or bones, but do this the day before. When cool skim off all the fat. Bring to the boil again the day you serve this soup and add the strips of meat to it. Allow only 1 minute of quick boiling. Remove the meat with a skimmer and add the thin strips of vegetables to the boiling stock. We can make a choice from cauliflower, spinach leaves, peas, French beans, leeks, carrots, and so on. In the gently boiling stock these vegetables are done in 8–10 minutes. Now we again add the strips of cooked meat blended with the monosodium glutamate, sherry, salt, pepper, and crushed cardamom seeds.

Serve the soup in four small Chinese soup bowls and serve with the Chinese spoons that go with these bowls. They are available in most shops all over Europe, and most of them are quite inexpensive.

And here are the two promised Russian recipes I was served in Kowloon.

Salianka (Russian Fish Soup)

for 6 servings:

not quite 4 cups fish stock	2 tablespoons capers
not quite 4 cups meat stock	1 large raw peeled beetroot or
1 generous tablespoon tomato	2 smaller ones, coarsely
purée	shredded
4 large fresh tomatoes cut	½ lemon, washed, unpeeled,
up in four	cut up in small pieces
1 fresh paprika cut up in	1 bay leaf
strips	2 cloves
2 sliced onions	3 drops tabasco sauce

The day before prepare a tasty meat stock with ¾ pound of cut-up pork meat and about 3 cups of water to which we add some soup vegetables, but no salt. With a cod's head or other suitable fish we prepare 3 cups of strong fish stock. Strain the fish stock, in which we still have the fish, or the cod's head, and add this clear stock to the meat stock. To this we now add all the ingredients indicated above with the exception of the tabasco sauce. Bring to the boil and continue to boil gently for a further 15 minutes.

Remove the flesh from the cod's head or the fish, and add it to the soup. Taste to see if salt is needed, but as the capers are rather salty be careful. Finally add the tabasco sauce.

If you would rather make a rich fish soup then add diced garden celery (fresh or canned), sliced fresh mushrooms, ¼ pound of boned raw fish, and 4–6 prawns cut up in strips. These added ingredients make the soup a delicious treat. In Kowloon they added fresh chopped parsley and a very generous amount of heavy cream just before serving.

If served with French bread this soup is a meal in itself.

A most exciting but rather expensive dish is

Farshmak (Meat Gratinée)

for 6 servings:

2 cooked chicken breasts, skinned, boned, and cut up in pieces

4 whole boiled sausages sliced

½ cup cooked ox tongue diced

1 crushed clove of garlic

½ pound pork meat thinly cut up in strips and boiled for 2 minutes only

3 hard-boiled eggs, quartered

2 pounds potatoes sliced and not over-cooked

1 fresh cucumber, sliced

1½ cups cheese sauce

4 tablespoons butter

First of all prepare the cheese sauce with butter, flour, and half milk and half stock or water with a meat cube. A helping of cream with a generous amount of cheese will add to the quality of this sauce.

Butter a fireproof dish liberally, using half of the 4 tablespoons of butter, and place in it all the ingredients listed except the eggs and the remaining butter, having first mixed all these ingredients with the raw cucumber slices but not yet blended them with the sauce.

When they are all in the fireproof dish lay on the quartered eggs and pour on the cheese sauce and dot the rest of the butter on the top.

The oven has already been on for 10 minutes, and so we can now cover the dish with aluminium foil and put it in the oven.

Let its content come to boiling-point, and when the sauce begins to simmer very gently we reduce the heat. Allow at least 20–30 minutes for the ingredients to become very hot. They should also be very creamy. Then remove the foil from the dish and put the oven full on again. Place the dish high in the oven or, if there is one, under the grill. In the immediate contact with the heat the surface of this dish should colour a golden yellow. Cover with further cheese and butter.

When arranging all the ingredients in this dish do not mix the quartered eggs with all the other things. They are neatly added to it shortly before we pour on the cheese sauce. Only then will they remain undamaged and give a nice colour to the *farshmak*.

There is no need to supply a first course with this dish as it is in itself a delicious but rather rich meal. A strong cup of coffee afterwards is all you are likely to want.

Now let us see what Japan has to offer.

JAPAN

THE flight from Hongkong-Kowloon to Tokyo when the moon is full is an unforgettable experience. The waiting plane lies so close to the seashore that the take-off is rather scaring, as are all the red warning lights on the hills surrounding Hongkong.

It is quite an experience in itself to fly over the snow-capped Fujiyama as it peeps through the clouds like a silver top, and the landing at Tokyo's airport is interesting. By now one has become accustomed to the bright smiles of the Chinese inhabitants of Kowloon, and so the smirk on the Japanese faces comes rather as a shock. Yet at the end of a few days you realize that the Japanese are friendly people and extremely polite. Tokyo is a most fascinating city, yet impossible to get to know. The street plans available give little or no help in finding your way. The city is like an enormous spider's web, and only its main streets are named. All the hundreds of smaller streets are name-less, so a tourist finds it difficult to find his way about. The main street is called Ginza and is so long that to the pedestrian it seems endless.

There are innumerable restaurants, snack-bars, and night-clubs in all these streets, both small and large. The hotels, both European and Japanese style, are expertly managed and the service is excellent.

In the Imperial Palace Hotel you have the old and the new combining in an antique building adjoining a most modern structure, and the fascinating part of this hotel is the basement shopping gallery where you can spend many hours shopping—and spending money.

The Japanese are very proud of their handicraft and spend hours on making their food look like exquisite miniatures. Colour and shape play an important part in their gastronomy, and much attention is given to flavouring.

Not only are their food titbits a pleasure to look upon, but even more attractive are the dishes, among which the bowls in all different sizes are the prettiest. The Japanese are masters of imagination in the domain of gastronomy, and most adept in the use of pineapple, stuffed olives, shrimps, chicken meat cut up in tiny strips or diced, eggs, Japanese soy sauce, cucumbers, dried mushrooms, and prunes with rice.

If a European cook were to try to prepare a Sushi, which is a raw fish and rice combination, she should have at least one Japanese ancestor in her family; otherwise the result might be disastrous.

The way they lay the table, too, is something one cannot but admire. The mats, doilies, dishes, and chopsticks are all so dainty. Elegant, too, is the table itself, which is usually low, oblong in size, and covered with mats, like the floors upon which one sits. You never enter a Japanese restaurant or hotel with shoes on, for this is just not done. They give you socks or slippers to wear, and you will feel quite at ease once you have got accustomed to it.

There are several Japanese dishes we can prepare in our countries, and the first of these I will give you is a mixed chicken and meat combination.

Genghis Khan Meal (Grilled Dish)

In Japan you will come across special Genghis Khan restaurants. The first thing you will notice on entering are the low tables with low wooden benches. The middle of these tables consists of a deep fireproof pot filled with charcoal. The top of the table is fitted out with a fireproof material. On the charcoal, which burns in an asbestos pot filled with sand, lies a beautiful hand-wrought gridiron.

On the table stands a bottle of Japanese soy sauce, another of saké (the Japanese wine), a bowl filled with a blend of paprika powder, salt, and cayenne pepper, another bowl filled with oil and provided with a little brush, and a tiny bowl with nutmeg and two metal chopsticks for each guest.

Before sitting down the female guest is given a white cook's apron and a big straw hat. This is to prevent her hair from getting greasy from the oil. The man also gets a big white cook's apron.

A nice geisha, who acts as your personal hostess, puts in front of you a plate upon which are placed, for two people:

4 very small pieces raw chicken breasts	2 slices lotus root
	4 slices aubergine
4 tiny pork collops (each piece of meat weighs about 30 grams	6 pieces white of a leek cut up in tiny rolls of ½ inch
2 pieces sirloin steak each of 30 grams	2 large brown mushrooms

First you grease the grill with oil and then do the same with some of the ingredients you are going to grill. For this we use the brush. Put the morsels on the hot iron bars and see that they do not brown too much. Turn, and after they are brown all over, allow about 6 minutes' cooking for all the ingredients except the small pieces of sirloin steak, which will be done far more quickly. Use for this the metal meat chopsticks, and if you are doing this for the first time the geisha will teach you how. Do not eat the grilled food until you have dipped each piece in the soy sauce and sprinkled it with the spices of your choice. With it you drink the saké out of miniature china cups.

This meal keeps you very busy, and it is indeed great fun. You can also prepare this type of food at home if you have a small stove to put in the middle of your table, a good well-greased omelet-pan, the spices, and the Japanese soy sauce. If you do not like saké, which is available in most European countries, replace it with dry sherry or white wine.

Another Japanese speciality is the

Yakitori (Grilled Chicken)

for 4 servings:

1 tender roaster divided in
four

A SAUCE PREPARED WITH
5 tablespoons soy sauce
¼ teaspoon ginger powder
¼ teaspoon demerara sugar
pinch cayenne pepper

pinch Ajinomoto
  (monosodium glutamate)
4 tablespoons oil

Marinate the pieces of chicken in the sauce you have made by blending well all the ingredients. Leave them in it for about 2 hours.

Heat the grill thoroughly and grease it with oil. Put the pieces of chicken in or on it in close contact with the heat. Brown well and allow about 15 minutes to be done. From time to time rub in some of the marinade sauce.

Serve little bowls with cooked rice garnished with grilled almond slices. Sliced almonds are on sale in plastic bags in most good grocers.

As good yet much different is the

Poached Chicken with Vegetables

for 4 servings:

½ boiling fowl divided in
small pieces with the
bones
1 can bamboo shoots
8 equal-sized carrots
15 equal-sized mushrooms,
fresh or dried
about 2 cups water
salt to taste
2 tablespoons Japanese soy
sauce (which contains
more salt than the Chinese
soy sauce)

a generous pinch ginger
powder
pinch cayenne pepper
a generous pinch demerara
sugar
1 generous tablespoon
cornflour

If in season
⅓ pound thin French beans
or pods
⅓ pound weighed peeled
green peas, not too small,
or 1 pack frozen peas

Barely cover the pieces of chicken with the water. Bring to the boil and skim the liquid several times in order to provide a clear stock. Reduce the heat and cover the pan.

Allow about 45 minutes for the chicken pieces to be done, but watch to see that the meat does not get overdone. This is important. Remove the chicken from the cooking liquid and put it aside. Remove all fat from the stock and bring to the boil again.

Add salt to taste, cayenne pepper, ginger powder, and demerara sugar. The vegetables should be cut up into fine strips, with the exception of the mushrooms and peas, and all added to the boiling chicken stock except the peas and the bamboo shoots.

Allow the shortest time possible for the vegetables to be done, as they must be crisp and should keep their colour. Now add the frozen peas and the cut-up bamboo shoots. They need only 5 minutes' cooking time.

While the cooking is taking place prepare a blend with the soy sauce, the cornflour, and as much stock as is needed to make a thick mixture. Stir into the vegetable-stock mixture and add the pieces of cooked chicken. Taste for salt.

The sauce should be only slightly thickened. It should be somewhere between a thick soup and a slightly thickened (with vegetables and cornflour) ragout. On the table place the bottle of soy sauce, the tomato ketchup, and, for those who like it, paprika powder.

The Japanese drink saké with this meal.

We cannot leave Japan without preparing the most important national dish, the

Sukiyaki (Meat-vegetable Frying Dish)

for 4 servings:

1 table cooking apparatus (electric or spirit stove)

1 not too shallow yet not too deep heavy iron pan

1 pound raw sirloin steak, cut up in paper-thin slices

4 pieces fat bacon without rind, each weighing roughly 30 grams

3 leeks well washed with the white cut up in rolls about 1 inch in length

6 medium carrots, cut up in long, thin strips

8 whole fresh mushrooms

8 slices raw aubergines, if available

instead of using chrysanthemum leaves use uncut celery leaves and bamboo shoots (canned) cut up once lengthwise

1 bottle with 2 cups very hot concentrated meat stock

1 bottle Japanese soy sauce

1 bowl with white sugar

For each guest

1 bowl with 1 raw egg in it

1 bowl with hot cooked rice

1 glass for the saké

Arranging all these ingredients is the principal work in which this dish involves us. You should roll up each thin slice of meat and put it in a circle on a straw tray covered with a plastic mat (to prevent the straw from getting soaked). Next to the meat arrange all the other ingredients as elegantly as you can, taking the colour effect into consideration. Heat one piece of fat bacon in the heavy iron pan on the cooking stove you have put in the middle of the table. When the bacon has melted and become very hot you start working.

In the fat roast some slices of meat to a dark brown, and add a spoon of soy sauce, 2 spoons of stock from the bottle, and a pinch of sugar. As the meat is so thin it is done in a few seconds. Divide among the bowls of your guests, who in the meantime have beaten up the eggs in their bowls. Coat the very hot meat with the beaten egg. Meanwhile add some vegetable to the frying-pan with mushrooms, soy sauce, stock, and again a pinch of sugar.

The rolls of leek need about 5 minutes to become crisp and very tasty.

You go on cooking meat and vegetable alternately. Frying at table is great fun, but it has one disadvantage for the hostess or the host, whoever is the cook, for he or she will not have much time to eat. You guests are so delighted with this freshly pre-pared food that they just go on eating and you cannot catch up with them.

Moreover, I have noticed that, however much meat I order, it is never enough, for the meat cut up in paper-thin slices dis-solves in one's mouth.

Every morsel of meat dipped in the beaten egg is eaten with some cooked rice. Needless to say, we fry with chopsticks and eat with them too. When they serve you a Sukiyaki in Japan your table has a personal geisha who prepares all these savoury titbits with great elegance and skill.

When I have guests for Sukiyaki I serve a glass of beer with it.

And finally here is the

Tempura (Deep-frying Fish Dish)

for 2 servings:

1 deep-frying pan with oil or vegetable fat
some slices aubergine

canned bamboo shoots sliced and well drained

BATTER MADE WITH

¼ pound half cornflakes finely crushed, half rice-flour
1–2 eggs

1 dessertspoon oil
water

FOR THE FISH MAKE A CHOICE FROM

4 de-frozen prawns, peeled and de-veined
8 small pieces raw eel
if available, raw calamary (inkfish) cut up in pieces

turbot or cod, fresh and boned
some big mussels

Start by preparing the batter and blend the crushed cornflakes with the rice-flour, the eggs, the oil, and as much water as is required to obtain a thick batter that will coat the fish thoroughly.

Let the oil or vegetable fat get hot in the deep-frying pan. The rest of the work is very easy.

We dip each piece of fish and vegetable in the batter and coat it well. Then we deep-fry it in the hot oil or fat, allowing only a few minutes to brown and get done.

Each guest has a bowl with a blend of half soy sauce and half stock in it. In this blend he dips the fried morsel. Personally I think this a most exciting fish meal.

One eats well in Japan, and the best part of their food is that it is always so freshly cooked.

Their sirloin steak called Kobebeef, after the city Kobe, where the cattle is specially fattened, is perfect. I never tasted better meat.

Chicken is not appreciated quite so much. But if they deep-fry a chicken it is just perfect. After turning over the chicken in beaten egg they roll it through a mixture of crushed cornflakes and herbs. These cornflakes make a wonderful crisp breading which is well worth trying out.

We now leave Japan for the 'new world,' and first to the United States.

FOURTH TOUR:
The United States
of America
and Mexico

I AM particularly delighted at the thought of writing this chapter—mainly owing to the fact that my latest visit to America took place just when I had started to write this book.

AMERICA

I HAVE twice visited the States, and altogether I spent two and a half months over there. In addition to New York and Washington, I was able to visit many other interesting places such as San Francisco, Los Angeles, New Orleans, and Chicago. My main object was to find out as much as possible about the way of life of the people and learn what I could about the food they eat.

I visited many places, but as friends had given to me a list of the 'gastronomic spots' in Fisherman's Wharf near San Francisco and in Hollywood and Santa Monica I made these special centres of interest. For those in search of good food and good recipes New Orleans is the very centre of 'high gastronomy.' Its restaurants offer top-class cooking and many new and exciting dishes. How could it be otherwise in a town where French and Spanish cuisine is combined with Creole cookery, with its knowledge of Italian herbs and other flavours? Is this gastronomy a grandchild of France or of Spain, and has it some Italian cousins? No one can tell, but I can assure you that I never tasted more thrilling dishes than during my ten days' stay in this wonderful town.

The cooks I met there were most friendly, and I am grateful to them for giving me their recipes and, more than this, for teaching me how to prepare them. Unfortunately, in the modern New Orleans hotels you are often served American cuisine, which is stereotyped throughout America. But the cooking in New Orleans' Vieux Carre (the old part of the town) is very different from normal American cooking.

I have the most wonderful memories of the many Polynesian restaurants all over America, where the food is most attractive and elegantly served.

If you stay in some of the larger American hotels you will find on a table in your bedroom a detailed breakfast menu. You can order your breakfast the evening before and state the precise hour you want it to be served in your room. Warm dishes are served on a trolley which sometimes carries a small heated oven in which you will find your hot dishes and your coffee or tea.

When staying in California you can order a fruit breakfast, and what wonderful fruit they serve you! This is not surprising, for Sunny Vale, in California, provides the United States and many other countries of the world with an abundance of fruit. Never did I encounter so many varieties of beautiful fruit as in California.

I liked the following snacks best of all.

Chicken or Meat Sandwich. Have ready two buttered slices of white bread. Arrange on each slice of bread a crisp, well-dried lettuce leaf. Prepare a blend with remainders of cooked chicken skinned and boned or some other kind of meat cut up in small strips (even canned chicken or meat can be used), as much mayonnaise with pepper and salt to taste as is needed to obtain a smooth spread.

To make it savoury in the American way, add some tomato ketchup and a generous amount of chopped parsley. Tabasco and mustard are usually on the table for those who want them.

Cut the slices of bread diagonally after being dressed. They can be prepared in advance, as the lettuce leaves protect the bread from becoming soggy.

Chicken and Egg Sandwich. This was one of my favourites. Prepare a smooth blend with cut-up cooked chicken meat (preferably the white meat), mashed hard-boiled eggs, mayonnaise, and chopped parsley with salt and pepper to taste. Some American cooks add chopped piccalilli to it, which gives a nice spicy flavour. Do not forget the lettuce leaves.

Egg Sandwich. A blend is prepared with mashed hard-boiled eggs, mayonnaise, Worcester Sauce, mustard, and chopped parsley. Lettuce leaves too.

Chicken Sandwich. A blend of chopped cooked chicken meat, chopped mushrooms, and capers with mustard and mayonnaise. Here, too, we use lettuce leaves.

Fish Sandwich. Well-drained canned tunafish is coarsely chopped and blended with chopped hard-boiled eggs, mayonnaise, chopped parsley, and/or chives. Spread out on buttered slices of bread covered with lettuce leaves.

Salmon Sandwich. Make a blend with well-drained canned salmon, shredded cucumber, and lettuce leaves (finely cut up in strips and well drained and dried), mayonnaise, and mustard. We also use lettuce leaves on the slices of bread.

Cream Cheese Sandwich. For this sandwich-spread we blend cream cheese with chopped stuffed olives, sweet-sour gherkins, syrup in which ginger has been preserved, pineapple (canned and well drained), and some dates or figs, both finely chopped. Arrange on slices of white bread covered with lettuce leaves. Add as finishing touch a little lemon juice.

Roquefort Sandwich. Blend Roquefort cheese with butter, red port, and cream in order to prepare a smooth, creamy spread.

Add to it some freshly ground black pepper and paprika powder, but no salt. For this sandwich we use rye bread or toast and no lettuce leaves.

Ham Sandwich. This is a very good spread and so easy to prepare. Blend together ham cut up in strips, mashed hard-boiled eggs, mayonnaise, tomato ketchup, and chopped parsley. Arrange on bread covered again with lettuce leaves.

What struck me most of all is the great amount of *vegetable sandwiches* which are ordered in all these bars. On buttered and lettuce-covered white or rye bread they arrange quite simply slices of tomatoes with fresh paprikas cut up in thin strips, radishes, and/or French celery also cut up in thin strips. They sometimes add mayonnaise to it, but very often do with only salt and pepper to taste. You can, if you care for it, have mustard and pickles served with these sandwiches.

And many Americans drink butter- or skimmed-milk with these sandwiches, probably to have animal proteins without fat.

A good warm snack is the

Hamburger. Prepare a ball of chopped raw steak and roast it so that the heart remains pinkish-red—that is, so that it is not completely done. Arrange on a scooped-out white roll and add chopped piccalilli. A simple yet good morsel.

You can do the same with the

Cheeseburger. Roast again a chopped steak shaped into a ball, not overdone please. At the same time melt two slices of cheese and arrange both cheese and steak-ball into a scooped-out white roll. Serve with mustard.

And here is another sandwich-spread:

Peanut-butter Sandwich. Fry slices of bacon until brittle. Blend with peanut butter in the following combination: 1 part of bacon and 2 parts of peanut butter. Add just a little mayonnaise and some soy sauce. Use this spread on rye bread.

The slices of bacon should be completely dry—not in the least greasy—before crushing them. Lean, not fat bacon must be used with the peanut butter.

And now the time has come to take a look at some real chicken dishes. The first is a chicken soup which fascinated me because of its pinkish colour.

Chicken Soup Biltmore

for 6 servings:

2 chicken legs (from a freshly boiled fowl)	5 large peeled tomatoes
7 cups chicken stock	1 generous tablespoon chopped green herbs
5 tablespoons coarsely chopped raw celery stalks (garden celery)	(parsley, chives, and others)
	1 small can tomato purée
5 tablespoons chopped raw carrots	½ lemon
	pepper and salt to taste

For this recipe we must prepare a savoury chicken broth the day before, taking care not to over-cook the boiling fowl. We use only the dark chicken meat, putting aside the two breast-pieces of the fowl to be used next day for another chicken dish. We also put aside 2 cups of the stock for the same purpose.

We skim off the fat from the remaining 5 cups of cold stock and drain it. Then bring it to the boil again and add the coarsely chopped vegetables. They will be done in less than 8 minutes. Next add the peeled tomatoes cut up in fine strips with the cut-up dark chicken meat. Allow a few minutes to get hot. Taste if there is enough salt and pepper and finally stir in the tomato purée blended with the lemon juice. For this use a wire whisk. Your Biltmore chicken soup will now be a beautiful red. Just before serving add the chopped green herbs.

With the two remaining breast-pieces we prepare the following dish:

Breast of Chicken Jerusalem

for 2 servings only:

2 breast-pieces of cooked
boiled chicken

LESS THAN 2 CUPS OF WHITE SAUCE MADE WITH

3 tablespoons butter	1 egg-yolk
3 tablespoons flour	2 tablespoons cream
less than 2 cups stock	lemon juice (optional)

FOR THE GARNISH

1 tiny can artichoke hearts	mushrooms
4–5 tablespoons cheese	salt and pepper to taste

Re-heat the pieces of chicken breasts in a saucepan with some stock. Cover the pan and reduce the heat to a minimum. The chicken should not be allowed to boil. Prepare in the meantime the white sauce and add as a finishing touch the egg-yolk beaten up with the cream and the lemon juice, if any. If you care for it you must use instead of the lemon juice some sherry or red port.

The sauce once blended with the egg-yolk and the cream should not be allowed to boil again.

Drain the artichoke hearts thoroughly and arrange them in a buttered oven-proof dish. On each heart we put 1 big mushroom, which we cover with a piece of cheese and a lump of butter. Put in the pre-heated oven and gratinate a golden colour. Remove the chicken meat from the stock and put it in a nice warm dish and cover with the creamy white sauce.

Serve both the dishes very hot, and serve with them very small boiled potatoes.

A really delicious chicken dish served to me in San Francisco is the

Chicken Lemon Soup

for 6 servings we use:

½ boiling fowl cooked in
7 cups water with ¼ pound
vegetables
pepper and salt to taste
1 garnished onion
pinch marjoram
pinch dill

a generous pinch paprika
powder
2 tablespoons uncooked rice
juice of 1 lemon
2 eggs
2 tablespoons chopped
parsley

Remove the fat from the boiling fowl before cooking. Bring the chicken to the boil in the water with all the listed ingredients except the rice, lemon, eggs and parsley. Skim the stock several times and allow the chicken to cook in the covered pan for about 1–1¼ hours. When cooked remove from the stock. Drain the stock through a sieve and let it cool a little. Skim off any remaining fat.

Bring to the boil again and add the rice. Allow about 15 minutes for the rice to be done. If you use instant rice only 6 minutes will be needed. Blend the lemon juice with the eggs and the chopped parsley and add them to the stock while beating briskly with a wire whisk. Before doing this, however, take the pan from the stove. If you do not serve the soup immediately see that it is kept warm on the lowest possible heat. Taste for salt and pepper. Serve with warm bread.

Again from San Francisco comes this recipe.

Chicken à la Ritz

for 4 servings:

2 halved spring chickens
salt and pepper to taste
2 tablespoons flour
½ cup butter
½ pound fresh mushrooms
3 tablespoons oil
5 sliced shallots

1 glass red wine or 1 smaller
  glass red port
½ cup cream
1 egg-yolk
2 tablespoons chopped
  parsley

Brown the butter in a saucepan and add to it the lightly flavoured chicken halves already salted and peppered. When they have browned add the sliced shallots and leave them to become a golden colour. Then add the red wine or the port. Allow 20 minutes for the chicken to be done.

Wash the mushrooms well and dry them as quickly as possible. Do not cut them up. Sauté them brown in the hot oil and then remove them with a skimmer. Add the mushrooms to the roasted chicken. While chicken and mushrooms go on cooking gently blend the egg-yolk with the cream. If you prefer you can use half the amount of cream.

Reduce the heat and stir in the blended egg and cream to the sauce. Work with a wire whisk, having removed the chicken halves and mushrooms to the side of the pan. See that the sauce is correctly salted and peppered. Serve immediately, as it must not come to the boil again, after having added the egg-cream blend.

This sauce is smooth and brown. Serve cooked rice with it.

In America they serve *wild rice* with this recipe. Wild rice not only looks different from our rice but the taste, too, is different. I have asked many an American cookery expert what precisely is this wild rice. Alas, all the answers were unsatisfactory. One told me it is a special type of rice of brown colour; another said it is a green vegetable now cultivated in American fields but which in earlier days grew wild. I regret to admit that I still do not know the right answer. I would compare its taste to that of Oriental 'bean sprouts.' Whatever its origin, the wild rice is prepared in exactly the same way as ordinary rice. Very often they blend this rice with chopped onions and chicken livers and add oregano. These rice grains are oblong, brownish in colour, and very tender.

Wild rice prepared as described above is often used as a stuffing, as you can see from the following recipe.

Boned Stuffed Squab (Spring Chicken)

for 2 servings:

1 boned squab (spring chicken)
1½ tablespoons wild or white rice
the liver and heart of the squab
1 small onion
1 tablespoon fresh chopped marjoram or oregano or ¼ teaspoon dried herbs
5 chopped mushrooms, fresh or canned
cayenne pepper and salt to taste
butter

FOR THE GARNISH
tiny artichoke hearts, canned
3 large potatoes scooped out into small round balls
some more mushrooms, canned or fresh, about ½ cup
1 tablespoon tomato ketchup

Prepare a forcemeat from the rice, already cooked, and the chopped onion, liver, heart, and 5 mushrooms all sautéed in a little butter. Add salt and cayenne pepper with the marjoram or oregano and stuff the boned squab. Sew or fasten with skewers.

Brown the butter in a casserole and let the squab brown too. Add some salt and cayenne pepper. To the sauce we add the raw potato balls with the fresh whole mushrooms. Let the squab continue roasting in the half-covered pan. Only 5 minutes before serving do we add the canned well-drained artichoke hearts and the canned mushrooms, if we have chosen them.

We serve this dish in the casserole it is prepared in. As a finishing touch the Americans often add some tomato ketchup and freshly ground black pepper.

As we have roasted potatoes with the chicken nothing else is served with it.

If you want to serve a simple hors d'oeuvre try the following recipe.

Perino Prawns

for 1 serving only:

1 slice hot toast
2 de-frozen large prawns
  shelled and de-veined
2 tablespoons lettuce leaves
  cut up in julienne
4 asparagus tips, canned
1 finely chopped shallot

1 generous tablespoon
  pinkish mayonnaise
1 dessertspoon coarsely
  chopped parsley
a slice of lemon
tomato ketchup or Worcester
Sauce

Blend the mayonnaise with some tomato ketchup to obtain the pinkish colour, and as flavouring add some Worcester Sauce. Butter the toast and cover with the julienne of lettuce leaves. Cut up the prawns lengthwise and arrange these halves on the lettuce leaves, and between each half we put one asparagus tip. Blend the mayonnaise with the chopped parsley and cover with it. Top with the slice of lemon and serve. Put the paprika powder and the black pepper on the table for use if required.

Before giving you recipes from New Orleans I might draw your attention to the much used *gumbo filé powder*. In the Creole cuisine it is absolutely a must.

This gumbo was brought to Louisiana by slaves coming from Africa. They had hidden these seeds in their clothes, and the seeds were planted first in the West Indies, from where they were later brought to Louisiana. They thrived and became known as *okra*. This filé powder is obtained from the pulverized dried leaves of an aromatic tree called sassafras (a laurel-like tree from North Africa). I was told that some fish powder is also contained in gumbo filé. Whatever the mixture is, its ingredients have given us a very savoury condiment.

Here is the first of the New Orleans recipes.

Chicken Gumbo

for 6 servings:

½ boned roaster divided into
6 small pieces
4 tablespoons flour
2 tablespoons lard, margarine,
or butter
1 large sliced onion
½ pound diced cooked ham
1 fresh Spanish pepper or 1
dried pepper
1 dessertspoon gumbo filé
powder

1 fresh stalk thyme or ¼
teaspoon dried thyme
1 tablespoon coarsely chopped
parsley
1 can tomatoes or 1 pound
peeled fresh tomatoes or 1
can concentrated tomato
purée
4 cups water
salt and pepper to taste

Separately

½ pound cooked rice

Prepare a dark-brown blend in a casserole with the browned lard, margarine, or butter and the flour. Stir constantly with a wooden spoon; let the flour brown gradually. As the flour begins to brown add to it the sliced onion, which should also brown. To this blend we finally add the six pieces of chicken, and when they are brown, and only then, add the whole well-washed fresh or dried Spanish pepper. Do not let it burst open as the seeds are much too hot. Now put in with the chicken the diced ham, with parsley, thyme, and gumbo filé powder and the tomatoes of our choice or the tomato purée. We have, of course, already peeled and cut up the fresh tomatoes into pieces. Stir the mixture and let it come gently to the boil and remain so for about 10 minutes. Do not cover the pan.

Bring to the boil 4 cups of water in a soup-pan and add all the browned ingredients from the casserole. Stir in with a wooden spoon, and when it has come to the boil again, cover the pan and reduce the heat; cook for 15–20 minutes for the pieces of chicken to be well done. The soup should simmer gently. During the last 5 minutes we add salt and freshly ground pepper to taste. The result of this cooking should be a thick dark-brown soup with a rich, spicy flavour. Finish with Worcester Sauce and tomato ketchup.

Serve this chicken gumbo in small soup-bowls and provide another bowl filled with cooked rice for each guest.

Some people prefer to eat the gumbo by alternating a spoonful of chicken soup with a spoonful of dry rice. Others add a little rice to each half-filled spoon of chicken gumbo. Personally I prefer the latter way.

In New Orleans they sometimes cook fresh okra in this soup. If it is available I would recommend you to try it. Okra is obtainable as long, hairy green pods which are cut up in strips, or very small green pods used whole. Okra reminds me of a broad bean, and the flavour is particularly delicate.

In the markets of New Orleans and all over Mexico you find an enormous variety of okra. Canned okra, if obtainable, is a satisfactory substitute for the fresh.

Although no chicken is used, I should like to tell you about another gumbo soup.

Gumbo Vegetable and Meat Soup

for 6 servings:

2 tablespoons lard
4 tablespoons flour
¾ pound soup vegetables
    among which spinach,
    green or white cabbage (or
    half of both), celeriac,
    watercress, and onion
2 tablespoons chopped fresh
    herbs, including thyme,
    tarragon, parsley, chives,
    marjoram, celery leaves

1 bay leaf
salt and pepper to taste
a few drops tabasco sauce
    (2–3 drops are enough)
5 cups liquid

Indispensable

1 *veal knuckle* or *the rind of* *a large piece of bacon* *and a ham bone*	1 *dessertspoon gumbo filé* *powder*
½ *pound pork meat cut up* *finely*	

Wash all the soup vegetables except the peeled onion and cut up finely. Cook them for just a few minutes in 1 cup of water and with the water still adhering to the vegetables. Drain, but take care to keep the boiling liquid. Let the fat get hot in a casserole and fry the small pieces of pork meat till golden brown. Add the chopped onion with all the fresh chopped green herbs, or, if necessary, dried herbs. But do not use more than ½ teaspoon of dried herbs.

When all these ingredients have turned brown, put in the gumbo filé powder and the flour with salt and pepper to taste. Pour in enough of the liquid from the vegetables to raise the volume to 5 cups, not more. Now add the veal knuckle, or the bone with the rind of bacon. Use all three if you have them. Bring to the boil, cover the pan, and reduce the heat. Allow 2 hours' simmering. Then remove the rind and the bone (or knuckle) and add the remainder of the pre-boiled soup vegetables. Let the soup come to the boil again and simmer for about 10 more minutes. Put in a few drops of tabasco sauce and taste to see that it is well salted and peppered.

Serve this gumbo soup in little bowls as for the previous recipe and do the same with the cooked rice, which is the accompaniment of every gumbo soup.

The gumbo oyster soup is a delicacy for oyster-lovers, but before serving be sure that none of your guests is allergic to oysters. Indeed, that also applies to other shellfish.

Gumbo Creole Oyster Soup Saint Antoine

for 4 servings:

8–12 oysters
1 large chopped onion
1 can tomato purée or 6
peeled large fresh tomatoes
with
1 generous tablespoon tomato
ketchup
1 dessertspoon gumbo filé
powder
a generous pinch dried
mixed herbs

½ pound celery stalks cut up
in small pieces
the contents of 1 can crab
meat
2 tablespoons butter
4 tablespoons flour
5 cups water
pepper and salt to taste

Brown the butter and sauté the onion till golden brown. Stir
in the flour and let it turn dark brown. Now add the mixed herbs
with the gumbo filé powder, the small pieces of celery, and pepper and salt to taste. Be careful with the salt as the oysters and

crab are naturally salty themselves. Never use an oyster that is dry.

We now pour the 5 cups of water on this blend and bring to the boil. Cover the pan and reduce the heat, but do not allow more than 10 minutes for cooking the pieces of celery. We have previously removed the oysters from their shells and have carefully kept the oyster liquid. We add both the oysters and their liquid, and the crab meat, divided into pieces, to the soup and allow 2–3 minutes for all these ingredients to get hot.

We also serve this gumbo soup in small bowls and with it tiny bowls of dry-cooked rice as before.

Place handy on the table the bottles with Worcester Sauce, tabasco sauce, and tomato ketchup.

Now for a real Creole chicken dish.

Chicken Creole with Rice

for 4 servings:

1 roaster chicken
1 can tomatoes or 1 can tomato purée or 5 large peeled fresh tomatoes with 1 generous tablespoon tomato ketchup
2 tablespoons sweet chili sauce
pinch chili powder

1 clove of garlic
2 coarsely sliced onions
1 bay leaf
3 tablespoons lard or butter
2 tablespoons flour
salt and pepper to taste
pinch mixed herbs
½ pound rice

Divide the roaster into four pieces. This chicken is not served in a sauce. It is garnished and later covered with a red, blended sauce. If this sauce turns out well we have succeeded in preparing a real Creole chicken dish.

Let the lard or butter turn hot and brown in a casserole. Sauté the chicken pieces till well brown. When this is done remove them from the fat and add the peeled sliced tomatoes (fresh or canned) to the casserole with the sliced onions, the clove of garlic, the bay leaf, the mixed herbs, and pepper and salt to taste. Stir in these ingredients in order to bring them into contact with the lard or butter and let them turn golden brown. By now all the liquid will have evaporated. Only then do we add, if any, the tomato purée or tomato ketchup. Stir once more and replace the pieces of chicken in the casserole. Sprinkle some salt over the pieces of chicken and place them to the side of the casserole. Add the flour to the vegetable-and-fat blend and stir. Put the chicken again in this blend, cover the pan, and allow about 25–30 minutes of gentle simmering. Stir now and then in order to prevent the mixture sticking to the bottom.

Enough liquid will develop in the covered casserole to obtain a well-thickened yet not sticky sauce.

As a finishing touch add the chili sauce blended with the chili powder and a lot of chopped parsley. We stir it in, and many a Creole cook will even add 2–3 drops of tabasco sauce. They like hot dishes very much. Taste before serving to see that it is well salted and peppered. Do not forget to serve the cooked rice with it.

Chicken Sandwich Piquant

for 8 slices of bread:

1 cup mayonnaise blended with 4–5 tablespoons grated horseradish
½ boiled chicken
3 firm fresh tomatoes (large size)

a generous pinch cayenne pepper
1 tablespoon cream (if any)
the heart of 1 lettuce

Prepare a blend with the mayonnaise, the fresh grated horseradish, the cayenne pepper, and the tablespoon of cream. If you use prepared horseradish cream from a jar you can omit the cream.

Butter 8 slices of bread. After washing and drying the lettuce heart thoroughly cut into julienne. The tomatoes are washed and dried and sliced unpeeled. Cover 4 slices of bread with the julienne of lettuce and a good helping of mayonnaise to which we have added slices of tomato. Then we cover with a generous layer of skinned, boned, and finely cut-up chicken meat. On all this we again put mayonnaise. Each garnished slice of bread is now covered with a buttered slice of bread. We now put the 4 sandwiches one upon the other, first covering the top surface of the first, second, and third sandwiches with mayonnaise. Fasten this 'tower' with four wooden skewers and stick upon each skewer a stuffed olive. Then with a very sharp knife we cut this tower into 4 equal parts, each of which remains fastened with an olive-garnished skewer. Four gourmets now have a wonderful snack to eat with their cocktails.

While still in New Orleans I got so fond of their chicken pilaff that I cannot leave it out.

Chicken Pilaff

for 4 servings:

1 small boiling fowl	breadcrumbs
4–6 cups water	1/3 cup butter
1/2 pound soup vegetables	pepper and salt to taste
2 extra large onions	1 bunch of dill, marjoram,
1/2 pound rice	parsley, celery, mint, and
2 egg-yolks	anything else you like

Boil the chicken and the soup vegetables in the water with the bunch of green herbs and salt and pepper to taste. Allow about 1½ hours, and when done, but not overdone, remove the chicken from the stock and sieve the stock. Let it cool and skim off all the fat. Bring to the boil about 1 cup of this stock with the rice and the two coarsely sliced onions added. Reduce the heat and let the rice dry-cook in the covered pan for about 17 minutes. Taste the stock for salt. In the meantime skin the chicken and divide it in four pieces. Remove the bunch of green herbs, generously butter a fireproof dish, and arrange the cooked rice-onion mixture in it. Put on the four pieces of chicken and see that the oven is at full heat.

Beat the egg-yolks with the pepper and mix with the bread-crumbs. Use as much as is needed to obtain a creamy blend which is sufficient to cover the top layer of this dish. We have not used all the butter, so we let the remainder turn a golden brown and pour it over the egg-breadcrumb blend. This dish must now brown in the hot oven. Then we serve it immediately.

The left-over stock we use the day afterwards for preparing a vegetable or vermicelli soup.

Vegetable Soup

In half-chicken stock and half-vegetable liquid (we need 5 cups of liquid) cook for about 8 minutes ½ cup of finely cut-up vegetables. Add to it meat balls prepared with sausagemeat, an egg, some breadcrumbs, pepper and salt to taste. We can also use canned meat balls if we wish to do so. The home-made balls are done in less than 5 minutes. Taste for salt and pepper before serving.

Vermicelli Soup

Bring 5 cups of chicken stock to the boil with, if necessary, water added to it. Stir in a packet or can of vermicelli soup. Finish this soup by adding two tablespoons of egg noodles. Allow 5 minutes' cooking time. Meat balls are also excellent in this soup.

And here is something quite different.

In New Orleans I had the pleasure of meeting some very famous restaurant owners, among whom were the proprietors of Saint Antoine, Chez Arnaud, and Brennan's. The owner of Brennan's restaurant gave me a most useful cookery book containing his own recipes. In one of the large American hotels in the modern quarter I met a French cook, René Nicolas. He too was most helpful, but I shall give the first word to Mrs. Germaine Cazenave Arnaud, who has followed the line of her famous father and now manages his restaurant. Germaine is a very keen woman who travels a lot and collects many interesting recipes, some of which she gave to me.

Oysters Bienville

In New Orleans oysters are eaten all the year round. But when the weather is very warm they are only served hot and are prepared in the oven in an interesting manner. They are greenish in colour and are called *Portuguese oysters*, the shells of which are rather large and fancifully shaped. I think that when served hot they taste just wonderful.

Although this book mainly concerns Gallina, I cannot describe the Creole cuisine without mentioning their oyster snacks.

For 4 servings we need:

12 Portuguese oysters (obtainable off-season in most countries)	breadcrumbs butter

WHITE WINE SAUCE PREPARED WITH

2 tablespoons butter	4 finely chopped mushrooms
1 tablespoon flour	pepper and salt to taste (but remember that oysters are already salty)
3 finely chopped shallots or 1 finely chopped onion	
½ cup shrimps or 4 de-frozen prawns	1 small glass white wine the oyster liquid

Carefully remove the top shells from the oysters. Pour off and reserve the liquid. We need an aluminium or other metal dish, which we fill ½ inch high with kitchen salt. On this salt we put the oysters, still in their bottom shells and with a piece of butter on top of each. We turn the oven full on and allow the oysters 3 minutes in the very hot oven and then remove.

To prepare the sauce put 2 tablespoons of melted butter in a saucepan and sauté the chopped shallots or the onion. Allow them to become golden brown, then add the chopped shrimps or prawns with the mushrooms and let these also brown. Finally stir in the flour and add as much oyster liquid and white wine as is needed to obtain a rather thick yet smooth blend. It should not 'run' when covering the oysters with it. Finally we cover these oysters with breadcrumbs and butter and let them gratinate in the oven or grill. Serve immediately in their shells. This dish will be sizzling hot, owing to the salt, which retains the heat.

Oysters are the gastronomic speciality of New Orleans and are generally served on these aluminium or other metal dishes. On the menu they are indicated with 3-3-3, which means that 3 of them are prepared à la Bienville, 3 à la Rockefeller (covered with cooked drained spinach blended with chopped shallots, flour, chopped parsley, butter, garlic, chopped anchovy, and some drops of absinthe), and 3 oysters Thermidor, which is quite simple to prepare.

As with the Bienville, we retain the oysters in their lower shells and place them on salt in the metal dish with some tomato ketchup and two fried slices of bacon on top. They are then baked sizzling hot in the oven and served.

Germaine Arnaud's second recipe is

Chicken-suprème en Papillotte

for 4 servings:

1 roaster halved
1 bunch of green stalks
1 garnished onion

about 2 cups water
pepper and salt to taste

FOR THE GARNISH
4–5 tablespoons butter
1 chopped onion
1½ tablespoons flour
½ pound ham finely cut up
½ pound small mushrooms
    halved

1 egg-yolk
the juice of ½ lemon or an
    equal amount of white
    wine

Bring the water to the boil with the two chicken halves, the bunch of green stalks, and the garnished onion. Add salt and pepper to taste and continue boiling for a few minutes. Then cover the pan and reduce the heat. The chicken halves should barely be covered with water. We allow about 15 minutes, but not more, for the chicken to be done. Probably less time will be required, for the chicken should not be overdone. The contrary is preferable. Drain and keep the stock after having checked to see that it is well salted and peppered. Bear in mind that we make a sauce with this stock and that the ham is itself already salted.

Skin and bone the chicken and divide the meat into not too small pieces. Using a saucepan, heat the butter to a golden colour. Sauté the chopped onion to a golden colour with the cut-up ham and the halved mushrooms. Stir and add the pieces of chicken. Blend with the flour and stir with a fork in order not to mash up the ingredients. We lighten this mixture with as much stock as is needed to prepare a well-thickened ragout. Now prepared a blend with the egg-yolk, the lemon juice, or the white wine. This blend we add to the ragout while stirring with a wire whisk.

We have ready four large pieces of wax-paper or aluminium foil. Cut them into a heart shape. In the middle of each piece put one quarter part of the ragout and fold the paper closely round it. Try to give them corrugated borders, for they keep more rigid that way.

Place these four papillottes on a buttered baking-pan in the hot oven. Allow 15–20 minutes to let this chicken ragout get sizzling hot. Serve the papillottes on the plates and cut them open lengthwise.

With it we eat pommes soufflées.

Pommes Soufflées (Soufflé Potatoes)

For this we use peeled and well-dried, rather large-sized potatoes. We cut them up into thin slices as long as a finger and about ½ inch broad. These soufflé potatoes are longer, broader, and much thinner than French-fried potatoes. Get the oil hot, but not too hot, in a deep-frying pan. The correct temperature for the whole period of frying is to start at about 320° Fahrenheit and increase very gradually. Drop the well-dried potatoes in the hot oil. We need only about 10–12 minutes for these soufflé potatoes to be done. As the word indicates, they should 'blow up' gradually. This can be obtained only by letting the temperature, too, rise gradually. Only in the last few minutes, when all liquid has been fried out of the potatoes, will they turn golden. Don't let them get dark brown. Serve on a napkin and for preference in a little basket.

Add salt shortly before serving, but not too much. If we do not serve these potatoes immediately they are likely to collapse.

Now we will have a look in Mr. Brennan's kitchen. In his restaurant you can have quite a thrilling experience. From nine o'clock in the morning his restaurant is open to people who care to come for breakfast. His menu is large and various, but I will give a few examples of the dishes he offers.

Eyeopener

A drink which, as its name implies, is calculated to open your eyes. It is prepared with brandy, bourbon whisky, gomma arabica (a syrupy sweet liquid), a little vanilla powder, and finally milk. Shake well and drink. Your eyes will be wide open in a very short space of time.

The real breakfast consists of

Eggs-Benedict

for 1 serving:

2 rusks	about ½ cup Hollandaise
2 thin slices grilled ham	sauce
2 poached eggs	

Butter the rusks and cover with the grilled slices of ham. Poach the eggs for about 10 minutes in boiling water with vinegar (and don't use too little) and salt. Trim the poached eggs and lay them on the ham and cover with the Hollandaise sauce.

Hollandaise Sauce. Original recipe from Brennan's cookery book for about 2 cups of sauce.

2 egg-yolks	salt and freshly ground pepper
¾ cup butter	to taste
2 tablespoons water or lean	the juice of ¼ lemon
stock	

Put a saucepan au-bain-Marie and allow the water or stock in the large pan to be near to boiling point but not boiling hard. With a wire whisk beat the egg-yolks in the little saucepan till frothy. While beating we add the two tablespoons of water or stock and continue beating. Then we add salt with pepper to taste and allow this egg froth to warm au-bain-Marie, but must not let it get hot. Still beating with the wire whisk, we add lump after lump of soft but unmelted butter. This butter must not be allowed to melt, for otherwise it will not thicken the sauce. It is, in fact, the main item in the successful making of a Hollandaise to see that the water is never allowed to get so hot that it melts the butter in the saucepan. When all the butter has been stirred in we taste for salt and pepper, adding more if required, and then we add as much lemon juice as we think suitable.

Before they serve you this egg-dish you will enjoy the grapefruit with which you start your breakfast. It is grilled. And how palatable are the rolls, buns, cheese, cold meat, jams, and marmalade that follow afterwards!

Here is a recipe in which Gallina plays only a secondary part.

Chicken Livers St. Pierre

for 2 servings:

about 6 tablespoons butter
½ finely cut-up fresh green paprika
2 chopped onions
a bit more than ½ pound whole well-washed chicken livers
2 generous tablespoons well washed and coarsely chopped mushrooms

¼ pound cooked Lima beans or cooked white or brown beans
1 Spanish pepper cut up finely but without any seeds
salt to taste
pinch cayenne pepper

Prepare this dish in a casserole that you can place on the table. Copper pans are ideal for this purpose. Let the butter turn golden and in it sauté the chopped onions with the half-paprika cut up in strips till golden brown. Then add all the other ingredients. Do not forget the salt and cayenne pepper and taste if the flavour of the dish is good. It should be rather hot. Heat well, and do not allow more than 10–15 minutes for the whole preparation of this dish. We work in an uncovered pan and stir with a kitchen fork.

Add some chopped parsley if you care for it and serve with dry-cooked rice. This dish is an excellent main course for 2 servings and, moreover, is very easy to prepare.

Here is another of Brennan's specialities.

Chicken Marchand de Vin

for 4 servings:

1 roaster divided in four
about 5 tablespoons vegetable
   oil

2 CUPS MARCHAND DE VIN SAUCE, FOR WHICH WE NEED

½ cup chopped mushrooms	2 tablespoons flour
½ cup finely cut-up ham	salt to taste
2 chopped shallots or 1	freshly ground pepper to taste
chopped onion	1 cup stock and the same
1 crushed clove of garlic	amount of red wine

Heat the oil in a casserole and brown the four pieces of chicken. Add salt to taste, cover the pan with the lid aslant, and allow 20–30 minutes for the pieces of chicken to be done.

In the meantime prepare the sauce as follows:

Marchand de Vin Sauce. Brown the butter and sauté the chopped mushrooms, the chopped onion or shallots, the clove of garlic, and the chopped ham till golden brown. Stir with a fork and add the flour, which should brown too. We increase this mixture with the hot stock and the red wine. Use as much liquid as is needed to prepare a creamy yet not too thick sauce. Add salt and pepper to taste, but check if the stock was already salted! If you use water with a meat cube instead of stock be very careful with salt.

Arrange the roasted pieces of chicken in a buttered fireproof dish (without any oil, of course) and pour the sauce over it. Put the dish in a hot oven and let it get very hot again.

I must also give you a recipe from the famous restaurant Saint Antoine. It is a very 'special' cup of coffee with which you are served as a tailpiece to your dinner.

Antoine's Café Brulot Diabolique

for 8 small cups:

1¼-inch-long piece cinnamon	5 big lumps sugar
7 cloves	2 small glasses of good brandy
the peel of ½ lemon, as thin as possible	about 2 cups coffee

Heat a copper saucepan on a spirit stove and then put in the cinnamon, cloves, lemon peel, and lumps of sugar, stirring briskly with a fork. When the sugar is melted pour in the brandy, having first poured it into a long metal spoon you have kept warmed for the purpose. Flambé the brandy and let it drip on the melted sugar with the spices. While stirring we pour the very hot coffee on it very slowly in order to assure that the lumps of sugar have melted completely and also to enable the spices to give their full flavour to this coffee 'diabolique.'

Divide it between the 8 tiny warmed mocha cups. Provide some extra sugar for the guests who like their coffee very sweet.

Another very good chicken recipe is the

Creole Omelet

for 2 servings:

*½ pound boiled chicken meat
for each person 2 pancakes,
prepared according to your
own recipe*

FOR THE SPICY, CREAMY SAUCE

*¼ cup lard, butter, or
vegetable margarine
1 chopped onion
¼ cup fresh or canned celery
stalks cut up in tiny pieces
1 finely cut-up slice celeriac
2 tablespoons coarsely
chopped parsley
¼ cup marshmallow diced
(optional)
½ aubergine sliced finely
2 peeled tomatoes*

*1 tablespoon tomato purée or
tomato ketchup
1 Spanish pepper fresh or
dried
1 tablespoon cornflour or
farina
a generous pinch gumbo filé
powder
2 drops tabasco sauce
2 cups stock or water
salt and cayenne pepper to
taste*

For the sauce we melt the butter or whatever fat we have chosen in a saucepan and sauté the chopped onion till golden brown. Now add the vegetables of our choice and stir with a wooden spoon. Allow to brown lightly. After that add the tomato purée or the tomato ketchup with the halved Spanish pepper (with all seeds removed carefully), the gumbo filé powder, the drops of tabasco sauce with pepper and salt to taste. Stir and let any superfluous amount of liquid evaporate on a high heat in the open pan.

Reduce the heat and allow the blend about 5 minutes to simmer in an open pan.

In the meantime we must prepare a smooth paste with the cornflour or farina and a little less than the 2 cups of stock or water. When all the liquid has evaporated we stir this into the thickened blend. Let this vegetable sauce come to the boil again, stir, and allow a gentle boiling on a very reduced heat. Taste for salt and pepper and also for flavour. It should be quite hot to the palate.

The pancakes are ready, and we have cut up in strips the skinned and boned chicken. Blend the meat with part of the sauce but do not use too much. Arrange little heaps on the middles of each pancake and roll them up. We use the remaining vegetable sauce as a garnish around these pancakes. Serve them with dry-cooked rice or fresh French bread.

And before leaving New Orleans just a few recipes from the French cook, René Nicolas.

Chicken Sauté New Orleans

for 4 servings:

1 roaster divided in four	1 glass white wine
2 tablespoons flour	salt and pepper to taste
4 tablespoons butter	1 bay leaf
1 tablespoon chopped shallots or onion	½ teaspoon coarsely dried thyme
1 crushed clove of garlic	½ cup stock or water
4 big mushrooms	4–8 oysters

Brown the butter in a casserole you can serve at table and sauté the well-floured pieces of chicken in it. They should become a good brown colour. Remove them from the butter, using a strainer, and sauté in the same butter the chopped shallots or onion with the crushed clove of garlic, the 4 mushrooms, the bay leaf, and the thyme. Let them turn light brown.

When done, add the remaining flour with the browned pieces of chicken and salt and pepper to taste. Stir and pour in the glass of wine and the stock or water. Cover the pan, reduce the heat, and allow about 30 minutes for the pieces of chicken to be done. Check and taste for salt. A few minutes before serving add the shelled oysters with their liquid. With this dish we serve dry-cooked rice, potato purée, or spaghetti.

Another recipe from Mr. René Nicolas and at the same time our last New Orleans recipe is the

Dixieland Chicken

for 6 servings:

1 large boned roaster
a deep-frying pan with oil or
lard

FOR THE MARINADE

½ cup chili sauce, preferably
the sweet variety
1 teaspoon salt

a generous pinch pepper
4 drops tabasco sauce

FOR THE COATING

1 cup flour
1 teaspoon salt
1 generous tablespoon paprika
powder
pinch cayenne pepper
1 tablespoon mustard

½ crushed clove of garlic
6 tablespoons grated
Parmesan cheese
2 eggs beaten with 2
tablespoons water

First skin the chicken and then cut up the 2 breast-pieces
lengthwise. Do the same with the legs, and the result is 8 pieces

of skinned and boned chicken. We put these pieces in the marinade we have prepared by blending all the listed ingredients. Allow 3 hours for the marinating in a covered bowl. Then remove the pieces of chicken, drain them, and dry in a cloth.

In the meantime we have prepared the coating for which we have blended all the ingredients. Roll every piece of chicken in it and get them well coated. The oil or lard in the deep-frying pan should be about 350° Fahrenheit. In it we fry these pieces of chicken a crisp brown, allowing about 6–10 minutes to be done. If the roaster is not very big and the meat tender about 5 minutes will do. It all depends on the bird.

Serve with green garden peas and French-fried potatoes.

We cannot, of course, leave America without having barbecued a chicken in the real American style—on a charcoal barbecue or grill.

Working on a barbecue in the garden is great fun, and I think it is indeed the most satisfactory way to prepare a chicken.

Barbecued Chicken Silver Fox

for 4 servings:

1 young roaster, halved
1 crushed clove of garlic
5 tablespoons olive oil

FOR THE MARINADE (BARBECUE SAUCE)

1 glass red wine	½ crushed clove of garlic
pepper and salt to taste	4 drops tabasco sauce
1 dessertspoon mustard	1 crushed bay leaf
1 sliced onion	3 tablespoons soy sauce
5 tablespoons oil	3 tablespoons tomato ketchup

And then
5–7 tablespoons stock

Marinate the chicken halves for at least 6 hours in the blended ingredients given for the marinade. Remove and drain the chicken but let it drain over the bowl in order to preserve the liquid. Thoroughly dry the chicken halves and rub them in the olive oil blended with the crushed clove of garlic. Arrange them on the charcoal grill or whatever grill you are using and put them as near as possible to the fire.

When well browned remove them away from the direct heat. While the grilling is taking place we have poured the marinade into a casserole and put it on the charcoal or in the grill. Let this get hot and then add the chicken halves to it. Allow 20 minutes for the post-cooking, but do not cover the pan. During the last 3 minutes we add the stock to the marinade.

In Washington they served this chicken in the casserole with its sauce and with rice on a side-dish. It was followed by a tasty dressed green salad. The dressing was flavoured and thickened with some cream, wine vinegar, mustard, and paprika powder.

Garnished and Gratinated Chicken Breasts

for 2 servings:

2 cooked chicken breasts from a boiling fowl, skinned and boned

1 small lightly cooked cauliflower

1 green paprika, parboiled 5 minutes and then cut up in strips

about 1 cup cheese sauce

Butter and well breadcrumb a fireproof dish and in it arrange the cauliflower, which must still be crisp and firm and divided into four pieces. On these we arrange the strips of paprika and cover them with the two chicken breasts. Finish this dish with the creamy cheese sauce.

We prepared the sauce with butter, flour, and, if possible, chicken stock. To make 1 cup stir in at least 3 tablespoons of grated Parmesan or Gruyère cheese. Allow this to get hot in the oven, putting it as near as possible to the heat (a grill is preferable). Cover with some extra grated cheese and lumps of butter and gratinate it a golden brown.

The cheese should melt and form a thick creamy cover to this chicken.

Serve at once with roasted potatoes or French bread.

And now we must leave America and follow Gallina through Mexico.

MEXICO

ONLY a poet can possibly do justice to this lovely, sunny country, and, alas, I am no poet. Instead I shall try to explain to you why I believe Mexico to be one of the countries of the future.

Efficiently run hotels and a cleverly conducted information service combine to attract an ever-increasing number of tourists. There is every reason why this should be so. Mexico City, the capital, is remarkable both for its artistic and architectural treasures and the vision of its modern town planning. The old quarters of the town are poor and down-at-heel, but in the new quarters there is a profusion of parks, wide avenues, and daringly sophisticated architecture. There are innumerable shopping centres, too, some of them cluttered and old-fashioned, others luxuriously modern in the latest tradition of plate glass and chromium. Attractive, too, are the markets, both covered and open, where the tourist can spend many a long hour watching the gay population making their purchases. Hours, also, can be spent in the churches and museums and in the various buildings that go to make the University.

There are a number of excursions within easy distance of the capital. The tourist bureaux organize excellent trips to places such as Taxco, the silver-mining town, where the colonial Spanish architecture prevails and modern building is forbidden, or to Cuernavaca, famous for the Diego Rivera frescoes in its Town Hall. Acapulco is a bather's and sun-worshipper's paradise, while the peninsula of Yucatan, with its capital Mérida and the Maya ruins at Chichien Itza, do not belie all that has been said and written about them.

How ever many showers may fall, they will never interfere with your walks, as the sun and the clear, dry air promptly dry your clothes. No one bothers to carry an umbrella, while the Mexican women and girls walk unconcerned in the rain in their full skirts and embroidered blouses. The people, too, are kind and gay and helpful, and everywhere there is evidence of Indian ancestry. I was particularly touched by the friendliness of the Mexicans, and rarely have I found cooks and restaurateurs so eager to share their secrets with me.

I had naturally expected to find in the Americas all manner of exotic fruits and vegetables that are unknown in Europe. I had not, however, expected to come across such a variety of chilies, fresh peppers, okras, melons, and pineapples.

It was an eyeopener, for instance, to discover that avocados were sold by the dozen, making them almost as cheap as potatoes. This abundance explained why they were used in practically every recipe. The same is true of the coconut, which is employed both ripe and unripe. The unripe nuts are used as receptacles for exotic chicken, fish, or fruit dishes, after the tops have been cut off and the fleshy centres scooped out. They are also used to hold iced rum or whisky. The importance of the brown bean in Mexican cooking was another revelation, as was the part played by the tortilla.

The Mexican tortilla is a tough, leathery pancake made from cornflour and water. It is used instead of bread and as part of innumerable dishes. I was told that only those who can claim some Indian blood really know how to make these tortillas. They are sold ready-made on stalls and in shops. Alternatively, the dough can be bought ready-mixed and the tortilla cooked at home. It is amusing to see how they acquire their paper thinness by being passed through what looks like a toy mangle. The tortilla is particularly good when combined with chicken, fish, or sea-food, although it is also excellent with vegetables or cut in strips in soup.

Seldom have I come across a country where the chicken is so cleverly prepared as in Mexico. Wherever I went, in famous and expensive restaurants or simple little eating-houses, without exception the chicken dish was always perfectly prepared.

Beer, too, is excellent in Mexico. This is hardly to be wondered at since many of the breweries are run by Germans.

The national drink is tequilla, a spirit prepared from cactus leaves, not unlike vodka. It can be mixed with other drinks and makes an excellent base for cocktails.

First of all I should like to give you three Mexican soups.

Potaje Frijol Bayo (Mexican Bean Soup)

for 6 servings:

1¼ pounds soaked dried beans	3 sliced onions
4 big potatoes	1 small white cabbage cut up in 8 pieces
the bone of a cooked ham or a veal knuckle	pepper and salt to taste
1 pound diced ham	2 tablespoons sweet chili sauce
6 large tomatoes	a dash Worcester Sauce
1 can tomato purée	8 cups water

The day before this soup is needed boil the ham bone or the knuckle in the water, allowing 2–3 hours' cooking time on a slow fire. Next day, having drained the stock, skim off the fat. Bring to the boil again and add all the ingredients except the ham, potatoes, chili sauce, and Worcester Sauce. Boil for a few minutes, then reduce the heat and simmer in a covered pan for about 1½ hours. Ten minutes before serving put in the diced ham and potatoes. Check for salt and pepper and add some extra cayenne pepper. Before serving add the savoury sauces. Personally I also use some lean bacon, diced, and a few drops of tabasco sauce.

I ate the Potaje Frijol in Mérida nearly every day and found it very acceptable in the very trying heat. An attraction of this soup is that all the vegetables are cut up very coarsely and the beans are not puréed, with the result that the ingredients retain their freshness and individuality.

Sopa de Pollo (Chicken Soup)

for 6 servings:

1 small or ½ a bigger boiling fowl cut up in small pieces
5 peeled tomatoes cut up in quarters
the well-washed giblets
1 unpeeled, well-washed, and thinly sliced lemon

1 tortilla, which can be replaced by one crisp baked pancake rolled up and cooled
salt to taste
a generous pinch cayenne pepper
7 cups water

Take off all the fat and boil the fowl in the water, with the pieces of tomatoes, lemon, coarsely chopped giblets, and salt to taste. Reduce the heat, cover the pan, and cook slowly for about 2 hours. Cut the rolled-up pancake first lengthwise and then in thin strips. Add them to the soup with the cayenne pepper. Taste for salt and check whether the fowl is tender in order that we can take off the meat with the spoon. In each soup dish we have some chicken meat and a slice of lemon. An easy-to-make and delicious soup.

Sopa Tartara (Tartare Soup)

for 6 servings:

1 small boiling fowl, halved
6 eggs
6 slices French bread
1 clove of garlic
½ pound canned, frozen, or fresh peas
2 tablespoons uncooked rice
1 sliced fresh paprika

1 tablespoon fresh oregano or marjoram or ¼ teaspoon dried
a generous pinch cayenne pepper
salt to taste
6–8 cups water

Boil the halved boiling fowl in the water with herbs and salt to taste. Skim and then reduce the heat. Cooking time in a covered pan is roughly 1½–2 hours. Remove the fowl, let the stock cool. Skim off all the fat and bring to the boil again. Add the peas with the paprika and the rice. Boil for a further 10 minutes on reduced heat. Taste for salt.

In the meantime skin and bone the cooked chicken. The meat is divided into not too small pieces. Put aside between two soup dishes.

Now let the stock come to the boil again and break in the raw eggs one by one. They should be ready-poached in about ten minutes. When the last egg is done we add the chicken meat and let the soup get hot again. Serve the soup as follows:

To each plate of soup we add 1 poached egg and a piece of chicken and serve with it a slice of buttered French bread rubbed with garlic.

In Mérida they cover each egg with some chili sauce, which makes it very hot and savoury.

And now I will give you a few quite different kinds of recipes, some of which are not connected with Gallina.

Camarones con Huevos Mérida (Prawns and Eggs Mérida)

for 4 servings:

1 chopped onion
2 big peeled tomatoes
1½ tablespoons tomato purée
or tomato ketchup
½ pound canned, frozen, or
fresh peas
4 eggs
frozen prawns (decide how
many of them to use)

a little salt
½ teaspoon freshly ground
pepper
1 tablespoon butter
1 tablespoon chopped herbs
(parsley, chives, or celery)
4 tablespoons oil

Let the oil get very hot in a fire- or flame-proof dish either on the stove or in the oven. Add to it the chopped onion, the peeled and coarsely cut-up tomatoes, the peas with the tomato purée or tomato ketchup. Cook as quickly as possible in an open dish, allowing only a few minutes. When the liquid has evaporated add the de-frozen, peeled, and lengthwise-cut prawns. Cover the pan and allow 5 minutes' cooking time. Remove the lid from the pan and add salt and pepper to taste and the butter, which must get very hot indeed.

Break the raw eggs in one at a time on it, pricking each egg-yolk. They should 'set' but not be hard-cooked. A creamy substance is correct. Remove the dish from the stove or oven, garnish with the chopped herbs, and serve immediately with cooked rice or bread, preferably hot French bread.

In a Mexican restaurant they will never serve cold or stale bread. It is always wrapped up in a napkin and very hot. Moreover, they use attractive straw baskets for serving it in.

Ensalada de Camarones (Shrimp Salad)

for 4 servings:

½ pound small shrimps or at least 6 frozen prawns cooked some minutes in water with a bunch of green and a pinch of mixed herbs (parsley, chives, etc.)

6 sliced sweet-sour gherkins

2 finely sliced peeled tomatoes

a lettuce heart

4 tablespoons mayonnaise blended with the juice of 1 lemon and 2 tablespoons tomato ketchup

pepper and salt to taste

2 tablespoons chopped parsley

1 generous tablespoon sweet chili sauce

1 fresh avocado peeled, stoned, and cut up in julienne (optional)

Garnish four wide-brimmed glasses with the julienne cut from the well-washed and dried lettuce heart and arrange the slices of tomatoes on it. Prepare a mixture with the prawns cut up lengthwise several times or the small shrimps, the slices of gherkins, the pink mayonnaise, chili sauce, and the julienne of avocado, if any. It is the avocado which gives the real Mexican touch to this salad.

Fill each glass with part of this blend and cover with the chopped parsley. One whole prawn or some shrimps make an attractive final garnish, while a slice of lemon attached to the brims of the glasses adds a very professional touch.

Ceviche Acapulco (Acapulco Fish Salad)

for 4 servings:

1 *pound boned, cooked, but still firm fish meat to your own choice*

1 *finely chopped onion*

½ *clove of garlic*

1 *tablespoon coarsely chopped parsley*

6 *sliced stuffed olives*

1 *fresh or dry seedless Spanish pepper (a small one) finely chopped*

½ *fresh green paprika cut up in julienne*

2 *peeled tomatoes cut up finely*

FOR THE SAUCE

4 *tablespoons tomato ketchup*

the juice of 1 lemon

a generous pinch sugar

¼ *teaspoon paprika powder*

2–3 *tablespoons sweet chili sauce*

4 *lettuce leaves washed and well dried*

Have four wide, shallow glasses ready and arrange a lettuce leaf in each. Prepare a blend with all the ingredients given for the salad. Use a fork for the blending in order not to damage the pieces of fish.

I strongly advise you to use fish with firm meat such as codfish, turbot, or brill. Do not over-cook. Divide this fish salad between the four glasses and pour over the sauce prepared with the listed ingredients.

If you would rather prepare a richer cocktail, then blend with the fish some shrimps and mushrooms with mussels or oysters. Serve with toast and butter.

Bacalao à la Campechana (Stockfish in Country Style)

for 4 servings:

1½ pounds soaked boned
stockfish

4 tablespoons oil

2 fresh paprikas, seedless and
cut up coarsely

1¼ pounds diced potatoes

1 red chili pepper cut
lengthwise without seeds

⅓ cup butter

1¼ pounds peeled halved
tomatoes

2 tablespoons coarsely
chopped parsley

1 clove of garlic

1 chopped onion

salt to taste

Heat the oil in a pan and add to it the fish with all the other ingredients except the potatoes, the parsley, and the butter. Sauté these ingredients in the oil, but do not let them colour. Add as much boiling water as is needed barely to cover these ingredients. Bring to the boil, cover the pan, and reduce the heat. Allow 20 minutes of very gentle simmering. Only then add the potatoes and the butter. Shake the pan in order to bring the potatoes to the bottom of it. Check to see if enough water is left to cook the diced potatoes for about 10 minutes. By then the liquid should have disappeared completely. We now have a very smooth fish mixture, which we put in a buttered fireproof dish. Cover with breadcrumbs and a generous amount of grated cheese. Pour over some melted butter and gratinate in the hot oven.

Nothing else is served with this dish, but we should garnish it with the parsley.

Now I will give you a good chicken recipe.

Gallina en Mostaza (Chicken in Mustard)

for 4 servings:

1 roaster	2 tablespoons lemon juice
⅓ cup butter	salt to taste
3 tablespoons flavoury mustard blended with ½ teaspoon paprika powder	

Quarter the roaster and rub it very generously with the mustard blend. Add a little salt. Pre-heat the oven, in which we have already put the roasting-pan with the butter, for about 10 minutes. When the butter is dark brown add the pieces of chicken to it. Let these pieces of chicken also brown and allow a further 25 minutes to be done. If necessary add some spoonfuls of hot water or stock, basting the chicken from drying out. When the pieces of chicken are brown I personally add some finely sliced carrots and one onion to the gravy. They give flavour and at the same time increase the liquid. Before serving the chicken work the gravy with the vegetables through a wire strainer. The vegetables will thicken the gravy, which can then be poured over the pieces of chicken.

With it serve boiled potatoes and fresh or canned celery. Heat canned celery in butter, but fresh celery we parboil and then braise in butter with lemon juice or Madeira.

The following is another way to prepare a Mexican chicken:

Gallina à la Mexicana (Chicken in the Mexican Way)

for 4 servings:

1 roaster
1 pound peeled and quartered
  tomatoes
1 sliced onion
1–2 crushed cloves of garlic
pinch cayenne pepper
2 hard-boiled eggs, chopped
  fine
2 tablespoons rum

¼ cup diced cooked ham
½ teaspoon mixed herbs
4 sweet-sour sliced gherkins
3 tablespoons shredded
  almonds
1 bay leaf
2 cloves
salt to taste

Put the quartered roaster in a pan, together with the tomatoes, onion, garlic, herbs, bay leaf, cloves, and salt to taste. Pour on some spoonfuls of water and bring to the boil. Reduce the heat in a covered pan, allowing about 25 minutes. When done remove the pieces of chicken with a skimmer and put them aside in a bowl. Let the liquid come to the boil again and add all the remaining ingredients, also the rum and the eggs. Stir.

In the open pan reduce the liquid as much as is required to obtain a thick vegetable mixture. Stir once in a while with a wooden spoon, thus preventing the tomatoes, onion, and all the other ingredients from sticking to the pan. Now replace the pieces of chicken and let them get hot again. Arrange in an attractive dish and cover with the thickened vegetable sauce. Taste for salt and add the cayenne pepper.

With this we eat

Arroz à la Mexicana (Mexican Rice)

for 4 servings:

¾ pound rice	3 tablespoons butter or oil
¼ teaspoon turmeric powder or a bit less saffron	pinch nutmeg
1 large chopped onion	2 tablespoons grated cheese

Heat the butter or oil and sauté the chopped onion with the turmeric powder or saffron to a golden-yellowish but not brown colour. Add the dry uncooked rice and stir. When the grains have turned light yellow add as much water as is needed to dry-cook the rice. To do this we cover the pan when the water boils, and then, on a very reduced heat, allow 17 minutes for the rice to be done. Only then add the cheese.

You can understand now why we use no fat in the preceding chicken dish. The rice furnishes sufficient butter or oil when the two dishes are eaten together.

Pechuga al Pastor con Puré (Chicken Breasts in the Pastor's Way with Mashed Potatoes)

for 2 servings:

2 chicken breasts	lettuce leaves
4 tablespoons oil	1 tomato
3 tablespoons sweet chili sauce	1 lemon
1 large diced onion	¼ cup butter
	salt and pepper to taste

Prepare a blend with the oil, the chili sauce, and the salt, with pepper to taste. Flatten the two chicken breasts as much as possible and dip them in the blend. They should be shiny and red all over.

First let the grill (or oven if you lack a grill) get hot. Put the two pieces of chicken as near as possible to the heat and let them brown.

Brown both sides, then reduce the heat a little and let the chicken grill for about 15–20 minutes. Baste occasionally with the remaining blend, using a little brush.

Garnish a dish with the lettuce leaves, washed and well dried, and arrange the pieces of chicken on it. Next add the raw slices of lemon and tomato. Serve mashed potatoes with it and the remaining chili sauce blended with the melted butter.

To serve this chicken in the traditional way we mix the sliced onion with ½ tablespoon of flour and fry them in hot oil till golden brown. Stir with a fork and work over a high heat.

It takes only a few minutes to brown onions in this way. Arrange them over the pieces of chicken.

Pollo Ranchera con Nata (Ranchera Chicken with Cream)

for 4 servings:

1 roaster divided into 6–8
  pieces
⅓ cup butter
1 finely chopped onion
1 fresh or dried whole
  Spanish pepper

1 fresh paprika
salt and pepper to taste
2 tablespoons sweet chili
  sauce
½ tablespoon cornflour
½ cup cream

GARNISH
2 tomatoes
8–10 olives

Brown the butter in a roasting-pan and add the pieces of chicken. Let them brown and then remove from the pan. In this butter sauté the finely chopped onion with the finely cut-up paprika, the whole Spanish pepper or (if halved) with all the seeds removed. This dish must be cooked until dark brown. Stir with a fork and do not reduce the heat.

When the correct colour is obtained return the pieces of chicken. Add salt and pepper to taste and pour the chili sauce with 1 tablespoon of water on it. Bring to the boil, cover the pan, and reduce the heat. Allow 25–30 minutes.

In the meantime prepare a blend with the cornflour and the cream. When the chicken is tender and nicely cooked again remove the pieces, and with the pan on a very low heat stir in the cream blend. Let the cornflour just thicken the sauce, nothing more. Allow 5 more minutes for this liaison to set. Stir occasionally, and finally pour this creamy dark brown sauce over the chicken arranged in a pre-heated dish.

Garnish the top with the sliced raw tomatoes, and the olives preferably stuffed. Serve with cooked rice or a bean purée.

And since I told you at the beginning of this chapter that the Mexicans have a delicious way with brown beans, here is a recipe using them.

Frijoles Refritos (Mexican Dried Beans)

for 6 servings:

1–1¼ pounds cooked brown beans

3 tablespoons lard

3 chopped onions

1 red paprika cut up in thin strips

a generous pinch paprika powder

3 tablespoons sweet chili sauce

pinch cayenne pepper

1 tablespoon fresh chopped marjoram or oregano, or ½ teaspoon if dried

salt to taste

Work the cooked dried beans through a wire strainer or use an electric mixer, but first see that the beans have been coarsely mashed. Keep aside the cooking liquid for later use. Heat the 3 tablespoons of lard in a pan and fry the chopped onions with the strips of paprika.

Add this blend and all the other ingredients to the puréed beans. If the blend is too dry or too sticky add some of the hot boiling liquid from the beans. This dish should have a creamy consistency like that of a well-prepared porridge. Its taste should be on the hot side.

We can also serve this brown bean dish with boiled chicken with a spicy tomato sauce, or with small pieces of boiled or roasted chicken blended only with tomato ketchup and lemon juice. These pieces of chicken we put in a pancake and roll it up. In Mexico they use the tortilla instead of a pancake for this dish.

On each separate plate we arrange the bean purée on lettuce leaves. Moreover, they serve Guacamole salad with these chicken-stuffed tortillas.

Guacamole (Avocado Salad)

3 fresh avocados peeled,
stoned, and finely cut up
4 firm tomatoes, peeled and
finely cut up
1 tiny Spanish pepper,
seedless, chopped
1 crushed clove of garlic

2 extremely finely chopped
onions
1 tablespoon chopped parsley
2–3 tablespoons cream
the juice of 1 lemon
pinch chili powder
pepper and salt to taste

Blend all the ingredients, but do not yet add the cream. Prepare a very smooth mixture which can best be made by using a pestle and mortar. Give it the creamy touch by adding as much cream as is needed. Taste for salt and pepper and also chili powder. This blend is also served with the stuffed chicken-tortillas.

The Guacamole is also used as an appetizer, spread out on

small round toasted pieces of rye bread. Top with grated cheese and serve with a drink.

And talking of drinks takes my thoughts back to Mexico, where I got to know quite a few of them.

Tequilla Sour. A mixture of 1 cocktail glass of tequilla, the juice of ½ a lemon, and ½ tablespoon of sugar. Instead of the tequilla, vodka can be used.

Calveta Sunset. A tumbler is put into a miniature ice-basket which is filled with cubes of ice dyed green. The plastic ice-basket is transparent and the green cubes look fairy-like.

This long drink is a mixture of crushed ice-cubes covered with 1 large glass of rum, the juice of 1 orange and 1 lemon, with the same quantity of pineapple juice and lime juice. This drink is garnished with 1 slice of orange, 1 slice of lemon, and one or more cocktail cherries.

Serve with straws.

I enjoyed many other drinks in Mexico City that were completely new to me. There were also dishes served in Polynesian restaurants that were unique.

For example, they serve gin in scooped-out unripe coconuts. They cut off the upper part of the nut and scrape out the small amount of coconut meat which lines the inside. The meat is left in the nut and a generous amount of gin is added, blended with sugar. The mixture is thoroughly stirred and is drunk through straws.

Even more attractive were the different rum drinks, served in beautiful glasses and topped with real fresh orchids of different colours.

Polynesian Chicken Curry

for 2 servings:

1 scooped-out unripe coconut
1 spring chicken divided into
4 pieces
¼ cup butter
1 chopped onion, not too
large
1 dessertspoon curry powder

½ bay leaf
1 clove
3 tablespoons grated coconut
5 tablespoons coconut milk
½ dessertspoon cornflour
salt and pepper to taste
juice of ½ lemon

Brown the butter in a pan and then put in the quartered spring chicken. Let the four pieces brown and add the curry powder with the chopped onion. Stir and let brown, then add the bay leaf, the clove, the grated coconut, with salt and pepper to taste. Bring to the boil, stirring all the time. Cover the pan, reduce the heat, and allow about 30–40 minutes for the chicken to be very well done. Then take the pieces out and remove the large bones.

To make the sauce blend the cornflour with the coconut milk and the lemon juice. Stir in the chicken sauce and thicken the mixture with the cornflour. Now put back the pieces of chicken and check to see if the dish is well salted and peppered.

In the Polynesian restaurants they put this ragout into scooped-out coconuts and serve dry-cooked rice and condimentos with it.

Condimentos (Spices). For this the Polynesian restaurateurs use a large glass dish in which are eight separate compartments. These are filled with finely chopped red cocktail cherries, finely chopped angelica, unsalted roasted peanuts, sautéed slices of bananas, grated cheese, parts of peeled grapefruit, mango chutney, and a sweet-sour sauce.

Salsa Agri-Dulca (Sweet-sour Sauce). Prepare this sauce by blending finely chopped seedless red chilis with a generous amount of demerara sugar, lemon juice, soy sauce, pepper and salt, with a little bit of crushed garlic and finally tomato ketchup.

Blend all these ingredients according to your taste.

I never use too many chopped chilis to start with, but add some more later on if necessary. This sauce is excellent for all kinds of hot dishes, but even with dry-cooked rice or spaghetti it makes a tasty and satisfying meal.

Combination Curry

for 4 servings:

½ cooked chicken
some de-frozen prawns
pieces lobster, crab, or salmon
   (freshly cooked or canned)
   —about ¾ pound

Work as described for the Polynesian curry with the difference that we sauté the chopped onion in the brown butter with the boiled pieces of chicken and all the fish and the parboiled prawns. Allow only a few minutes for the sautéing, as all the ingredients are already cooked. This curry with its meat-fish combination is outstanding in my opinion. It is served with rice and condimentos.

We now leave Mexico and cross the Atlantic to Egypt and North Africa.

FIFTH TOUR:
Egypt and North Africa

Now we come to two countries which in more peaceful days I visited regularly. Whoever has seen the tombs of the Pharaohs or the pyramids at Giza, Memphis, or Sakkara will agree with me that they belong to the great moments in a traveller's life.

Even a trip up the Nile or a visit by car to the great ruins is a revelation. Where else is the sky so strangely blue, the air so clear, the mosques and minarets so dazzlingly white or golden cream, as in the old quarters of Cairo? Cairo's citadel with its triple-domed mosque is probably unique. In the narrow streets there is an incessant coming and going of people. In the dark little shops are wonderful displays of those handicrafts that are such an integral part of Arab life. If one is fortunate enough to stay in hotels on the banks of the Nile, then the life on its waters unrolls itself like the most charming of fairy tales. Equally fascinating are the highways leading out of the capital, on which camels, mules, donkeys, and horses are still the principal means of transport.

When in Cairo a visit to the Cairo Tower is a must. Its topmost storey contains a restaurant on a revolving platform. In under twenty minutes one can see the whole of Cairo.

EGYPT

In Egyptian gastronomy the chief roles are played by lamb and mutton. The chicken is not highly regarded, but the pigeon is considered a great delicacy.

Khoobz Mahleb, the national bread, resembles the Indian chapati in that it is used, among other things, as a receptacle for other food such as meat, rissoles, vegetables, and sweet mixtures. The possibilities are endless.

The Egyptians are fond also of creamy spreads made from a variety of ingredients and similar to the American 'dips.' For these they use aubergines, white beans, salmon roe, mince, to mention only a few.

The koftas and kebabs must be sampled, while yoghurt is a great favourite. Since we are in a Mohammedan country pork is taboo. Stuffed pigeons are much in demand, as are also lamb and mutton prepared with fruit, vegetables, and nuts. Egyptian cooks are clever with fish. To my surprise the people drink a great deal of whisky. Street stalls do a thriving trade in food cooked while you watch and usually served with the national bread.

The visitor will be offered many excellent rice dishes.

Riz Daoud Pacha (Pacha Rice)

for 4 servings:

6 tablespoons nuts peeled and finely chopped (make your own choice)

6 tablespoons soaked (in hot water) and swilled raisins

1 clove of garlic

¼ teaspoon turmeric powder or a generous pinch saffron

¼ pound thick vermicelli

½ pound rice

pepper and salt to taste

1 finely chopped onion

½ pound finely cut-up chicken livers

pinch thyme

pinch coriander

pinch basil

pinch cayenne pepper

3 tablespoons butter or 3 tablespoons oil, and moreover 1 extra tablespoon oil

First let the butter or oil get hot but not browned. Sauté in it until golden the chopped onion with the chopped chicken livers. Add the crushed clove of garlic with all the herbs and spices. Stir, and only then add the finely chopped nuts (I use almonds), the swilled and well-drained raisins with the uncooked rice (do not wash). Pour as much water on it as is needed to dry-cook the rice. Bring to the boil and allow 17 minutes only on a reduced heat in a covered pan. This rice is yellow in colour and very shiny. Previously we have broken up the thick vermicelli and soaked it for about 3 minutes in boiling water, having drained and run cold water over it. Heat the extra table-spoon of oil in an omelet-pan and when hot fry the vermicelli. Allow 5 minutes of sautéing in the open omelet-pan. When the rice is done we stir in the golden-coloured vermicelli with a fork. Allow this combination 5 more minutes of cooking in order to blend well.

This is a very savoury dish which is worth while trying out. It is used either as a main dish or with koftas or kebabs.

It is also much used as a stuffing for turkey, pigeon, or chicken. Then we allow only 15 minutes for the rice to be done. It should go on cooking while roasting the bird.

Egyptian Chicken Riz Daoud Pacha

for 4 servings:

1 roaster	½ cup butter
Riz Daoud Pacha for the	1 garnished onion
stuffing	pepper and salt to taste

Salt the inside of the chicken lightly as the rice is already salted. Brown the butter in the roasting-pan in a very hot oven and then add the roaster to it, well stuffed with the rice.

We have, of course, fastened the chicken with skewers or sewed it.

Let the roaster brown in the hot oven and then cook for about 30–40 minutes. Reduce the heat if necessary and baste from time to time with the gravy to which, after the roaster has browned, we have added the garnished onion. If a small roaster is used less time is required for the roasting.

When I roast a chicken in the oven I allow full heat for the first 10–15 minutes and do not mind if the gravy sticks to the pan and turns very, very dark brown. I loosen this brown thick substance on the bottom of the roasting-pan just before reducing the heat and adding some spoonfuls of hot water or hot stock. Stir with a fork. This gravy will be a rich brown colour and very tasty.

Divide this roaster into four portions and add some of the stuffing to each plate. Before serving squeeze the onion juice into the sauce.

With this chicken we serve the following salad.

Salad Cairo. Cut up slices of cooked beetroot, slices of cucumber and tomatoes, into finger-long strips. Arrange them elegantly in a bowl, taking the colours into account. Sprinkle with a mixture made with fresh coarsely chopped basil, dill, and parsley. Do not be too sparing with these green herbs as they give the real flavour of the salad.

Prepare a dressing with ground-nut oil, sweetened lemon juice, or lime if available, salt, and cayenne pepper. Pour the dressing over the salad 5–8 minutes before serving.

As I have already said, I greatly enjoyed the creamy spreads the Egyptians use with bread, raw vegetables, or fruit. Here is one of them.

Baba Ganoug Hommosia (Spicy Vegetable Mixture)

4 *aubergines*	4–5 *tablespoons oil*
2 *small fresh Spanish peppers,*	*cayenne pepper and salt to*
red or green	*taste*
1 *clove of garlic*	*pinch crushed coriander seed*
2 *big onions or 10 shallots,*	*pinch basil*
chopped very finely	*pinch dill*
2–3 *tablespoons vinegar or*	
lemon juice	

Rub in the aubergines with oil and arrange them on a greased baking-pan. Turn the oven full on for about 10 minutes and then put the baking-pan in it. Let the aubergines brown first, then well cover the whole pan with a piece of aluminium foil. Allow at least 45 minutes for the aubergines to get very well done. They should be quite creamy. Remove from the stove and put in a bowl. Mince them in an electric mixer or pass through a Chinese strainer. Then blend the aubergine purée with all the listed ingredients in order to obtain a creamy but not too thick spread. Should its consistency be too thick add some extra oil or stock.

Taste to see that the mixture is spicy and a little bit sour. You will enjoy dipping pieces of hot bread into it.

A rather unusual combination is the

Foul (A Broad Bean Dish)

for 4 servings:

¾ pound cooked white beans
(these should be well
cooked) or 1 can broad
beans

FOR THE SAUCE

3 finely chopped onions
1 chopped clove of garlic
4 tablespoons oil
2 tablespoons tomato ketchup
½ teaspoon paprika powder
pinch cayenne pepper

1 tablespoon flour
3–4 tablespoons lemon juice
the boiling liquid of the
white beans or, when using
the broad beans, some stock

Boil the broad beans to a very soft consistency. The broad beans whether canned or bottled should also be cooked very tender. Do not use the liquid from the can or bottle to cook, but use stock—it tastes better. Then prepare the sauce.

Fry the chopped onions with the clove of garlic in the hot oil until golden. I use 2 cloves of garlic, but in Egypt they use even more. Remove the pan from the heat and add the blend made from the tomato ketchup, the flour, and the lemon juice.

Keep stirring and add the paprika powder with the cayenne pepper. Taste to see if enough salt has been added to this mixture.

While stirring bring to the boil and add as much stock or boiling liquid as is needed to obtain a creamy yet not too thick sauce. Put the white or the broad beans into a bowl and pour over the sauce. Blend the sauce well with the beans. You can eat this vegetable dish either cold or warm.

If cold serve with kebab of chicken or mutton.

Kebab (Meat on Skewers)

for 4 servings:

1 small skinned and boned spring chicken or 1 pound mutton cut up in squares
4 very small laurel leaves

4 onions sliced very thickly or
4 whole shallots
4–8 halved tomatoes

A BLEND OF
8 tablespoons oil
pinch dill

pinch coriander or mint
pepper and salt to taste

Divide the chicken into 8–12 pieces, all of about the same size. Put them in the oil, mixed with the listed ingredients. Let the pieces of chicken or squares of mutton marinate for about 1 hour.

Fill each skewer alternately with pieces of the meat, tomato halves, slices of onion or a whole shallot, and 1 laurel leaf. The quantity of onions and tomatoes will depend on how many skewers you decorate. Personally I choose very long skewers. Each of them is sufficient for one person.

Rub the remaining oil blend into the ingredients on these skewers and cook in a hot grill or oven. Put them as near as possible to the heat, and when nicely brown allow about another 10 minutes' cooking. This depends on the size of the chicken or mutton. Garnish each skewer with chopped parsley, dill, or mint.

Kofta (Mutton Rolls)

for 4 servings:

1 pound minced mutton or, if you prefer, half mutton and half beef
1 finely chopped onion
1 chopped clove of garlic
salt to taste
1 raw egg

a very generous pinch basil, thyme, sage, and dill or mint
4–5 tablespoons breadcrumbs
a generous pinch cayenne pepper

Thoroughly blend all the listed ingredients and make the mixture into sausage-shaped rolls. Flour each roll and roast in an omelet-pan in very hot oil to a dark brown. When done serve with the Foul (white bean dish, p. 312).

These rolls can also be put on skewers and grilled a dark brown. Sprinkle them with some extra chopped mint.

Tamiah (White Bean Cookies)

for 4 servings:

¾ pound white beans not cooked but coarsely ground in a liquidizer or in an electric coffee mill
1 tablespoon flour
2 cloves of garlic, crushed
1 big finely chopped onion

a generous pinch cayenne pepper
salt to taste
½ teaspoon dill
oil
lemon juice

Prepare a blend with the white bean powder and all the listed ingredients. Add as much oil and lemon juice as necessary to give the required sour taste and to obtain the correct consistency to make into flat cookies about the size of a round tea biscuit, but twice as thick.

Use ground-nut oil for the deep-frying. Brown the cookies in the hot oil, and when done they will come floating to the surface. Remove with a strainer and drain. Serve cold or warm with:

Saffron Chicken

for 4 servings:

1 quartered roaster	½ teaspoon dill
3 tablespoons oil blended with	½ teaspoon saffron
pinch cayenne pepper	1 teaspoon turmeric powder
salt to taste	¼ cup fat or butter

Turn the oven full on, and when well heated brown the butter or fat in a roasting-pan. Rub the blended oil into the chicken and place the four pieces in the pan to cook. Baste once in a while and allow about 20 minutes to be done. The saffron and the turmeric powder will give this chicken a beautiful yellowish-brown colour.

Serve with the Tamiah or the Riz Daoud Pacha.

Finally here is one of my favourite exotic dishes which was so well prepared in Cairo.

Mussaka Semiramis (Egyptian Meat-vegetable Dish)

for 6 servings:

1½ *pounds coarsely minced mutton* or *lamb*
1 *big finely chopped onion*
1 *raw egg*
a *generous pinch dill*
a *generous pinch sage*

a *generous pinch coriander and a generous pinch thyme*
salt and pepper to taste
3 *tablespoons oil*

VEGETABLES

4 *sliced aubergines*
2 *red paprikas cut up in strips*
½ *pound firm peeled quartered tomatoes*
some more pepper and salt to taste

¼ *cup butter*
¾ *cup grated cheese (of your own choice)*
breadcrumbs
lumps of butter
pinch allspice
pinch paprika powder

Heat the oil in an omelet-pan and fry the onions with all the given herbs and spices until a golden colour. Reduce the heat and add the chopped mutton or lamb with salt and pepper to taste. Do not overlook that we are also using salt in the vegetables. Remove the pan from the heat, add the beaten raw egg, and stir well. Put this mixture in a bowl.

Using the same omelet-pan, turn the butter to a golden colour. Sauté all the vegetables in it until they are also a golden brown. Add the allspice and the paprika powder with salt and pepper to taste. Stir once more.

Prepare an attractive fireproof dish well greased and breadcrumbed. Fill it alternately with the vegetables and the meat. The top layer should be of vegetables covered with breadcrumbs, grated cheese, and some extra lumps of butter. Place in a hot oven and cook until the top layer is a nice golden brown.

This dish must be served very hot with cooked rice.

Alas, the chicken does not play an important part in the Egyptian cuisine, and so we will leave this country and go to North Africa, where Gallina is much more popular.

NORTH AFRICA

IT has always been a joy for me to visit Algeria and Morocco. Algiers, Bou Saada, Biskra, Ghardaia, Constantine, Casablanca, Rabat, Fez, Marrakesh are happy hunting grounds with their fascinating mingling of European and Arab cultures. The climate, moreover, is extremely agreeable if one goes to Africa to find sunshine, dream under the palm trees, and let the restless world go by.

Both in Algeria and in Morocco I learnt a great deal about gastronomy. Where else are herbs and spices so skilfully used?

Where else are they grown in such abundance and so profitably, giving, as they do, a livelihood to so many people?

The narrow streets of the Casbah in Algiers, of the Medina (Arab quarter) and of the Mella (Jewish quarter) of Casablanca are filled with the heady, disturbing aroma of the herbs and spices used in the cooking.

The Arabs are simple yet skilful cooks and do wonders with a home-made grill over a charcoal fire, using the simplest ingredients such as a handful of fresh vegetables and a few pieces of meat.

The most famous of their herb-spice mixture is the Ras el Hanout I have already described (p. 28) in my chapter on Herbs and Spices.

In the Souks, or spice markets—an item on every tourist's programme—you are overwhelmed by the variety and pungency of the scents. Nowhere else have I seen so many donkeys loaded with mint leaves.

The varieties of paprika and curry powders are numberless, and I was interested to learn how important a part is played by mint in both savoury and sweet recipes. Aniseed and absinthe, too, are widely used. Rose-water is another item in the Arab kitchen. It is not only used for desserts, but is also offered to guests in which to wash their fingers before picking up the roast or grilled lamb, mutton, or a wonderful 'bastilla' pie, made of puff-pastry and stuffed with raisins, almonds, honey, sugar, herbs, spices, and pigeons.

I still remember nostalgically my first diffa, or Arab dinner party, held late one evening, in an oasis under the rustling palm trees. I sat on the floor covered with Persian rugs, and the main dish was a mechoui, or lamb roasted whole, prepared by Berber cooks.

These Berbers as well as the Touaregs (the blue men) are, with the Arabs, past-masters in the art of preparing their own special oil blend needed for successful grilling.

This contains ⅓ of butter blended with ⅔ of oil, preferably ground-nut. To this is added Ras el Hanout, which if necessary we can replace by using a mixture of curry powder, basil, mar-

joram, allspice, together with coarsely ground peanuts or almonds, fresh chopped herbs, some soaked parboiled and well-
drained raisins, lemon juice, and honey. This is a mixture in
which both sweet and spicy flavours are mingled. Incidentally,
this mixture is not only used when roasting whole animals or
birds, but also employed when preparing such vegetables as tomatoes, aubergines, and marshmallows.

But since we are not likely to grill a whole lamb or sheep let
us prepare an Algerian chicken.

Choua de Poulet (Algerian Chicken)

for 4 servings:

1 tender roaster, halved
cooking salt

A MIXTURE FROM

4 tablespoons creamy butter	*1 teaspoon curry powder*
6 tablespoons oil	*pinch thyme*
2 tablespoons ground almonds	*pinch turmeric powder*
2 tablespoons raisins (swilled	*pinch mixed herbs* or *allspice*
in hot water)	*1½ tablespoons chopped green*
2 tablespoons lemon juice	*herbs, including mint*
a generous pinch cayenne	
pepper	

Prepare and blend the mixture the day before you need to use
it. Rub this mixture into the halved roaster, but before doing so
salt the chicken. Turn the oven full on for 10 minutes in advance, put the chicken on an oiled baking-pan, and let it brown.
Reduce the heat a little and allow about 25 minutes for the
grilling. Needless to say, a genuine grill does this work much
more efficiently than an oven. Rub the oil-butter mixture into
the heart and liver and then grill and stuff the roaster with them.
When grilling in an oven put the chicken on the grid in the
toasting-pan and do not shut the door tight. Allow the steam to
escape as it would do from a real grill.

The colour of the chicken will be a golden brown, owing to the blend of curry powder and turmeric. While grilling occasionally rub in some more of the mixture.

With the Choua chicken we serve cooked rice and place on the table a little dish with caraway seeds mixed with salt and black pepper.

If you care for a very tasty Algerian salad try this one.

Salade aux Pommes Douces, aux Tomates et Poivrons (Apple-tomato-paprika Salad)

for 4 servings:

2 sweet apples, washed, cored, and quartered

4 large, peeled, quartered tomatoes without seeds and liquid

2 paprikas cut up finely in julienne

1 large sliced onion

1 crushed clove of garlic

pepper and salt to taste

4–5 tablespoons oil

the juice of 1 lemon

2 tablespoons chopped parsley, chives, and mint

Heat the oil in an omelet-pan and fry to a golden brown all the listed ingredients, except the chopped fresh herbs (leave the skin on the apples). Let the liquid evaporate as quickly as possible and allow 5 minutes for all these ingredients to be done.

Arrange in a glass dish with the frying-oil and if necessary add salt and cayenne pepper to taste. Let cool completely before adding the lemon juice. Only then top with the chopped herbs.

It is principally the combination of sweet apples with paprika and tomatoes which gives a special flavour to this salad. In Algeria they add a little chili powder and a few caraway seeds.

The Moroccan way of preparing a cucumber salad is somewhat exotic.

Salade de Concombres (Cucumber Salad)

for 4 servings:

1 large fresh cucumber with little seeds	1 large crushed bay leaf
	salt to taste
5 tablespoons vinegar	1 tablespoon sugar
2 tablespoons oil	

Peel the cucumber and shred it very coarsely. Having pressed out the liquid mix the cucumber with all the listed ingredients. Allow to macerate for 5 minutes then serve. This sugar-vinegar combination is a particularly happy choice with grilled meat or fish dishes.

A very typical chicken soup is called Harira. This soup is usually eaten by the Mohammedans during Ramadan, when it is prepared without meat. Taken at any other time meat can be used.

Harira (Moroccan Soup)

for 6 servings for two days:

1 old boiling fowl without
any fat left on
the giblets, which should be
ground
1 teaspoon curry powder
4 rusks
1 pound finely chopped
mutton or lamb
1 large finely chopped onion
2 generous tablespoons
coarsely chopped parsley
1 pound weighed, shelled,
uncooked broad beans or
¾ pound soaked lentils
(soak 2 hours only) or 1
pound soaked white beans
(overnight)

pepper and salt to taste
a generous pinch ginger
powder
¼ teaspoon coriander seeds
a generous pinch saffron or
some more turmeric
6 large tomatoes
1½ tablespoons rice
2 tablespoons butter
10–12 cups water

Bring the chicken to the boil with 8 cups of water, the chopped onion, the uncooked broad beans, the lentils or white beans, pepper and salt and ginger powder to taste, the saffron or turmeric, and the coriander seeds. Allow 2–2½ hours of gentle boiling on a reduced heat.

In the meantime prepare a creamy blend with the ground giblets and the lamb or mutton, the 4 rusks, the curry powder, the butter, and salt and pepper to taste. Prepare balls the size of walnuts with this mixture.

Put 3 cups of boiling water in a pan with the peeled quartered tomatoes and the rice. Boil gently and add the meat balls one after another. Let the water continue to boil very gently for 8 minutes and then remove the meat balls and put them in a bowl. Reduce the heat, cover the pan, and allow a further 30 minutes on a very low heat for the tomatoes and the rice to be cooked.

Check to see if the boiling fowl is done. Remove from the pan and allow the stock with the beans or lentils to cool. In the meantime skin the fowl and cut into not too small pieces. Remove the superfluous fat from the cooked stock and put the pan again on the stove. Bring the stock to the boil, add the meat balls with the rice-tomato liquid and the pieces of chicken. Taste for salt and pepper.

Before serving add some more cayenne pepper and the chopped green herbs.

This soup is food and drink at the same time. Please do be rather generous when using turmeric-ginger powder and curry powder. These spices, like the saffron, give the authentic flavour to this Harira.

In Algeria they mix the uncooked rice with some yeast, which gives a most attractive appearance to the soup.

Here is another chicken recipe.

Poulet au Piment à l'Oudina (Oudina's Pimento Chicken)

for 2 servings:

1 *roaster*	1 *egg-yolk*
2 *fresh very tiny Spanish pimentos (chilis)*	1 *well-beaten egg-white*
	pinch curry powder
2 *tablespoons thick honey or 1 tablespoon honey blended with 1 tablespoon demerara sugar*	*the juice of ½ lemon*
	½ cup olive oil blended with ½ tablespoon dried sage

Halve the roaster as described for the Pollo alla Diavolo on page 82. Prepare a mixture with the honey, with or without sugar, the lemon juice, and the two well-washed but whole Spanish pimentos. Finally add to this mixture the stiffly beaten egg-white with the egg-yolk. When we have thoroughly flattened the roaster we carefully loosen the skin covering the breast with our fingers. Divide the prepared mixture into two half-portions. Take care that in each portion you put one Spanish pepper. Fill each breast and cover with the skin. Rub salt and oil blended with sage into the chicken halves.

Thoroughly pre-heat the grill and put the roaster as near as possible into immediate contact with the heat.

Let this brown and allow 20–25 minutes' cooking time. From time to time rub the oil into the chicken.

While the grilling takes place prepare a dry-cooked rice and have one peeled banana ready for each person. Using 2 tablespoons of butter, fry and brown over the whole bananas, adding 1 tablespoon of honey, a pinch of freshly ground pepper, and ¼ teaspoon of curry powder.

Arrange some of the cooked rice on each plate and place a portion of chicken on top garnished with the fried banana.

If you think this is too rich a dish, remove the whole Spanish pepper from the stuffing before eating.

This dish has a deliciously sweet-spicy flavour.

Tajine de Légumes Saida (Saida's Vegetable Stew)

for 4 servings:

3 large onions peeled and sliced	a generous pinch turmeric
2 paprikas without seeds, coarsely cut up	a generous pinch curry powder
8 not too big potatoes peeled and quartered	a generous pinch hot paprika powder
4 large tomatoes peeled and halved	pinch thyme
¾ pound half-lean half-fat lamb or mutton, diced	pinch basil
4 tablespoons oil	a generous pinch crushed caraway seeds
2 tablespoons butter	1 generous tablespoon chopped mint
	salt and pepper to taste

Saida showed me how she prepared this stew in an earthenware pot over a charcoal fire. Very slowly, with much 'feel' for the cooking, she gently stewed the vegetables and meat. First she browned all the ingredients in the hot oil with the herbs and spices. She then relaxed, squatted on the floor, and said, "Now I have a good hour to rest—how wonderful!"

This is the way we all should work, taking all the time needed to stew very gently. Use an ordinary saucepan and heat the oil and the butter. In this we brown the diced meat with the vegetables, the potatoes, and the herbs and spices, leaving the tomatoes until later.

Reserve the mint. Let all the ingredients brown and the water evaporate. When they are well browned add the tomatoes, stir, cover the pan, and reduce the heat. The tomatoes provide the necessary liquid. Allow the stew to become creamy rather than watery. This will need 50–60 minutes' cooking. Before serving add the chopped mint and taste for salt and pepper.

Here is another very exotic dish.

Djaja Mammra (Stuffed Chicken)

for 4 servings:

1 heavy roaster
not quite ½ cup butter
1 garnished onion

FOR THE STUFFING

40 grams swilled drained raisins
30 grams cooked rice
2 tablespoons butter
1 small finely chopped onion
½ teaspoon ginger powder
pinch curry powder
pinch turmeric powder
pinch basil
pinch thyme
pepper and salt to taste
1 tablespoon golden honey
1 tablespoon lemon juice
1 hard-boiled mashed egg

Mix all the ingredients listed for the stuffing, but do not forget to taste for salt and pepper. When blending, the rice must still be warm, for in this way it will absorb all the flavours more easily. Loosen the skin of the roaster from the breast and stuff the mixture between the skin and the meat. Rub the outside of the chicken with a little salt and fasten with skewers or sew it up.

Have a pan ready and put in the roaster. Pour over enough water to reach half-way up the chicken. Bring the water to the boil and let this water evaporate in the open pan. While the water boils add the ½ cup of butter.

As the water evaporates the butter and the roaster will brown and the chicken will be half done. Now brown the roaster on all sides and turn the stuffed part to the bottom of the pan. Cover the pan aslant, reduce the heat, and allow about another 20 minutes, but watch to see if the chicken is ready earlier as the time needed will depend on how young the roaster is and also on its weight.

While the bird is cooking add a garnished onion for extra flavour. The butter will not burn as the onion will provide sufficient moisture.

Carve the roaster, serving some of the stuffing with each helping.

In the Algerian restaurants they serve warm white bread with it rubbed with a blend of oil and crushed garlic.

To be sure to get the right flavour into the stuffing it is important that you should not use the herbs and spices alone. You must add enough salt and even cayenne pepper to give it the right balance.

Tajine de Poulet au Citron (Lemon Chicken Stew)

for 4 servings:

1 tender boiling fowl with no fat left on it	bunch green stalks
about 4 cups water with salt to taste	4 tablespoons oil
	4 tablespoons butter

FOR THE GARNISH

1 lemon

¼ cup raisins

pinch saffron

1 teaspoon pepper

1 teaspoon curry powder

pinch allspice

1 teaspoon salt

¼ teaspoon sugar

Two days before preparing this dish we must semi-quarter the lemon by cutting only half-way through the fruit so that the lower part remains untouched. Have a large jam-pot ready and put the quartered lemon into it with all the ingredients listed for the garnish. Put a lid on the pot, shake, and leave to macerate for 48 hours. Remove all the fat from the boiling fowl, put the fowl into a pan, and add as much water as is necessary to cover three-quarters of its height. Add salt to taste, keeping in mind that the lemon garnish we use later has also been salted. Add the bunch of green stalks to the water and 4 tablespoons of oil, and bring to the boil. Reduce the heat, cover the pan, and allow about 1 hour for cooking.

Remove the lid from the pan and turn the heat full on. The water should now evaporate completely, and this will take about 20–30 minutes. The flesh of a medium-sized boiling fowl should be ready and tender by now. The fowl will be rather shiny because of the added oil.

Turn the oven full on and finish the chicken as follows:

Add 4 tablespoons of butter to a fireproof dish and put it into the hot oven, allowing the butter to brown. Then put the cooked, drained fowl into the dish and add the lemon blend from the jam-pot, having first strained it through a sieve. The lemon will still retain some liquid in the pot, and this liquid must be kept for later use.

Fowl and lemon should now brown and roast for a short time only. During this time, which may be from 10 to 20 minutes, depending on how tender the fowl was, we baste with the brown butter. Before serving we add the remaining lemon liquid from the pot to this butter.

Serve with cooked rice or potatoes but nothing else.

If I am to talk to you about Algerian and Moroccan dishes I cannot possibly leave out their national dish, couscous.

The couscous can be bought in well-provided food-shops in most European capitals and is sold in plastic bags. It is made from semolina rolled into tiny pearls. The Arab cooks prepare the semolina pearls with oil, but as it is a very time-consuming work we use ready-made couscous for our dish.

To heat it we use a steamer with a cloth over the holes to prevent the couscous from falling through. We serve a stew with it prepared from chicken and/or lamb and a variety of vegetables.

Couscous (Algerian Semolina)

for 6–8 servings:

1 bag ready-made couscous
4 tablespoons butter

FOR THE STEW

4 cups water
pepper and salt to taste
½ pound dried chick peas
soaked overnight or canned
chick peas
¾ pound diced mutton or
lamb
1 boiling fowl cut up in 8
pieces without any fat left
on
3 big quartered onions
10 small whole carrots or 2
large diced carrots
4 halved turnips
1 not too big vegetable
marrow thickly sliced

canned artichoke hearts
(optional)
if available: ¼ pound
weighed, shelled, fresh broad
beans or green peas
½ white cabbage coarsely cut
up
4 nice dark-red firm tomatoes
½ teaspoon turmeric powder
pinch saffron
a generous pinch crushed
coriander seeds
pinch ground pimento
4–6 tablespoons butter

Let the 4–6 tablespoons of butter get golden in a stock-pot and sauté the pieces of chicken, the diced mutton or lamb, the drained soaked dried chick peas, all the fresh vegetables, and the herbs with spices and salt and pepper to taste.

Do not use the canned artichokes or chick peas at this stage. Add the water and let it come to the boil. Cover the pan and reduce the heat, allowing about 1 hour. When the pieces of chicken are tender the other ingredients will also be done. If we use canned vegetables we add them shortly before serving. Taste for salt and pepper. Add some extra freshly ground pepper.

Remove all the ingredients from the stock with a skimmer and arrange them around the steamed couscous, to which we have added the 4 tablespoons of butter, stirring it in with a fork in order not to mash up the semolina pearls. Serve cups of stock separately.

Lentilles du Souk (Market Lentil-pot)

for 4 servings:

1¼ pounds lentils washed and soaked for 2 hours only	1 fresh or dried small whole Spanish pepper
1¼ pounds peeled, quartered tomatoes	1 teaspoon paprika powder salt and pepper to taste
2½ tablespoons chopped parsley	1 crushed clove of garlic
2½ tablespoons chopped mint	4 tablespoons butter or vegetable fat
2 large, sliced onions	

First brown the butter or fat in an uncovered pan and then add the onion slices, the garlic, tomatoes, Spanish pepper, and the paprika powder, and cook until they turn a golden brown. Then add the well-drained lentils and bring to the boil. Add salt and pepper to taste and see that the bottom of the pan is covered with some liquid. Cover the pan and reduce the heat.

The lentils should cook in as little water as possible, but should more be needed then use the water in which they were soaked very sparingly, a tablespoon at a time. Allow about 35–45 minutes only for cooking. Check for salt and pepper. Add the coarsely chopped fresh herbs when the lentils have been taken from the fire. This dish is supposed to be served rather dry; by no means should it be soggy. Eat it with boiled potatoes and some roast mutton or lamb. Be generous with garlic when roasting the meat.

And to end up with here is a very typical Algerian dish.

Tajine aux Feves (Broad Bean Stew)

for 6 servings:

2 pounds lamb or mutton cut up in rather big dice
3–4 pounds broad beans weighed, shelled
about 6–7 tablespoons olive oil
½ teaspoon ginger powder
a generous pinch freshly ground pepper
salt to taste
pinch saffron or ¼ teaspoon turmeric powder
1 crushed clove of garlic
2 chopped onions
a generous pinch crushed coriander seeds
water

Mix all the ingredients with the exception of the meat, the garlic, the onions, and the broad beans. Crush very finely in a mortar with pestle. Blend in gradually from 5–7 tablespoons of water. Let this mixture come to the boil in a saucepan, stir, and add the meat, which has been covered for about 15 minutes with the chopped onions and the garlic. When it boils thoroughly cover the pan and reduce the heat. Allow to simmer gently on a low heat until the meat is tender and done. In the meantime cook the broad beans, but check in order not to over-cook them. Use enough water for the boiling. The beans should remain firm. Drain well and add them to the stew. Allow some more minutes of stewing in a covered pan. Check before serving for salt and pepper. If possible serve in the pan in which the meat has been cooked.

Rice or potatoes can be served with it, but are not essential. In Algiers we drank the national red wine with it.

Good-bye, Africa, and good-bye to all the other countries we have visited on this tour. We leave each other, but not before adding some desserts to this long list of recipes.

Some Sweet Advice

RATHER tired and replete from touring around the world, we have come to the end of our journey. Yet I cannot say good-bye to you without giving you some 'sweet' advice. I shall not try to describe all the desserts I have tasted on my different tours. Many of them are much too sweet and too heavy to suit the average taste, and, moreover, many of them are very complicated to prepare. I will therefore confine myself to telling you about desserts you might perhaps like to try out.

First a dessert I like very much.

Omelet Française (French Omelet)

use for this omelet per serving:

2 eggs	2 tablespoons milk or water
pinch salt	1 tablespoon butter
1 tablespoon sugar	

Brown the butter in an omelet-pan which should be neither too large nor too small. It should be about the size of the omelet you are going to prepare in it. A pan of about 8 inches in diameter serves for 2–3 eggs.

Using a fork, beat the eggs lightly and add all the other ingredients. Personally I use 2 tablespoons of water for 2 eggs. I think that with water we obtain a lighter and fluffier batter than with milk.

The butter in the omelet-pan must become hot and a little brown. Pour in the omelet batter and shake the pan up and down from right to left.

With a palette knife lift the edges of the omelet and let the liquid from the middle run to the hot bottom of the pan. Keep shaking the pan in order to allow the omelet to set evenly. If working efficiently the cooking of an omelet takes no longer than 2–3 minutes. Work on a high heat.

The correct consistency of an omelet can be compared to a 'creamy' scrambled-egg dish.

When the omelet is cooked, slip it on to a warm dish and at the same time fold it in two.

Never try to prepare an omelet with more than 6 eggs, which are sufficient for three persons. This is the maximum size you can comfortably cook an omelet. When the pan becomes too heavy and the omelet too large both are difficult to handle.

This was the recipe for a simple French omelet. Here follows another version:

Omelet Soufflé (Soufflé Omelet)

for 1 serving:

2 egg-yolks	2 tablespoons butter
2 well-beaten egg-whites	less than ½ cup sugar
pinch salt	

Prepare the batter with the egg-yolks and ¼ cup of sugar. Beat till foamy. Add a pinch of salt with the two stiffly beaten egg-whites. Blend lightly. Pour this batter in the omelet-pan in which the butter has turned hot and golden.

Prepare this omelet as indicated for the simple French omelet.

Remember that a batter with beaten egg-whites is apt to turn too brown, so keep shaking the pan while cooking a soufflé omelet. It takes longer to cook than the French omelet. The top of this omelet should be very creamy.

Slip the cooked omelet on a hot dish and fold in two. Sprinkle with the remaining sugar and caramelize the top of the omelet with a poker you have heated on a high gas-flame.

Serve immediately.

Omelet Varieties

Omelet Flambée (Flambéed Omelet). When you have cooked the ordinary or the soufflé omelet put it on a very hot dish. Pour over some brandy, armagnac, or rum, and light. Let the flame go out slowly and serve.

We can successfully flambée an omelet only if both the dish and the omelet are very hot. Otherwise the alcoholic liquors will not burn. To be on the safe side many cooks pre-heat the alcoholic liquors to make sure that the omelet will flambée well.

Omelet aux Fruits (Fruit Omelet). For 2 persons marinate about ⅓ cup of a fresh or a well-drained canned macedoine of fruits in sugar blended with kirsch or maraschino for about 30 minutes.

Cut the canned or fresh fruit up finely before marinating. When the omelet is cooked stuff it with the fruits before folding in two. Heat the stuffed omelet thoroughly before serving.

And here from France is a very simple yet delicious dessert.

Compôte de Pommes (Apple Stew)

for 4 servings:

2 pounds sweet apples (do not use cooking apples as they collapse while cooking)
1 cup water

the peel of 1 lemon
½ cup sugar (which depends on your taste)

Core the apples, peel, and quarter. Bring the water with the lemon peel and the sugar to the boil. Add the apples immediately and shake the pan up and down. When the last quarters of the apples are added, remove them to the bottom of the pan. The sooner these quartered apples come into contact with the boiling liquid the sooner they are done.

Personally I love lemon, and so I always add the juice of half a lemon to the water before boiling. Moreover, lemon juice prevents the apples from discolouring. The liquid should evaporate while cooking in the open pan. One of the charms of this sweet is that it leaves us tender and undamaged apples that are sweet-sour to the taste.

Apple Stew with Cream. Prepare a cream with 2 cups of sweet strawberry syrup blended with ½ cup of water, ¼ cup of semolina, 1–2 egg-yolks, and the beaten egg-whites. Boil the syrup with the water (sugar is superfluous, as the syrup is sweet) and drop in the semolina. Let it drop into the liquid like raindrops, stir well, and the semolina will thicken the liquid.

Use a wire whisk for stirring in the stiffly beaten egg-whites lightly blended with the egg-yolks. Work on a very reduced heat and keep stirring until the eggs and semolina turn creamy. Eat this cream with the Apple Stew.

Apples with Ginger-vanilla Cream. Prepare a fluffy cream with 2 cups of milk, 3 tablespoons of sweetened vanilla custard powder, and 1 or 2 eggs (again we beat the egg-whites). Pour on the stewed apples and let cool. Garnish with whipped cream blended with some finely sliced syrup ginger balls.

Gâteau aux Pommes (Apple Pie)

Use a 9-inch pie-dish with a 1-inch-high rim.

½ pound pastry flour	*pinch salt*
2 eggs	*the apple stew given above to*
7 tablespoons butter	*be used for the filling*
2 generous tablespoons sugar	

Blend first the soft creamy butter with the egg-yolks, sugar, and salt. Work well until a smooth mixture is obtained. Only then add the stiffly beaten egg-whites and add the flour little by little. Work with a pastry blender or, as I do for preference, with the fingers, for hand temperature is ideal for the making of good pastry.

After having obtained a homogeneous and somewhat elastic dough, shape it into a ball, cover with a cloth, and allow it 30 minutes to rest.

Meanwhile butter and breadcrumb the pie-dish and also the rim. We have already cooked the apples, which for this purpose should be absolutely dry. Evaporate all the liquid and blend this apple stew with 2 tablespoons of chopped almonds, 2–3 tablespoons of currant jelly or red jam, and 1–2 tablespoons biscuit crumbs.

Line the pie-dish with the thinly rolled-out dough, taking care that the dough also covers three-quarters of the height of the ring. Put the apple stew on top of the dough. Turn on the oven for a full 10 minutes in advance. When fully heated put in the pie-dish and allow 25 minutes of baking in a heat of 350° Fahrenheit. Then reduce to 185°–200° Fahrenheit and allow another 25–30 minutes. Prick the pie with a thin pin to see if the dough is done. The pin should come out completely dry and very hot. Only then remove the dish from the oven and leave it to cool.

You can garnish this apple pie with whipped cream and cocktail cherries.

Here is a nice pudding I learned to prepare in India.

Pineapple-rice Composition

for 5 servings:

3 cups milk
½ cup rice
1 generous tablespoon
cornflour
1 egg
5–6 tablespoons grated
coconut
4 finger-thick slices pineapple,
fresh or canned (but then
well drained)

½ cup sugar
½ cup heavy cream
the juice of 1 lemon or 2
limes
1 teaspoon turmeric
powder

Bring the milk with the sugar to the boil and add the rice with the turmeric powder. Allow the boiling to go on for some minutes and then cover the pan and reduce the heat. Give 50–60 minutes of gentle boiling for the rice to be done.

Meanwhile cut up into thin strips the fresh or the canned and well-drained slices of pineapple. Prepare a blend with the cornflour, the grated coconut, the beaten egg-yolk, and the stiffly whipped egg-white. When well blended stir in 1 tablespoon of cold milk and the lemon or lime juice.

During the last 10 minutes add this cornflour blend with the pineapple to the cooked rice. On a reduced heat let the mixture set until a creamy homogeneous result is obtained.

Put it into a dish rinsed with cold water and allow it to cool. This delicious dish is served with heavy cream, which is not whipped.

And from Austria comes this

Kaiserschmarrn (Emperor Pancake)

for 2 servings:

4 eggs	1/4 cup swilled raisins, drained
1/3 cup sugar	pinch salt
1/4 cup cream or milk	3–4 tablespoons butter
1/2 cup flour	

Beat the egg-yolks to froth with the sugar. Add the flour, the well-drained raisins, the cream or milk, a pinch of salt, and finally the stiffly beaten egg-whites. Blend them in with a wire whisk.

Brown part of the butter in an omelet-pan and add the batter. Cook on one side until golden brown. When the top side of the pancake is set turn with a spatula. Add some more butter and let this side cook and also turn golden brown. Now comes the Austrian finishing touch. With two forks tear this pancake into pieces, not too small. Leave this for some more minutes in the omelet-pan on a very reduced heat and sprinkle with some extra sugar. Slip on to a hot dish and serve with Pflaumenröster, as beneath.

Pflaumenröster (Prune Stew)

for 2 servings:

about 1 pound fresh prunes: if these are not available use dried prunes pre-soaked	1¼-inch-long piece of cinnamon
about 1/2 cup demerara sugar according to your taste	the peel of 1/2 lemon
2 cloves	2 tablespoons butter
	very little water

Halve and stone the washed fresh or soaked dried prunes. Bring them to the boil with only the adhering water and add all the listed ingredients, the butter included.

Reduce the heat and in a covered pan allow the time required to cook these prunes to a very creamy consistency. With both fresh and dried fruit the cooking liquid should evaporate completely. Serve these creamy stewed prunes only when cooled.

Here is another Austrian dessert I love very much.

Salzburger Nockerln (Salzburger Egg Dish)

for 6 servings:

7 stiffly beaten egg-whites	pinch salt
5 egg-yolks	4 tablespoons butter
¼ cup flour	about ¾ cup milk
¾ cup sugar	

Heat the milk with the butter in an oblong fireproof glass dish in a hot oven, but do not let it come to the boil. Shake the dish in order that the hot milk with the butter will coat all the sides.

In the meantime briskly beat the egg-whites. Prepare in a bowl a creamy blend with the egg-yolks and the sugar. Add the flour with the pinch of salt little by little and finally stir in the beaten egg-whites. With two spoons shape this blend into 3 oblong but not too high 'snowballs.' Put them into the hot milk-and-butter blend and place them in the oven.

Reduce the heat and allow about 15–18 minutes for this dish to set in the covered dish. Check to see if the balls are cooked, then remove the lid from the fireproof dish, and turn up the heat. Put these Nockerln in immediate contact with the heat and let them turn a golden colour, but do not let them turn brown.

Serve immediately.

And to prepare quite a different dessert we go to Algeria.

Pannequet Arabe (Arabian Pancake)

for 6 servings:

3 eggs

¾ pound wheat-flour

a generous pinch salt

about ⅓ cup sugar

2 tablespoons mixed spices
(use ground cinnamon,
nutmeg, ginger, clove, and
allspice)

1 dessertspoon baking powder

1 dessertspoon oil

2 cups very strong cold coffee

a little more than ¼ cup
milk

50 grams dates, stoned and
halved

3 tablespoons chopped mixed
candied fruits, among which
are orange rinds

4 tablespoons butter or
vegetable fat

Blend the flour, eggs, baking powder, mixed spices, salt, sugar, and oil. When well blended pour in as much coffee and milk as is needed to obtain a creamy yet not too thin batter. Let it stand for a few minutes and then stir again in order to be sure that the batter is creamy enough. Only then add the dates and the mixed chopped candied fruit.

In a not too small omelet-pan heat 1 tablespoon of butter to a golden brown. Cook half the amount of batter first on one side to a golden brown and then, when the pancake is somewhat set, turn it over with a spatula and allow the other side to brown. Before cooking the second side add another 1 tablespoon of butter. When folding this pancake sprinkle some extra white or brown castor sugar on it. Divide this pancake in three pieces and slip them on the hot plates. Keep warm and cook the second pancake. Serve immediately.

Personally, when preparing these very delicious pancakes, I use two omelet-pans, in order to prepare six servings at the same time.

Pineapple Salad

for 6 servings:

1 fresh pineapple	1 grapefruit
about ¾ cup cane sugar	1 bag bigarreaux (candied
1 generous glass kirsch,	cherries)
maraschino, or cointreau	

Peel the pineapple, but peel it less thickly than you would do when cutting it up for dessert. The object is not to cut out all the hard brown pits as you would do normally. Neither must we cut out the 'stalk.' Having lightly peeled the pineapple, we cut it up into paper-thin slices, working with a very sharp knife, preferably with a sharp saw-knife.

Heap up the slices and put in a bowl. Pour over the chosen liquor. Personally I think maraschino or kirsch is best, but in Mexico they very often use rum. Add the sugar, cover the bowl, and allow two hours of marinating. Arrange the slices of pineapple overlapping on a nice flat glass dish, garnish with the grapefruit segments and the bigarreaux.

Serve with the sugar-bowl and the bottle of kirsch, maraschino, or cointreau.

Hollandse Custardvla (Dutch Custard Cream)

for 4 servings:

3 cups milk	2 eggs
4 tablespoons sweetened	½ cup cream
custard powder	

Bring the milk to the boil. Blend the egg-yolks with the custard, the stiffly beaten egg-whites, and three extra tablespoons of cold milk. When the milk boils stir in this blend with a wire whisk. Reduce the heat, but go on stirring well with the wire whisk until the blend is set.

Remove the pan from the stove, but keep on stirring for several minutes to prevent the eggs from curdling.

Check for sugar and then pour this cream in a water-rinsed dish. Allow to cool and garnish with whipped cream before serving.

English Fruit Loaf

30 grams almonds (chopped)	¾ pound flour
1 bag glacé cherries, cut up finely (about 1 ounce)	¾ cup butter
	5 eggs, the whites of which are briskly beaten
1 generous tablespoon candied orange and lemon rinds	¾ cup sugar
½ cup sultanas (swilled in hot water)	pinch salt
	2 tablespoons flour

Blend the fruit with the peeled chopped almonds, the pinch of salt, and the 2 tablespoons of flour. Cream the egg-yolks, the sugar, and the butter in a bowl till soft and fluffy. Then add gradually the flour with the fruit and the almond blend. Work until a homogeneous mixture is obtained and whisk in the beaten egg-whites. Put into a well-greased, breadcrumbed loaf-pan and place in a pre-heated, but not too hot, oven for about 25 minutes. Then reduce the heat and allow a further 1½–1¾ hours. Check with a knitting needle that the loaf is done. The knitting needle should come out very hot and completely dry. Let this fruit loaf cool in the open, turned-off oven.

Mousse de Semoule au Kirsch et aux Fruits
(Swiss Semolina Fruit Mousse)

for 4 servings:

the juice of 4 large juicy oranges	4 eggs
	½ cup cream
enough water to make, with the juice, about 2 cups of liquid	about ⅓ cup semolina
	½ cup sugar
	1–2 tablespoons kirsch

Bring the water mixed with the fruit juice to the boil. In the meantime lightly beat the egg-yolks with the sugar. Beat the egg-whites very briskly. Add the semolina to the water-orange juice mixture. Stir in with a wire whisk. Allow about 8 minutes for the semolina to thicken, but keep on stirring with the wire whisk.

Remove the pan from the heat and add the egg-yolk and sugar blend. Stir with the wire whisk, and only then add the beaten egg-whites.

Replace the pan on a high heat and beat energetically with a wire whisk. Beat well, and be on the alert for the moment the mousse shows the slightest tendency to come to the boil. You must then take the pan off the heat. Stir in the kirsch and continue beating for 1 minute.

Pour this mousse into a water-rinsed glass dish, let it cool and set, and then put it into the refrigerator. Take it out only some minutes before serving.

And the last 'sweet' offering I can make in this all-too-short chapter comes from Italy.

Zabaglone (Italian Egg Dessert)

for 3 servings:

3 egg-yolks	the rind of ¼ lemon
⅓ cup sugar	a little stick of vanilla (1
about 2 cups white wine (the	inch long)
Italian Marsala is best)	

This zabaglone can be prepared au-bain-Marie, but we can also prepare it in a pan on the electric or gas stove. But if we do so we shall have to work very quickly and beat well. It is anyhow the quickest way and is real fun to prepare.

Beat the egg-yolks with the sugar in the saucepan until frothy. Then stir in the warmed but not hot wine, to which we have added the lemon rind and the stick of vanilla. Leave the pan on a high heat and beat very hard with a wire whisk. Do not stop until the egg-blend thickens and turns very frothy. Go on beating. This blend should rise, and only then remove the pan from the stove. But go on beating! Divide this zabaglone between three glasses. First pour into each glass some froth and then the cream itself. Serve immediately. A well-beaten zabaglone is supposed to run over the glass.

Time has now come to say au revoir to you. May you enjoy these recipes and try out some of them.

Epilogue

This is the end of my book. To travel again, if only in thought, through all the countries I have learned to know so well has been a great joy to me. I believe that there are three ways in which one travels. The first consists of preparing a tour and getting to know a country through books and travel literature and with the assistance of travel agencies. The second is the tour itself, which is so often rushed and hectic but fascinating, if somewhat tiring. The third is to sit down quietly and write an account of what you have experienced.

It is of the utmost importance that one should go to a great deal of trouble in the preparation of a tour, since much of its success will depend on how well one knows one's subject. If you have read it up thoroughly beforehand there is little of interest that you are likely to overlook.

On such a tour one gets to know so many people, and some of them do not just remain ships that pass in the night. As a result of my tours I have made many friends and have forged ties of friendship with people of different races and civilizations that have become very precious to me, proving that there can indeed be friendship and understanding between men and women of all races and all beliefs.

As I wrote of the discoveries I made on my travels all these memories came flooding back. The subject need not be gastronomy or even Gallina, for, whatever may be your interests, if you have pursued them in your travels you will again be on the road as you write about them. So it has been for me.

All the countries of the world are not included in this book, for I have written only about those which I have actually visited. But I intend to travel again, and in the near future hope to offer a further selection of recipes.

And now I must bid farewell to you . . . and to my book. It has become rather dear to me, and if it finds its way into your kitchen, and even into your heart, I shall consider myself very fortunate.

Index

Pommes frites (Belgian fried potatoes), 58–59
Pommes frites à ma manière
(French-fried potatoes my way),
59–60
Pommes Parisiennes (Parisian potatoes), 159
Pommes soufflées (soufflé potatoes),
278
Pork:
meat and vegetable soup, 242–43
sweet-sour, 241–42
PORTUGAL, 97–103
chicken:
in pie-crust, 102–3
in *piri-piri* sauce, 99–100
with green peas, 101–2
soup with chicken, 98–99
Potaje frijol bayo (Mexican bean
soup), 291–92
Potatoes:
and cauliflower, curried, 214
Belgian-fried, 58–59
French-fried, 59–60
Greek way, 194–95
mashed, 94–95, 151
paprika, 145
Parisian, 159
roast, 133–34
soufflé, 278
Poule-au-pot (*poule Henri IV*), 39–
40
Poulet à la crème (creamy chicken),
46–47
Poulet au piment à l'Oudina (Oudina's pimento chicken, 323–24
Poulet au 'vert' (green chicken), 60–
61
Poulet belle époque (Edwardian
chicken), 162
Poulet Casanova (chicken Casanova),
156–57
Poulet-champignon à l'estragon
(chicken-mushrooms with tarragon sauce), 47–48
Poulet froid à la gelée (cold chicken
in aspic), 42–44
Poulet sauté chasseur (hunters'
chicken), 50–51
Prawns:
and eggs Mérida, 294
-in-the-net, 227
Perino, 266

Prune stew, 338–39
Psarosoupe (fish soup), 196–97
Puddings:
chicken, 179
Dutch custard cream, 341–42
fruit mousse, Swiss semolina, 343
Italian egg dessert, 344
pineapple-rice composition, 337
Puré de patata (mashed potatoes),
94–95

Quatre épices, 28

Ragout of spring chickens, 122–23
Ranchera chicken with cream, 302
Ras el hanout, 28
Red: beetroot salad with horseradish,
171
lacquered duck, 235–36
mayonnaise, 57
Rice:
Belvedère, 228–30
chicken pilaff, 188
-dish, 48–49
Dutch, 69
exotic, 71–72
fried, 240
Greek, 192
Indian, 220
Mexican, 300
pacha, 309–10
vegetable dish, 152–53
wild, 264
with chicken, 96–97
See also Paella
Risi (rice), 192
Riz daoud pacha (pacha rice), 309–
10
Roast chicken:
accompaniments, 67
in aspic, 43
in beer-batter, 125–26
Dutch, 66–67
stuffed (Turkish), 203–4
with sausage-meat stuffing, 185–86
Roast potatoes, 133–34
Roman chicken, 84–85
Roquefort sandwich, 258–59
Rosemary, 21
Russian fish soup, 243–44

Saffron, 26–27
chicken, 315
Sage, 21